T0068712

Mood Prep 101

MOOD PREP 101

A Parent's Guide to Preventing Depression and Anxiety in College-Bound Teens

Carol Landau, Ph.D.

OXFORD
UNIVERSITY PRESS

OXFORD
UNIVERSITY PRESS

Oxford University Press is a department of the University of Oxford. It furthers
the University's objective of excellence in research, scholarship, and education
by publishing worldwide. Oxford is a registered trade mark of Oxford University
Press in the UK and certain other countries.

Published in the United States of America by Oxford University Press
198 Madison Avenue, New York, NY 10016, United States of America.

© Oxford University Press 2020

All rights reserved. No part of this publication may be reproduced, stored in
a retrieval system, or transmitted, in any form or by any means, without the
prior permission in writing of Oxford University Press, or as expressly permitted
by law, by license, or under terms agreed with the appropriate reproduction
rights organization. Inquiries concerning reproduction outside the scope of the
above should be sent to the Rights Department, Oxford University Press, at the
address above.

You must not circulate this work in any other form
and you must impose this same condition on any acquirer.

Library of Congress Cataloging-in-Publication Data
Names: Landau, Carol, author.
Title: Mood prep 101 : a parent's guide to preventing depression and
anxiety in college-bound teens / Carol Landau, Ph.D.
Other titles: Mood prep one zero one
Description: New York : Oxford University Press, 2020. |
Includes bibliographical references and index.
Identifiers: LCCN 2019052828 (print) | LCCN 2019052829 (ebook) |
ISBN 9780190914301 (paperback) | ISBN 9780190914325 (epub) |
ISBN 9780190914332
Subjects: LCSH: Anxiety in adolescence. | Depression in adolescence. |
Teenagers—Services for. | Parenting. | Parent and teenager.
Classification: LCC BF724.3.A57 L36 2020 (print) | LCC BF724.3.A57 (ebook) |
DDC 155.5/1246—dc23
LC record available at https://lccn.loc.gov/2019052828
LC ebook record available at https://lccn.loc.gov/2019052829

This book is not intended as a substitute for the medical advice. Readers should consult
with a physician or mental health professional in matters relating to their health. Neither
the publisher nor the author is engaged in rendering professional advice or services to the
individual reader. Neither the author nor the publisher shall be liable or responsible for any
damage allegedly arising from any information or suggestion in this book.

The names and identifying details in this book have been changed in order to protect the
identities of any patients and their families and to protect their confidentiality. For example,
the names, hometowns, as well as the professions of the patients' parents have been
deliberately altered.

9 8 7 6 5 4 3 2 1

Printed by LSC Communications, United States of America

For David

John, Missy, and Julia, Rob and Alice

With Love

And in memory of Alice and Henry Landau

CONTENTS

PART III. Vulnerabilities and Strategies for Change

PART IV. Changing Times: Campus Life, Depression, and Anxiety

ACKNOWLEDGMENTS

Creating this book has been a family project. I thank my son, Robert Landau Ames, and my husband, David Ames, for their support, encouragement, and invaluable assistance in editing the manuscript. David has also always been available, with reassuring words and many cups of coffee. My sisters, Rosemarie Helmbrecht and Vicki Landau, read portions of the book and provided helpful feedback. My daughter-in-law, Melissa Urban Ames, a member of the Rhode Island Board of the American Foundation for Suicide Prevention, pointed me toward resources in the area of suicide prevention. My sister-in-law, Kristen Tsangaris Landau, provided me with thought-provoking ideas and reading materials, as did my nieces, Megan Helmbrecht, Hope Helmbrecht Krom, and Stacy Helmbrecht Wilson.

It would be hard to find more supportive colleagues than those in the Division of General Internal Medicine in the Department of Medicine at the Alpert Medical School, Brown University, my academic home/family for most of my career. I would like to thank Division Chiefs, Kelly McGarry, Angela Caliendo, Mark Fagan and Michele Cyr; and Chair of Medicine, Louis Rice. Thanks to everyone in the division, especially, Kate Cahill, Seth Clark, Rebekah Gardner, Jennifer Jeremiah, Dominick Tammaro, and Elizabeth Toll for their support. Thanks also to Steven Wartman and especially Colin Harrington, my gifted teaching partner in the psychiatry and psychology in primary care curriculum for the past 18 years. I have been fortunate to work with such a group of committed, talented, and humorous people and have benefitted enormously from teaching residents in primary care internal medicine.

My colleagues from the Department of Psychiatry and Human Behavior, Amy Bach, Steven Barreto, Debra Herman, and Marjorie Weishaar, have been sources of guidance and clinical wisdom. I thank the Beckwith Family Foundation for supporting my work in depression prevention. Thank you also to Kathryn McClure, Karen George, and Vanna Thlang for assisting in preparation of the manuscript.

The Office of Women in Medicine and Science at Brown, including Carey Baker, Kathleen Haslam, Katharine Sharkey, and Debra Abeshaus, has long been a place for me to find mutual mentoring and professional development. I am also grateful for dear friends, relatives, and colleagues: John Winthrop Ames, Julia Ames, Dottie Bianco, Laura Brady, Vanessa Britto, Elda Dawber, Betty Fielder, Philip Hall, Aleta Bok Johnson, Ferdinand Jones, Hester Kaplan, Carol Levine, David Levine, Susan Loar, Anne Moulton, Sherri Nelson, Adam Pallant, Alice Rha, Michael Sikorski, Maria Suarez, Marion Wachtenheim, Gabrielle Warshay, and Marin Warshay.

Many faculty and clinicians from around the country have been generous with their time in discussing the issue of depression and anxiety in college students. Thanks go to Randy Auerbach, Claire Cafaro, Aaron Krasnow, Kathleen Jenkins, Barbara McCrady, Victor Schwartz, Amy Wasserbauer, and Sharlene Wolchik. Kathleen Moss, Executive Director of LEAD Pittsburgh, shared materials from their program for preventing anxiety and depression. Stacey Colino and I collaborated earlier on a project on body dissatisfaction and I am indebted to her for some of the ideas in Chapter 6.

Belinda Johnson, former Director of Psychological Services at Brown, has been an indispensable source of wisdom, clinical judgment, clarity, and support. She has been extremely generous in sharing her knowledge and experience in student mental health. This is a much better book due to Belinda's ongoing involvement. Along with our dear friend, Iris Shuey, a psychiatrist who died in 2011, we spent countless hours discussing depression and anxiety along with many other topics.

The patients in my practice and at Rhode Island Hospital have been a daily source of inspiration.

It was a very good day when I met my editor at Oxford University Press, Sarah Harrington, who ushered the idea of the book through to its completion, with good advice and a wise perspective. Thanks also to Jerri Hurlbutt for her precise and valuable copy editing.

WHAT REMAINS

My mother, Alice Landau, died just after I completed this manuscript. She was always extremely supportive of my family and my career and, as an avid reader, she was very interested in my writing. Before she died, she was aware that the book was done and even shared the good news with her devoted caregivers, Jacynth Campbell, Dorothy Hewan, Rhodene (Michi) Mullings, and Pearl Hoeksema. My mother and my father, Henry Landau, came to the United States after World War II in order to start a new life of peace, freedom, and opportunity. Among their many accomplishments, they created a successful homebuilding and development business in Ann Arbor, Michigan and encouraged my sisters, my brother, Rick Landau, and me to attend college so that we could pursue our academic interests and establish careers. There was never any question about their dedication to our education. They instilled in me the values emphasized in this book—family and education—and those values will remain.

Providence, February, 2020

ABOUT THE AUTHOR

Carol Landau, Ph.D., is Clinical Professor of Psychiatry and Human Behavior and Medicine at the Alpert Medical School, Brown University, and a consulting clinical psychologist and lecturer. She is Co-Director of Psychology and Psychiatry in Primary Care in the Department of Medicine. She is senior author of three previous books and was an editor and contributor to *Brown Child Adolescent and Behavior Letter*. Dr. Landau is a member of the Senior Advisory Council for the Office of Women in Medicine and Science at Brown and is a past president of the Rhode Island Psychological Association.

Dr. Landau graduated cum laude from Brown University with honors in American Civilization. After working for 2 years in a psychiatric hospital, she returned to her studies and received her doctorate from the University of Rhode Island, where she was a University Fellow. She completed her residency in clinical psychology at Brown Medical School and then joined the faculty in the Department of Psychiatry and Human Behavior, where she served as Chair of the Clinical Appointments, Reappointments and Promotions Committee. Dr. Landau also maintains an independent practice in consultation and psychotherapy.

Dr. Landau has received numerous awards for her writing and teaching, including the Excellence in Teaching Award, the highest honor bestowed on Brown Medical School clinical faculty, and an award from the Beckwith Family Foundation for Teaching in Internal Medicine. Her work has also been recognized by the Rhode Island Medical Women's Association and the journal *Psychosomatic Medicine*.

Dr. Landau has served as an expert on depression for the American Psychological Association's Office of Public Affairs for many years. She has commented on depression for *The Wall Street Journal*, *US News and World Report*, the *International Business Times*, and *The New York Times*. Online, she was a contributor to *iVillage* and now contributes to *Healthywomen.org*.

Most recently, she has shared her expertise on the topic of hidden depression, or "smiling depression," with *Yahoo News*. She has also written about perfectionism on *HuffPost*, alcohol and stress reduction for *CNN.com*, and depression and suicide in college students for *The Providence Journal*. Her videos about comfort eating and the dangers of fad diets were produced by KnowMoreTV and are available on YouTube. Dr. Landau has given workshops and presentations on depression and student mental health to the Society for General Internal Medicine, the Higher Education Consultants Association, and the American Association of Medical Colleges, as well as at numerous colleges and universities and community organizations.

Originally from Michigan, Dr. Landau moved to Rhode Island to attend college and fell in love with the architecture, beaches, and people of Rhode Island, where she lives with her husband. More information on Dr. Landau's work and research is available at http://www.carollandau.com.

PART I

*Depression and Anxiety
in College Students*

How Parents Can Help

CHAPTER 1

Empowering Yourself to Support Your Teen and Prevent Depression and Anxiety

[Parents can provide] the warm cocoon of security wrapped around their children. [They can communicate] "You will always have someone there for you. You can strike out into the world, secure in that love, secure that love will find you."
—Ruth Ware, *The Death of Mrs. Westaway*

I f you are worried about your teenager going off to college, you are not alone. Despite the excitement and high hopes, you may be concerned about many issues; depression and anxiety are among the most troubling. Maybe you've seen the reports about how the rates of depression in young people are rising and that college counseling centers are overwhelmed. You might be aware of the controversy surrounding the novel and subsequent Netflix series *13 Reasons Why* or have read about or seen the Tony award-winning Broadway plays *Dear Evan Hansen* and *Fun Home*, both of which deal with depression, social anxiety, suicide, and family dynamics. You could also have more personal concerns—a family history of a mood or anxiety disorder or a teenager who has shown some symptoms of extreme sadness and worry. These are all understandable. Whatever your reason for reading this book, you will find the knowledge, support, and tools to help your teen, yourself, and your family.

The statistics on depression in college students are sobering. Current estimates vary, but at least 13% of students suffer or have suffered from at least one major depressive episode; many more may not have a formal diagnosis but still experience some symptoms of depression, like hopelessness and negativity. According to the Anxiety and Depression Association of America, anxiety disorders are the most commonly diagnosed mental health conditions, and among adolescents, the rate is 31.9%. Anxiety and depression are not equal-opportunity conditions: women significantly outnumber men in both categories.

Overall, this generation (sometimes called *Gen Z*) are more likely than previous ones to report that their mental health is poor. There are many reasons for this, including financial problems, family separations, gun violence, and sexual assault. In a study by the Pew Research Center, 70% of today's teens report that anxiety and depression are major concerns of their peers, whether or not they personally suffer from the conditions. A survey by the American Psychological Association found that 90% of today's teens report at least one physical or emotional symptom that they feel is stress related. These are troubling times. At the same time, Gen Z is significantly more likely to seek professional help. Depression and anxiety in college are not only mental health problems; they are major barriers to learning. The symptoms—inability to think clearly, negative thoughts and emotions, and worrying—also interfere with education—all the more reason for us to devote our energies to prevention and treatment.

A FAMILY-CENTERED APPROACH

You know your child better than anyone. It's important not to forget that, especially during the tumultuous teenage years. The philosophy of this book is not that you can perfect your child or turn her into an individual who will be totally immune from depression, anxiety, or the stresses of life. Instead, the book will combine my expertise with the latest psychological research and evidence-based treatment, and provide you with ideas, tools, and communication strategies that you can select to help you while raising your teenager.

Because every child is unique, there is no "one size fits all" approach here. Just as I will describe how cognitive flexibility is helpful to students, this book embraces the value of your flexibility as a parent. There is no one way to be a good parent, but rather this book can provide a collaborative process of using the material, combined with your best judgment and good communication with your teen.

Your family is the best source of security for children. "In everyone's life, at some time, our inner fire goes out. It is then burst into flame by an encounter with another human being. We should all be thankful for those people who rekindle the inner spirit." This quote, attributed to Albert Schweitzer, twentieth-century theologian and humanitarian, is especially true with respect to depression and anxiety, and for teenagers the support begins at home. Warm, consistent family support has been shown to be a powerful, positive force for everything from self-regulation to mood management to fostering positive relationships. Don't forget that you have the power to assist your teenager in a myriad of ways. We can't control what happens to them, but we can provide the reassurance and unfailing support that each child deserves.

HOW TO USE THIS BOOK

The goals of this book are to help parents and teens understand depression and anxiety and their symptoms, and to find ways to prevent them. The book is divided into four sections. First, I review adolescent development, depression, and anxiety and then share ideas for helping your teen develop a strong emotional foundation before going off to college. Next, I look at characteristics that are common to people who are vulnerable to anxiety and depression and review strategies to change these factors. Finally, I will give you a sense of what teens will experience on today's campuses.

This book focuses on preventing and managing the whole array of problems associated with depressed mood and anxiety, as well as the clinical conditions like major depressive episode (MDE), persistent depressive disorder, social anxiety disorder, and generalized anxiety disorder, which Chapter 3 describes.

A comment about the word *prevention*: people often falsely assume that preventing depression and anxiety is like putting fluoride in the water to eliminate cavities, but there is no parallel type of prevention for psychiatric disorders. I wish I could give you a magic formula that would make your child invulnerable and would prevent anxiety and depression entirely. Even if, as a society, we devoted the necessary resources to improving child and adolescent mental health, there would still be other factors at play, like genetic predisposition, poverty, unexpected losses, and severe stress. Moreover, some sadness and worry are part of the human condition. Despite these factors, you have a lot of power to help your teen.

This book is based not only on my clinical experience and research but also on the results of major efforts at preventing depression, especially the Institute of Medicine's (IoM's) 2009 "Report on Preventing Mental, Emotional, and Behavioral Disorders Among Young People: Progress and Possibilities." The report concludes that reducing risk factors, including vulnerabilities in the way teens think, learning coping skills, managing and tolerating distress, reducing family conflict, and developing relaxation and meditation skills—all the material included in this book, can be effective. Blending my clinical work with evidence-based strategies and the IoM consensus, I have created a roadmap for parents who want to prevent or minimize the effects of depression and anxiety in their teenage children.

We must help teens have a strong family foundation from which to face the stresses of college and adult life. As parents, you can lower the risk of your teen developing depression or anxiety by sending them off in strength, helping them develop positive traits associated with resilience and psychological health, and by teaching them skills to help lessen negative behaviors and thinking patterns associated with depression (see Chapters 4 through 10, in Part II). If you see some of the cognitive vulnerabilities to depression and anxiety, such as perfectionism, in your teen, you can help her adapt in a healthier fashion, as outlined in Chapter 12, and at some point, you can talk with her about what to expect during college. Sometimes college brings very positive changes, with freedom and opportunities galore. Other times, college is not a perfect fit, and that's okay; you will be there for your child to talk about it. She needs to know that some students become depressed or anxious and that there will be many ways to get help if she does.

Another aspect of preventing major depression is early identification and intervention. If we identify early symptoms of depression and anxiety, we can intervene before, during, and even after college in order to prevent the development of a disorder, like clinical depression or an MDE. We can reduce the effects of social anxiety disorder. Even if teens do end up developing an MDE, they will be less likely to relapse if they undergo optimal treatment, especially if it includes social support. You can help your child with depressed or anxious symptoms at any age by monitoring them and keeping the lines of communication open. It's also important to understand that even if your student does become anxious or depressed, there is still hope for them to do well, academically and psychologically, in college, especially with early identification and treatment.

This book includes all these types of prevention, based, in part, on the pioneering work of numerous psychologists who have been developing and evaluating effective, preventive strategies for over 30 years. We've known for even longer than that that anxiety and depression can be treated successfully. Our teenagers can benefit from what we have learned about preventing these conditions during college when parents provide the foundation and skills early on.

Each of the chapters that follow will provide you with the best information we have on managing emotions, changing behavior and thought patterns, and maintaining psychological health. All of these can help you and your teen. The information is primarily for you as a parent and, whatever your teen may say, parents are still the most powerful role models in their children's lives, so demonstrating healthy communication, attitudes, and behavior is crucial. You might want to talk with them about what you have learned or you might want to share the book with them. Although many teens say that they don't want more information and would prefer that you listen to them, every person is different, and education specifically about depression may be extremely helpful. There is also a chapter on communication skills (see Chapter 4), which may help you overcome what you perceive to be your teen's disinterest. Teens are hypersensitive and at times hypercritical, so this can be a challenge. You'll want to do the best you can, while understanding that you are not perfect. There will be times when you don't live up to your own ideals, but even these missteps can lead to fruitful conversations. Chapter 12 on perfectionism explores this issue.

Each chapter contains tips on educating, communicating, and demonstrating the relevant material. Moreover, because many issues surrounding teen depression and anxiety—pressure to achieve at all costs, lack of sleep, materialism, concerns about the future, discrimination—are reflections of problems in our culture, this book will also discuss the areas in which you can advocate for improvements in schools, colleges, and communities regarding mental health services and the other issues that we will explore. There are resources relating to the subject of each chapter at the end of the book, including material from governmental and professional organizations.

I do not advise that you and your spouse or partner sit down with your teen at the dinner table and start a lecture on depression and anxiety prevention after reading this book. Lecturing does not work! Instead, I want you to be informed and ready to seize other opportunities to engage with your teen as they arise. There are times when communication with your teen just seems to flow and they are as open to your views as you are to theirs. My hope is that this book will help you participate in these moments with a new perspective.

Over the past 30 years, I have treated students who are struggling psychologically, from many high schools, colleges, and universities in Rhode Island and Massachusetts, spending hundreds of hours meeting with them and their parents. I have enjoyed close relationships with several college counseling centers and with high school guidance counselors, and I have served as an informal consultant to many deans and mental health professionals at local universities. I also teach seminars on depression, behavior change, and development at the Alpert Medical School at

Brown University. Most of all, I have listened carefully to the concerns of teens and their parents. These experiences are the most powerful sources of knowledge, humility, and inspiration I have known, and have informed my work as a psychotherapist and educator and, ultimately, the content of this book. I realize how fortunate I am to be able to engage in these relationships every day.

A FEW WORDS ABOUT VOCABULARY

I will use the words *parent, mother, father, spouse,* and *partner* to reflect the diversity of family structures. I define a family as a group of people who are consistently committed to supporting and cherishing one another for the long term. This definition does not depend on gender, sexual orientation, or legal marital status. Raising children can be the most challenging and rewarding experience of our lives, so the more support you can get, the better. But that support is not limited to legal marriage or a biological family. I tend to use the terms *young women* and *young men* when referring to college students, but because I view younger teenagers as *girls* and *boys,* there will be points in this book when I refer to them as such without intending any disrespect. I alternate using the feminine and masculine pronouns and also use the singular pronoun *they* to reflect gender diversity.

THERE WILL BE NO BLAME HERE

You can be an excellent, caring parent and your teen may still fall victim to depression. There are too many other factors involved—biological, social, economic, and academic, just to name a few—for me to guarantee that your student won't become depressed. I don't want to blame or instill guilt in parents if a teen becomes depressed. I remember the days when mental health professionals would blame parents, especially mothers, for everything from depression to schizophrenia to autism, and I want none of that! As the psychiatrist Dwight Evans wrote, "The fact is 100% of teenagers would probably be depressed if parental perfection were the only way to prevent it."[1] We all make mistakes, even if we try our best. We need to be kind to ourselves, accept, and learn from our mistakes. Blame and shame

1. Dwight L. Evans & Andrews, L. W. *If Your Adolescent Has Depression or Bipolar Disorder: An Essential Resource for Parents* (Adolescent Mental Health Initiative). New York: Oxford University Press, 2005, p. 25.

interfere with that process. If your teen becomes depressed or has had a depressive episode, you still have the power to help her.

Support and listening are themes that run throughout the book. If you reflect on your life and difficult times, you'll remember how meaningful and affirming it feels to have someone who is there for you and listens in a non-judgmental fashion. It is also possible, though, that you did not have a supportive family of origin; because of that possibility, I have included a chapter about reflecting on your own childhood in order to better understand any challenges to parenting that may result from it (see Chapter 10). In this light, it is also worth noting another reason that a family-focused approach is the best for preventing depression: Some research suggests that up to 50% of the parents who bring their children for treatment are themselves depressed, so my hope is that you, too, will benefit directly from all of this material.[2]

I've written this book to help parents in different situations; you can use it to help you with high school students and college students, and with younger teens as well. If your teen is doing well but you want them to be prepared for the changes and potential stresses of college, the book has material on development and coping skills. If your child has some symptoms of depression or anxiety but is getting by, the book will help you distinguish between sadness and worry and clinical depressive or anxiety disorders. If he is being treated, you will find information about how to be supportive and how to access help on campuses. These are all aspects of prevention. The material is evidenced based, which is to say that it is derived from solid psychological research and presented within the context of my clinical experience with students and their families.

If you have a spouse, partner, or co-parent, it is preferable that you both read the book and talk about it in order to be more consistent. It might also be helpful to discuss it with friends and relatives. I hope that this book will be shared with high school teachers and guidance counselors as well as college faculty and staff. All of these professionals make enormous contributions to adolescent health and well-being.

WHY ME, WHY NOW?

My clinical work is a blend of many traditions and disciplines. My interest in family dynamics and my commitment to helping families grew from my first job as a social caseworker in a psychiatric hospital. I was able to observe

---

2. Evans & Andrews, *If Your Adolescent Has Depression or Bipolar Disorder*. pp. 3–39.

skilled psychiatric social workers interview over 500 families under severe stress. I learned that empathic listening, validation, and direct communication could make an enormous difference.

Graduate school, especially my studies with James Prochaska, allowed me to learn techniques of cognitive and behavior therapy and short-term psychodynamic therapy. During my psychological residency, I was supervised by David Barlow, who shared his expertise in treating anxiety and his commitment to evidence-based therapies. During graduate school and residency, I was also surrounded by highly motivated and creative students, many of whom are still friends. In my current therapy practice, I collaborate with each patient or family to create a unique plan, using therapeutic strategies with a focus on family dynamics. My use of distress tolerance and distraction skills began with reading the work of Susan Nolen-Hoeksena, whose groundbreaking research emphasized the need to combat rumination with distraction. Then my exposure to dialectical behavior therapy (DBT), developed by Marsha Linehan, provided both theoretical and practical material of enormous importance. Before then, too many psychotherapists, myself included, focused on change alone rather than on the acceptance that there will be some distress in life. Originally created to help patients diagnosed with borderline personality disorder, I have found that the clinical and educational skills DBT offers are extremely helpful to almost all patients. My colleague from our psychology residency, Steven Hayes, also emphasized acceptance when he created acceptance and commitment therapy (ACT).

For many years, I have also followed Jon Kabat-Zinn, Jack Kornfield, and other leaders in mindfulness meditation training. Kabat Zinn developed the mindfulness-based stress reduction (MBSR) program. Although many people have utilized mindfulness and meditation skills, Kabat-Zinn was instrumental in introducing the skills to the mainstream medical community. I have used his principles and teaching materials in my education of residents in internal medicine and medicine-pediatrics. My son, Robert Landau Ames, also introduced me to other forms of meditation.

I am passionately committed to the three areas of my career: psychotherapy, teaching, and writing for the general public. I view engaging in psychotherapy, especially with young adults, as a privilege. Many of the stories in the book describe my work with teenagers or young adults and their parents. This reflects my philosophy of family-oriented care, and in some situations, the severity of the presenting problem. I see many students alone as well. In addition to my clinical practice, I teach primary care internal medicine and medicine-pediatrics residents at the medical school at Brown, where our curriculum covers developmental psychology, psychiatric diagnoses including depression and anxiety, and behavioral self-management. I am proud to be part of our program in primary care internal medicine that has graduated several hundred well-trained and caring physicians. I have also treated doctors in training who suffer from depression and anxiety. More recently, I received a grant to develop a curriculum to prevent depression in young physicians. In addition, my family life has provided me with additionally informative experience. My husband is a college chaplain who worked at Brown for many years, so I have also gotten to know students who experienced psychological problems or a crisis and turned to a chaplain rather than a mental health professional. As a mother, I understand the challenges of communicating with teenagers. All these elements of my background have helped me appreciate the nuances of effective treatment and preventive strategies, as well as how students tend to react to their parents' attempts at communication and intervention.

This book is the culmination of my commitment to psychological community education. Even before graduate school, when I had a job as a community mental health outreach worker, I believed that psychological research should be shared with as many people as possible. I have delivered papers and seminars in community settings, written for many family-oriented magazines (sadly, many are gone now) and, more recently, websites, and also authored or coauthored three previous books. Now that we face a worldwide crisis of depression and anxiety in adolescence and in college, my hope is that you and your family will benefit from the knowledge I have gained over these years.

REMEMBER: YOU ARE NOT ALONE

Depression and anxiety are struggles for many families, but as a society we often treat them as shameful secrets. As a result, many parents and teens suffer in silence and fear. Isolation is not only sad, it can be terrifying. The musical *Dear Evan Hansen* addresses adolescent anxiety and depression by following two families, the Hansens and the Murphys. One of the most poignant songs is "Anybody Have a Map?" in which Heidi Hansen, Evan's mother, is upset and alone after having attempted to give Evan an energetic pep talk—but instead created mutual frustration. Meanwhile, Cynthia Murphy cannot seem to convince her son Connor to go to school and he storms away. The song reveals the fears and needs of many parents facing the psychological problems of their teens: "The scary truth is I'm flying blind and I'm making this up as I go." Continue reading the book: you will not be flying blind.

CHAPTER 2

Adolescent Development

Myths and Realities

Many children grow through adolescence with no ripples whatever and land smoothly and predictably in the adult world with both feet on the ground. Some who have stumbled and bumbled through childhood suddenly burst into bloom. Most shake, steady themselves, zigzag, fight, retreat, pick up, take new bearings, and finally find their own true balance.
—Stella Chess, MD

Before we examine the specific topics of depression and anxiety in college, let's look at the basics of adolescent development. There are, of course, entire books and courses devoted to this topic, but this chapter will give an overview of some of the most important issues. Our understanding of adolescence is changing all the time as different social norms develop and neuroscience research explodes with new knowledge. If your child is nearing adolescence, you are probably wondering what to expect; if your child is already a teenager you're probably asking, "Why is this happening?" and "Is this normal?" We will start to examine these questions here and look at them in greater depth in subsequent chapters.

Prior to the late nineteenth century, societies tended to view adolescents as miniature adults. G. Stanley Hall, the first president of the American Psychological Association, began the psychological study of adolescence, in the late 1890s. The first known use of the word *teenager* occurred in 1921. While Sigmund Freud outlined stages of psychosexual development, he focused on childhood. His youngest child, Anna Freud, was one of the founders of child psychoanalysis. It wasn't until the mid-twentieth century that the idea of a specific developmental stage of adolescence was more clearly delineated.

Erik Erikson was a brilliant development theorist who, with his wife Joan Erikson, published detailed articles on lifespan development. In his eight stages of psychosocial development, Erikson identified specific psychosocial crises, that, when resolved, resulted in a successful developmental task tied to each stage. Erikson and other theorists believed that the stages occurred in a predetermined order and that each stage built on the previous one. Other theorists have suggested that although there is some truth to Erikson's stages, development is not quite so linear and predictable.

Today, we understand that teens are creating a conscious sense of self that is developed in part by interactions with others. In other words, they are beginning the task of answering the question "Who am I?" If you think about the establishment of identity that way, it is an enormous challenge with a number of parts. An individual doesn't have one single, all-encompassing identity but rather physical, social, occupational, romantic, moral, and other identities. Adolescence, then, is an exciting and complicated time.

Jeffrey Arnett has further identified ages 18–24 as a stage of "emerging adulthood" between adolescence and adulthood. According to Arnett, emerging adulthood, which includes most college students, is characterized by instability, self-focus, and identity exploration. Arnett notes that individuals in this age group do not view themselves as "young adults" because in industrialized countries they tend to be unmarried and still in the process of education.

Adding to this complexity is the difficulty of establishing a clear identity if a teen comes from a group that the dominant culture has tended to marginalize in some way. For example, a teen from a racial minority, one who is a recent immigrant, or a lesbian, gay, transgender, questioning or queer (LGBTQ) teenager may struggle more with questions of identity. Given that identity forms in part by interaction, for teens who are "different," relating to people from the dominant culture who are critical or hostile can impede these teens' natural growth and development.

Adolescence was once defined by age, from 13 to 18 years, after the onset of puberty. Now, however, girls reach puberty by age 11 and boys reach it by age 12, on average. Puberty is a long process that includes a surge in the sexual hormones, estrogen and testosterone. These hormones cause physical changes, allowing the maturation of the reproductive organs and the development of such secondary sex characteristics as pubic hair as well as larger breasts and hips for girls and more muscle mass and facial hair for boys. Puberty also causes growth spurts, although not at a precise, predictable age. Adolescence may be marked physically by puberty, but development is a more complicated process involving social, moral, and cognitive changes. It culminates in young adulthood.

Despite ongoing changes in society's views of adolescence, a number of myths persist and cloud our understanding of today's teenagers. You may have bought into some of the myths of adolescence. Like all myths, each one has a kernel of truth but does not accurately represent the whole picture. We don't want to reduce teens to a stereotype, so we need to examine these myths with a critical eye.

NINE MYTHS ABOUT ADOLESCENCE

Myth #1: Teens only care about their friends.

It is true that friends may become the top priority for teens during their teenage years. It is likely that they will be a lot less interested in their parents and want to spend more time with their friends if things are going well. That doesn't necessarily mean that teenagers do not need or value their parents, though. Teens still tend to identify their parents as their most important supports, whether or not they have many friends. They turn to their parents when they are confused, hurt, or experiencing stress. They often want advice, but because they want to see themselves as independent, some teens may not ask for it, even as they are receiving it from a parent indirectly.

Your teen may make strong, long-lasting friendships, but that's not always the case during adolescence. Some teens are more introverted, and many teens have some conflict with friends. They still need you, their parent; they will learn about relationships from you; and they may want to share their concerns about friends from time to time.

In addition, 80% of children have siblings. We read a lot about sibling rivalry, but in reality, siblings can be another source of support, especially in dealing with and sharing complaints about a variety of topics (even you!). Relationships with cousins, grandparents, extended family, and close family friends can also continue to be sustaining relationships during the teen years. Teachers, coaches, and mentors in a job setting or volunteer organization can have an enormous impact on adolescents. Peers are therefore only one part of the adolescent picture, though they're certainly an important one.

Myth #2: If teens storm off or are quiet and sullen, they don't want to talk to you. They want and need to be on their own.

Not completely. Even if they are too upset to do so during a single exchange, your teen may still want to talk to you. As we will discuss, and as you may well remember, teens are not totally in control of their emotions. They usually do want you to inquire about their day, their friends, and their ideas and opinions, even if they aren't ready to share them at the moment. You may need to be patient and try again later. Timing is important, but availability is even more important. Saying something like "Okay, well, I'm around when you want to talk" may be helpful. Parents are the adults and need to keep the door open. Consistent, warm, and available parents will usually hear from their teens sooner or later.

Teens do need some privacy, though, especially when it comes to friends. They may not tell you about a party where alcohol was served, drugs were used, or there was a lot of sexual activity going on. This is indeed deception by omission and is quite common. They will usually be more likely to share with you when something important or dangerous has happened if you let them know that you will do your best not to lecture them and will listen. If you hear about a public incident, you might try to engage your teen in a general discussion of the issue, whether it is drugs or alcohol, unwanted pregnancy, or even sexual assault. That way you can hear their concerns and express yours without it becoming personal and therefore threatening.

Many of the teens I see are not only afraid of punishment but also concerned that they will upset their parents. In the Netflix series *13 Reasons Why*, Clay, one of the main characters, reveals in court testimony that he attended a party and took ecstasy with his friends. This is a surprise to his father, who later asks Clay, "Why is it that kids don't tell their parents anything, ever? . . . Are you afraid we won't understand? . . . So you're protecting your secrets." To this Clay proposes an alternative: "Or we're protecting you." Most often this is related to sex, drugs, and alcohol, but my patient Eileen, a 19-year-old college junior, was afraid to reveal to her parents that her boyfriend had broken up with her because she knew that her father would become irate and she would have to manage his emotions in addition to her own. In light of cases like Eileen's, it's important to try to keep your emotions in check if you want to know more from your teen. Moreover, communication is a two-way street. It is an interaction in which the unique chemistry between you and your teen affects your behavior as well. If you become extremely upset when your teen walks away from you, you will succeed in making both of you feel worse and impinge on his sense of privacy and growing autonomy. Chapter 10, on self-reflection, will help you learn how your psychological issues and vulnerabilities, family of origin, and culture may affect your parenting and your communication.

Older models of adolescent development described the adolescent stage as culminating in "separation," defined as detachment from parents, and also viewed conflict as a typical step in that process. More recent theories acknowledge that although teens need to experiment with and then adopt increasing levels of autonomy, their attachment to their families of origin can and should be ongoing, but in new, less immediate ways.

Myth #3: It is impossible to set limits on teens in today's world.

The world is undeniably more complicated than ever, especially given the widespread influence of the Internet and social media. We all know stories about preteens who can override parental controls on their computers and movie streaming services. Setting limits about sex, alcohol, drugs, and curfews still matters, no matter how difficult it may be. Setting limits on social media in particular is critically important.

Setting limits needs to start early and doesn't necessarily mean having endless arguments. Research suggests there are two important issues in limit-setting. First, it is important to monitor your teen. The word *monitor* may have negative connotations for you, and it is even more likely that it will for your teen, but what I am suggesting is to keep track of them in different ways. You can't set limits if you don't know what is going on. It is dangerous out there, and adolescents tend to underestimate risks. One option, for example, is to insist that your teen check in by cell phone. You can decide that they will lose privileges if they refuse to check in or do not answer when you call. In addition, smartphones can work both ways: Some parents track their teens' smart phones (it is preferable, though not technologically necessary, to do this with the teen's knowledge). Do not fall for the "Chloe's parents will be home so I may stay there overnight" ploy either! May stay there? You'll need to confirm this with Chloe's parents before allowing this overnight stay.

This relationship of accountability works both ways: Your teen needs to know where you are as well. I have seen some families where the parents decide that their teens' increasing autonomy means more parental freedom. This may work to a certain extent, but teens still need to know that parents are available to feel secure. Some parents justify their absences as "laissez-faire" parenting, but this approach does not usually come to a good end. It's that unsupervised house where the out-of-control parties are held.

Your style of setting limits is key. As we will discuss Chapter 4, on communication, you will want to model rational decision-making and listening skills, and your way of setting limits should be part of that process. An authoritative, but not authoritarian, style of parenting works best. Authoritative parents use explanations, listening, and persuasion. They set firm guidelines and limits, but their style also involves warmth, and involvement and allows teens to have some independence. Such parents try to provide support for increasing autonomy, but do so gradually. In contrast, the authoritarian parenting style is a restrictive, punitive approach that demands complete respect and obedience. This situation often leads to teens who later have trouble making decisions, regret the ones they were pressured to make, or rebel against their parents' rigidity. Indulgent parents do not set limits and, in many ways, allow their children to run the family. Usually these teens don't learn about limits and can run into problems with peers and teachers when they do face limits. In contrast, research suggests that the children of authoritative parents have greater self-esteem, a buffer to depression.

I do not mean to suggest that setting firm limits within a rational, warm parenting style is easy. It's not easy at all; normal features of adolescent development make setting limits with teens a challenge in several ways. Teens like to show off their newly found skills of argumentation and they may try to engage you in a protracted debate. While some debates, say about politics, music, and so on, may be enjoyable at times, you need to be clear that the limits you set in the name of safety are not up for debate. If you find yourself waffling when your teen persists in asking you about attending an activity, you don't have to say yes or no right away. You can say something like "I am not sure. I need to think." If you have a spouse or partner, you can add that you want to involve them. You can buy some time to think it over; but you need to be clear that you are in charge. Even if your teen struggles against them, limits are an expression of your values and your desire for your child to be safe.

It is also true that teens will not tell parents everything. They may omit many important details. Nonetheless, explaining your reasoning and your values makes sense; it gives your teen an opportunity to begin to internalize them and, ultimately, understand your reasoning.

Myth #4: You can keep family secrets from teenagers.

Not many. They tend to know what's going on at home. They are sort of like the song about Santa Claus, "They see you when you're sleeping; They know when you're awake." Teens can read your nonverbal communication, they listen, and they talk with other relatives. It's best to be as honest as possible, especially when the issue affects the whole family. You may need to discuss difficult topics like divorce and separation, substance abuse, and other serious illnesses over time and with questions answered. At the same time, you, too, have a right to some privacy, so you do not need to reveal everything. In addition, there may be details that would be harmful for your teen to know; this depends somewhat on his age. We will also explore this is in Chapter 4, on communication.

Some of the secrets you would like to keep, such as a family history of depression or substance abuse, are actually critically important to share. If a teen is struggling with symptoms of depression, knowing these secrets will help him understand more about the extended family and may help him feel less alone. Moreover, mental health professionals need this information to help them with their diagnosis.

Myth #5: School is the most important environment for helping a teen identify career interests and aspirations.

Not so—you are. School can be part of a team that supports your teen's dreams and hopes and prepare them academically. However, educators, like all of us, have strengths and weaknesses. To be sure, there are many exceptional, dedicated teachers and school counselors, but they may be overloaded or your teen may just not connect well with them. You, on the other hand are perfectly positioned to listen to, understand, and inspire your teen. A study at Harvard University education by Nancy Hill, Ming-te Wang and Jacquelynne Eccles found that three factors of parenting predicted achievement in teenagers: some autonomy and independence, warmth, and support for their dreams and aspirations. These results echo the authoritative parenting style. These same parental attributes can provide a strong family foundation for preventing or coping with depression.

In addition, supporting long-term career and other goals can give teens a sense of meaning and purpose, and these can improve coping with the stresses of adolescence. Meaning can come in many forms—career aspirations, work (paid or volunteer), caring for a family member, political engagement, and religious, spiritual, or ethical beliefs. These meaningful activities also engage teens at a moral level, move them away from being overly self-involved, and provide an orientation toward the future.

Myth #6: But really, isn't adolescent development all about hormones?

Not completely. When most people say this, they are referring to the sex hormones.

Puberty refers to the physical changes caused by hormonal changes; *development* is a more encompassing term. Let's look first at the issue of hormones and puberty. The sex hormones are only one type of 50 types of hormones that regulate all parts of biological systems. The multiple physical changes of puberty, combined with self-consciousness, can feel overwhelming to teens at times.

Mood changes are part of puberty, but they are not the whole story. They are also a result of brain development. The hormonal and neurological systems of our bodies are closely linked. Different parts of the brain mature at different ages. The prefrontal cortex (PFC) plays a role in mood, attention, and impulse control and doesn't fully mature until about age 24. Meanwhile, the amygdala, a walnut-shaped structure deep in the brain, matures earlier. The amygdala is part of the limbic system and is associated with impulses, emotion, and aggression. Researchers believe that the PFC needs to "come online" in order to regulate the amygdala, and until then, impulsivity and emotionality dominate. The amygdala is also associated with the automatic fear response that is, in general, protective—we need to know when we are under threat—but anxious individuals' brains overrespond and also have a fear response to the unexpected.

I stay away from comments like "Watch out—it's their raging hormones" for other reasons as well. In reality, we all feel surges of emotions at times. I've noticed that teenage boys are often criticized for any misbehavior by invoking testosterone. Women hear similar comments about "estrogen" throughout adulthood. Even recently, I've been in meetings where the lone man in attendance says something like "Whoa, there is too much estrogen in this room!" None of us wants to be reduced to hormones.

With hormones fueling some of development, it is clear that teens can use their parents' guidance. In her brilliant memoir, *Lab Girl*, Hope Jahren compares a teenager to a tree: "My tree had also been a teenager. It went through a ten-year period where it grew wildly, with little regard for the future. Between ages ten and twenty, it would double in size, and it was often ill-prepared for the new challenges and responsibilities that came with such height. It strove to keep up with its peers and occasionally dared to outdo them."[1]

1. Hope Jahren. *Lab Girl*. New York: Alfred A. Knopf, 2016, p. 27.

Myth #7: Teenagers are in constant state of risk-taking, intensity, and drama.

Teens often get a bad reputation based on our worst fears. We watch and read about drinking, rude behavior, out-of-control sexuality, and other varieties of risk-taking, and it is true that these things happen sometimes. But not all the time. Most adolescents work hard in school, at work, or both and care deeply about their families and about society.

Psychologists are in part responsible for this negative attitude. G. Stanley Hall popularized a term used by his colleague, William Burnham, labeling adolescence as a time of *Sturm und Drang*, a German phrase meaning "storm and stress" that was first used to describe the proto-Romantic eighteenth-century German literature and philosophy. Hall believed that teens will typically have conflict with parents, engage in risky behavior, and experience disruptions in their moods. These characterizations have continued to be themes in some developmental texts and certainly the mass media. The comedian John Oliver revealed how the view of teens as an out-of-control, irrational mass is promulgated by showing a series of video clips from local news broadcasts that included teens smoking Smarties candies, eating cotton balls, and crashing into fences on purpose, as if these were all teen trends rather than newsworthy exceptions. Although there is some truth to storm and stress, it doesn't represent all of adolescence.

As for conflict, some is an expected part of the process of adolescence, but only 20–25% of teens report severe conflict with their parents. Conflict is typical because teens need to test limits, but also establish more autonomy and become less dependent. Severe family conflict, however, is one of the factors that can disrupt development and so merits concern. And, as you'll see in Chapter 4, we can learn and teach strategies for assertive, not aggressive, patterns of interaction.

In contrast, the eminent cognitive social psychologist Alfred Bandura pointed out long ago that we don't want to create a self-fulfilling hypothesis. If teens and parents believe that risk-taking behavior is the hallmark of adolescence, it may well become a reality. He wrote, "I have often been struck by the fact that most parents, who are experiencing positive and rewarding relationships with their pre-adolescent children are, nevertheless, waiting apprehensively and bracing themselves for the stormy adolescent period. Such vigilance can very easily create a small turbulence at least."[2]

2. Alfred Bandura. The stormy decade: Fact or fiction? *Psychology in the Schools*, 1(3), 224–231, 1964, pp. 230–231.

Jeffrey Arnett also reviewed the field and found that in at least four areas—hazardous driving, substance abuse (with the exception of marijuana), crime, and unprotected sex—compared to 1990, today's teens are taking fewer risks. The causes for these changes are unclear but may be related in part to public policy, like the increase in the drinking age from 18 to 21, and public education efforts.

Myth #8: Teens (and all of us) are either "normal" or "crazy."

It's very common to hear a parent ask, "Is this normal?" It's a reasonable question and we all use that term now and then. But there is an underlying false dichotomy at work here—that people are either "normal" or "crazy" or, to use other pejorative labels, "abnormal," " psycho," and so on. The better question is, "Does my teen need help?" I believe in psychiatric diagnoses, but the idea that it's a question of "normal" versus "abnormal" is one reason people who need it do not seek help. Less than half of teens who have psychological disorders receive treatment. If teens believe that consulting a mental health professional or taking medication means they are "crazy," they will be resistant to getting the help they need because of their desire to fit in with their peers. In reality, psychiatric problems are on a continuum from mild to severe. In addition, the steadily increasing rates of depression and anxiety in teens are so high that if not "normal" they are certainly common. In addition, many teens who do not have a formal psychiatric diagnosis can benefit from help. Teens who are experiencing life changes, family problems, and learning differences all can benefit from counseling. Just as having the flu during the winter months is "normal," it does not mean that we wouldn't seek medical attention if we had a particularly bad case of it.

Myth #9: There is only one path through adolescence.

No matter what the development theory is of "normal adolescence," there are always individual differences based on culture, education, minority status, and income. And then there is the major role of gender. Young women and men alike can suffer from prescribed gender roles that are emphasized during adolescence. Teen development presents different challenges for boys than for girls that can have negative implications for depression. For teenage boys, the required traditional masculine role results in their loss of an emotional vocabulary and creates emotional disconnection. For girls, although we are teaching and encouraging them to be independent, ambitious, and career minded, they are still all too often being evaluated by their appearance. This leads to alienation and a disconnection from their bodies as well as from other girls.

YOUNG WOMEN: BODY DISSATISFACTION

Adolescence brings a set of biological, psychological, and social changes and the three realms interact. Puberty brings biological changes to girls and boys. For boys, deeper voice development and more muscle mass are consistent with a positive male body image. Therefore, most boys tend to feel more positive and have increased self-confidence about their bodies during puberty. Girls, on the other hand, develop wider hips and fuller breasts. Although this body type was part of the female ideal in years past, currently there is a "thin but buxom" ideal for female desirability. During adolescence, many girls focus intensely on appearance in general and, specifically, on their bodies. Body dissatisfaction is a result of the pressure to attain the unattainable. Even the most recent studies of teenage girls confirm that although they feel much more freedom to create and reach for their goals, they continue to feel judged as a sexual object or feel unsafe as a girl. If you think this is an outdated concern, consider this: In 2019, the American Civil Liberties Union (ACLU) of Wisconsin filed a suit against a school system because, "According to parents and students, in March 2018, cheer coaches at the annual Tremper High School cheer banquet—featuring over 150 people in attendance—distributed offensive and objectifying awards to female cheerleaders, including the 'Big Boobie' award and the 'Big Booty' award."[3]

Feeling bad about her body and appearance also can make a teen feel discouraged, and it can take a toll on her confidence. Tracy, a high school senior, summed it up for me one day: "Not matter what else I do, my bad body image is like, kept in a net on the ceiling. I try to keep it up there, but it can drop down on me at any time." We will explore ways to counter body dissatisfaction in Chapter 6, on healthy bodies and self-regulation.

3. ACLU Wisconsin. ACLU sends demand letter to stop sexual harassment in Kenosha Unified School District, February 21, 2019. Retrieved from https://www.aclu-wi.org/en/press-releases/aclu-sends-demand-letter-stop-sexual-harassment-kenosha-unified-school-district

Boys are hit hard by psychological expectations of adolescence, though in a different way. Boys are expected to become the traditionally "masculine" psychological type as soon as they reach puberty. This involves a repression of emotions, a lack of attention to empathy, and a certain detachment from people in general. For boys, this leads to a loss of close friendships. The kinder relationships between some preteen boys must change overnight into a back-slapping "bro," teasing, and taunting type of relationship.

Men are encouraged to become traditionally masculine by the same social and media forces that pressure women to have a thin ideal body type. In addition, institutions such as some fraternities, sports teams, and the military have traditionally enforced these behaviors. Psychologically, men lose the ability to become connected and receive social support. If they have been hurt or even traumatized, they are discouraged from talking things through. Thus, they lose a valuable opportunity to heal. Dehumanizing women can also be part of the toxic process, as the scandals in those same institutions reveal.

And it gets more complicated. Homophobia plays a big part in the over-emphasis on traditional male behavior. Don MacPherson, an activist, and former NFL player Wade Davis, Jr. testified to Congress after a scandal at the University of Colorado and other colleges where sex with women was used as a recruitment tool. Davis reported, "Masculinity is a performance. It's an act. We don't raise boys to be men. We raise boys to not be women or gay men. We don't affirm what a loving man is. . . . We're not supposed to be effeminate or care, love or be sensitive, and it's all utter BS because we are all these things." Davis and others have suggested that the root of homophobia is sexism. Gay men are "framed as being 'feminine,' as being 'weak,' as being 'less than a man'— which is the language of how we talk about women."[4]

In a fascinating study by Michael Kimmel, boys from a wide range of backgrounds were asked what made a "good man" and what made a "real man." A good man's attributes: "integrity, honor, being responsible, being a good provider, doing the right thing, putting others first, caring and standing up for the little guy." In contrast, a real man must "never cry, be strong, don't show your feelings, play through pain, suck it up, power, aggression, win at all costs, be responsible, get rich and get

4. Wade Davis, cited in Dastagir, A. Men pay a steep price when it comes to masculinity. *USA Today*, March 31, 2017.

laid."[5] The only overlap is the importance of being responsible. Moreover, the boys listed their father, coaches, male friends, and older brothers as the primary teachers of what "real men" are.[6] Thus, boys are severely instructed to lose their most human characteristics or risk being labeled a sissy, gay, or, worse, "like a girl."

I believe that the gender difference in diagnosed depression, where women outnumber men at the rate of 2:1 is real, yet I also believe that it is in part due to the consequences of prescribed traditional masculinity. Girls tend to be diagnosed with conditions that are "internalized," like depression and anxiety, whereas men are diagnosed with "externalizing" conditions, like substance abuse and behavior problems. If a boy is told that it is unmanly to cry or show sadness, he will resort to indirect expressions of emotion. He might try to repress emotions, smoke cigarettes, or drink to make himself feel better. These types of self-medication can lead to addictive or self-destructive behaviors, where the gender difference is reversed and men outnumber women. In childhood, boys have higher rates of diagnosed depression than girls; this trend reverses in adolescence. Some see this as a result of the repressive effects of school systems on young boys, but it is also possible that by the time they are in their teens, boys learn to stifle any direct expression of sadness, but in so doing create additional layers of difficulties and defenses which are manifest, for example, in higher rates of drinking. We will explore these issues more in Chapter 4, on communication, and Chapter 7, on healthy boundaries.

The price of body dissatisfaction in women and prescribed traditional masculinity in men is that teens may be punished or criticized for being themselves; they must conform to some fixed, outdated gender roles. These fixed roles go against one of the basic goals of adolescent development, identified early on by Erik Erikson: establishing a strong and authentic identity. The many forces that can lead to depression in teens are worsened by the pressure to conform, rather than create a unique identity. It is incumbent on all of us to free our teens from prescribed roles that deny them their individual and beautiful combinations of human qualities.

Despite these forces, I have also been impressed by the strengths of many teenagers. They have amazing internal resources. Daniel Siegel, the author of numerous books about adolescence, has pointed out that adolescents have four extremely positive characteristics: novelty seeking,

5. Michael Kimmel, Masculinity and our common humanity: "Real" men versus "good" men, in Way, N., Gilligan C., and Noguera, P. (Eds.), *The Crisis of Connection: Roots Consequences and Solutions*. New York: New York University Press, 2018, pp. 173–174.
6. Michael Kimmel, Masculinity and our common humanity, pp. 173–174.

social engagement, emotional intensity, and creativity. I am also struck by their curiosity, exuberance, and flexibility and by their desire to innovate—these are some reasons why I enjoy working with them.

Another strength of many teens is their interest in right and wrong, and they tend to have strong opinions about fairness. Adolescent moral development is in part a result of increasing cognitive and social development. Moral development is a process in which teens develop attitudes and behaviors toward others that are based on values, principles, and ethics of caring. Moral development is a crucial building block of adolescence. Lawrence Kohlberg extended the work of cognitive theorist Jean Piaget and suggested that there were stages of moral development, based in part on the ability to think independently. One relevant stage for adolescents is the conventional stage, characterized by an acceptance of society's norms about right and wrong, even when there are no immediate consequences for obedience or disobedience as there were in an earlier stage. The post-conventional stage occurs when an individual moves beyond conventional norms and considers abstract ethical principles. Social psychologist Carol Gilligan later criticized Kohlberg's theories because they were only tested in boys; she argued that women approached ethical problems differently from men, writing that women have an "ethics of care" based on personal context. She later wrote that she believed that this ethic of care "was not inherently limited to females, but it was certainly more common among her female participants. Therefore, the ethic of care was not designed to replace Kohlberg's theory of morality, but rather to complement it."[7] Similar to some critiques of Erikson's stages, I believe that Kohlberg's stages of moral development may also be more variable based on gender, experience, economic status, and other factors.

The major influencers of moral development are parents, other family members, teachers, and members of the clergy, as well as religious and educational institutions and the larger sociopolitical environment. It is clear that a positive relationship with parents is related to moral motivation and that parents who encourage questioning and thinking about moral development facilitate growth during adolescence and beyond. During adolescence, peer influences on moral development begin to play a larger role.

Trauma, death of a parent, and exposure to daily fear and violence can interfere with acceptance of the larger society's rules. Uri Bronfenbrenner has emphasized the role of social context and suggested that all individuals

7. Carol Gilligan, in Ball, L. Profile: Carol Gilligan, *Psychology's Feminist Voices*, 2010. Retrieved from http://www.feministvoices.com/carol-gilligan/

can slip back to an earlier moral orientation of self-interest when there is a breakdown of the familiar social order, as in war or a natural disaster. Bronfenbrenner's interest in social influences led him to be a cofounder of the Head Start program.

Teenagers are acutely aware of hypocrisy. They can tease out a contradiction between stated values and behavior. The "hidden curriculum," a term coined in 1968, refers to unwritten, unofficial attitudes, values, and behaviors that may conflict with the formal curriculum.[8] For example, what do teenagers learn when their school has a stated policy of empathic learning, yet bullies are not punished? Or what are teenagers to make of the rule of law in the face of the violence committed against young African American men by police? These and similar contradictions do not go on unnoticed by adolescents.

One of the criticisms of today's teens and college students is that they care only about financial success. This trend is somewhat understandable since it occurred after the global economic crash of 2008. It also seems clear that teens are reflecting the materialism of the current dominant culture. The cost of college and student debt is another factor. If we push our teens toward a small group of colleges and they continue to view undergraduate education as just another step on a ladder to attaining a very specific job or graduate school, then they are sacrificing an important developmental part of the college experience: self-exploration. The college experience can be a time for emerging adults to clarify their values, critically analyze them, and act on them. We will discuss moral development in college and the issue of service learning and community involvement in Chapter 15.

Overall, then, adolescence is both a challenging and exciting time of life. There are many reasons to maintain an optimistic view of development, which will avoid Bandura's self-fulfilling prophecy hypothesis. You can appreciate the time you have to watch your child grow and change, try out a whole new range of ideas and identities, and eventually emerge with a new, consolidated sense of identity. Granted, there may be some difficult days, but there are not many more rewarding experiences.

As your teen matures, a great time of transition occurs when he leaves home. Those fortunate enough to attend college face numerous challenges. They must learn to take charge of their courses, schedules, nutrition, sleep, social lives, and safety when they move away from home. They need to give up some of the facades of high school and explore more meaningful aspects

8. Phillip Jackson. *Life in Classrooms*. New York: Holt, Rinehart and Winston, 1968, p. 33.

of their personalities. And, they need to learn to manage their moods without the constant assistance of their families or high school friends. In short, this is a time to explore identity and consolidate self-regulation.

The next chapter explores depression, anxiety, and other conditions that interfere with adolescent development. This may sound scary, but you must remember this: No matter what, you *can* provide your teen with the security and support to make a successful transition to adulthood. As Victor Schwartz, Medical Director of the Jed Foundation states, "College is challenging; it can be hard, with some aches and pains, but most people get through it OK."[9] This can be true whether or not your student develops anxiety or depression. The connection with a caring family is the best foundation for adulthood and pushes back against the forces that separate us all.

9. Victor Schwartz, Personal communication, June 20, 2019.

CHAPTER 3

Traveling Companions

Adolescent Depression and Anxiety in Many Forms

The concern about the prevalence of depression and anxiety during college is not new. Richard Kadison, Chief of Mental Health Services at Harvard, sounded the alarm in 2004 that colleges were unequipped to treat the large number of students with psychological problems. Since that time, as discussed earlier, the mental health of college students continues to be a major issue. The American College Health Association reported in 2016 that although the college students they surveyed tended to be in good physical health, their mental health was poor. Over 35% of students reported feeling so depressed that they found it hard to function for a period of time during the previous year.

People use the word *depression* in a number of ways. I find it helpful to think of depression as being on a continuum--from least to most severe--as a state, a symptom, or a disorder. Everyone has a bad day or experience, a state of sadness now and then. It is human to respond with sadness to a loss or significant disappointment. If sadness continues over time for most of the day, it may be a symptom of a larger disorder[1], including a major depressive disorder (MDD). A major depressive episode (MDE) is a period of time when a person has the symptoms of a major depressive disorder (MDD). Similarly, the word "anxiety" can mean anything from mild worry

---

1. American Psychiatric Association. (2013). *Diagnostic and Statistical Manual of Mental Disorders, 5th Edition*. DSM-5 5th Edition, Washington DC: American Psychiatric Association.

to a clinical disorder like generalized anxiety disorder or social anxiety disorder. Severity, duration, interference with daily functioning and the presence of other symptoms are factors that distinguish ordinary sadness or worry from the depressive or anxiety-based syndromes.

My experience as an educator, therapist, and consultant is consistent with the statistical trend that all types of depression and anxiety in young people are on the increase. At the same time, working with them in therapy is enormously rewarding. I am delighted when I receive updates from former patients, long after they have left treatment. I received a short email from Jeff, now aged 32, "Working as a real estate developer, traveling a lot for my company, started dating a girl I met on Bumble. Thanks!" Jeff was never a man of many words, so this is enough to make me smile.

Many years ago, neither of us was smiling. When Jeff trudged into my office waiting room one December morning, he had that empty look that makes me worry. It seemed to take him forever just to walk the few steps from the waiting room into my office. He said he hadn't slept well and looked rumpled and forlorn; his jeans and parka were dirty, his T-shirt stained, and his sneakers drenched by melting snow. Jeff clearly hadn't been taking care of himself. His eyes were downcast; his speech was slow, and he sighed a lot as he started to tell me his story. Football had been Jeff's whole life. He had been a star receiver on his high school team in Texas. He told me that the book and television series *Friday Night Lights* were totally accurate in depicting Texas communities completely consumed by football. Jeff had been very excited to come to college and play, but he injured his knee during his sophomore year. Now he was going to be benched for a long time because he needed surgery. At the same time, his girlfriend from home, who had gone to another college, had broken up with him. After suffering physical pain came this major loss and disappointment. "Maybe I could have taken one or the other, but not both." Jeff was unable to concentrate on his classes and felt worthless. Like many people with depression, Jeff's thinking was distorted; he couldn't see any other positive aspects of his life, now that he was alone and off the team. These negative distortions caused Jeff to be preoccupied with worries and with concerns about his future.

If we examine Jeff's story, we can see that he was not just feeling sad or down for a few days; his depression was interfering with his functioning. Jeff was in fact suffering from an MDE—persistent sadness, hopelessness, loss of energy, poor sleep, and a decrease in concentration, with anxious features. These symptoms had persisted for more than 2 weeks, in fact, for several months.

WHAT IS A MAJOR DEPRESSIVE EPISODE (MDE)?

If your teen has been consistently depressed or irritable *or* has lost pleasure in daily activities (or both) for at least 2 weeks, it's possible that she is suffering from an MDE. Irritability is a frequently reported symptom of an MDE in adolescents. These symptoms represent a change from previous moods or behavior and interfere with functioning. Other signs of an MDE include the following:

- Marked weight loss, or change in appetite
- Sleeping too much or too little
- Lethargy or fatigue, loss of energy
- Feelings of worthlessness or excessive or inappropriate guilt
- Cloudy or indecisive thinking
- Recurrent thoughts of death, plans of suicide, or a suicide attempt
- Feeling restless or slowed down

To be diagnosed with an MDE, a person doesn't have to experience all of the symptoms every day but rather depressed mood or loss of interest and five of the other symptoms most of the time during the previous 2 weeks. Especially with teens, there may be aches or pains, headaches, cramps, or digestive problems without a clear physical cause. Other terms for an MDE are *clinical depression* or *major depression*. Even if a teen doesn't meet the criteria for an MDE, the existence of many of these symptoms and signs are enough to cause concern, especially if we are committed to preventing clinical depression.

After I explained my thought that he was suffering a major depression, Jeff replied, "I don't think so. My dad has that." I hear this type of comment a lot. His father had suffered debilitating periodic depressive episodes throughout Jeff's life but had never received any treatment. Jeff's father was usually quietly withdrawn, speaking very little, but at times he would explode in anger and several times had hit Jeff's mother. Jeff was, in fact, determined not to be like his father. I backed off a bit and asked Jeff to look at the checklist for depression. I also remembered the long list of people who have talked publicly about their depression, so I mentioned that Duane "the Rock" Johnson and NFL Hall of Famer and TV commentator Terry Bradshaw, both of whom had suffered from depression after they stopped playing football. Understanding that depression was common and that he had suffered two major losses helped Jeff see that he could be depressed and still be different from his dad. At age 19, many students want to avoid being like their parents, so I explained that Jeff's father's resistance to getting help was probably more relevant to his dysfunction than the depression itself. I then described how cognitive behavior therapy (CBT) could facilitate Jeff's overall rehabilitation. Jeff grew more motivated to engage in treatment and later requested a consultation for antidepressant medication as well.

Jeff's mother had struggled with opiate addiction but had gotten sober when Jeff was 12. When he wasn't playing football, Jeff had tended toward sadness but never had other symptoms before his injury. ("That's one reason I loved the game; it got me out of the house.") After about 12 weeks of CBT and taking an antidepressant, Jeff started to gain weight and sleep better. And our therapy helped him think differently. He began to examine other parts of his life that could make him feel worthwhile again. He was a hard-working student; his professors and other students tended to enjoy his comments in class. Contrary to the stereotype of the tough football player, Jeff had a sweetness and a kind sense of humor when he started to feel better. He also began to feel more hopeful that he could play football again after surgery and rehabilitation and maybe date again. We will look at CBT in detail in Chapter 11.

I asked Jeff whether he had suffered any concussions or other head injuries, but he said he hadn't had any and downplayed the risks of playing football. I have strong feelings about the damage football and other contact sports can inflict on young players (especially the resulting chronic traumatic encephalopathy), but I decided that treating Jeff's current MDE was more important than continuing to address and possibly disagree about the concussion issue. As it turned out, he played for another season but then became more involved in studying business.

When you consider Jeff's serious and disabling symptoms, you can see why it is so frustrating for a depressed teen when he hears someone say, "Just pull yourself together and move on," or "Think about others who are worse off than you are." It's not at all that easy. Depression is a serious condition. As one of my grad school professors liked to say, "We don't tell a person with a broken leg to just try walking on it; we treat it."

Jeff is one of many adolescents who suffers from an MDE. His story is relatively straightforward, but diagnosing depression can be a little tricky with teens because they may not express sadness; they may instead express it as irritability, or complain of a headache, stomach pain, or vague aches and pains. Sometimes, the major symptom is a feeling of emptiness rather than sadness. In my experience, emptiness is often a sign of a more serious depression. In other cases, depressed teens will become defiant and oppositional or irritable and cranky. The social butterfly and video game player may stop doing both and stay up late watching movies. Teens may also complain that life is meaningless or boring. Jeff was not suicidal, but suicidal thoughts and actions can be part of depression, again revealing that depression is a serious illness.

Jeff was at risk for depression because of his history of paternal depression, his mother's previous opiate misuse, and the loss of his favorite pastime. I have seen many students from different backgrounds having similar trajectories. They start college with some specific goals, only to encounter a barrier or suffer another loss and begin to experience symptoms of depression and anxiety. Often symptoms and conditions develop in the first or second year of college; many of the stories I share in this book fit this pattern.

The statistics on adolescent depression keep getting worse. Overall, a World Health Organization study found that 35% of full-time students in eight countries screened positive for at least one lifetime mental health disorder and 18.5 % met the criteria for a major depression during the previous 12 months. Estimates vary, but a 2017 review of national surveys of teens in the United States, aged 12 to 17, with a huge sample of 101,685, revealed that the current rate of major depression is 13.6% among males and a whopping 36.1% among females. The prevalence of MDE is highest among multiracial adolescents and Native Americans. Most studies show that teenage girls are diagnosed with depression at least twice as often as boys and that this difference continues throughout adulthood. This gender difference is a consistent finding across cultures, though experts don't agree on the causes of this difference. Women outnumber men when it comes to the anxiety disorders as well. We know that anxiety is often a precursor to depression.

Depression doesn't travel alone, either; usually (more than two-thirds of the time) another psychological condition, like substance use, attention deficit disorder (ADD), behavior problems, and especially anxiety, accompanies it. In some studies, depression and anxiety coexist for all ethnic groups about 50% of the time.

Anxiety disorders are also increasing as an individual diagnosis, with over 31% of teens having an anxiety disorder, according to The National Institute of Mental Health (NIMH). The vast majority of students seen at college counseling centers describe symptoms of anxiety or depression according to a survey by the Association for University and College Counseling Center Directors Annual Survey.

At one time, experts described depression and anxiety as "two sides of the same coin" because they both create profoundly negative emotions and worry. John Moe, journalist and host of the podcast *The Hilarious World of Depression*, called depression and anxiety the "Hall and Oates" of psychological disorders (though I think he needs an update, like Jay Z and Beyoncé). It is clear that there is a lot of overlap between the two conditions.

We can be a bit more precise about the differences between depression and anxiety. One model of the two conditions suggests that we look at negative emotion, positive emotion, and physiological arousal. Using this model, we can see that depression involves high negative emotion and low positive emotion. Anxiety also involves high negative emotion but is also characterized by high physiological arousal and worry. Therefore, the strategies to decrease negative emotion will help teens with depression and anxiety. Anxious teens will also need to pay special attention to calming physiological arousal, which we will discuss in Chapters 6 and 8.

It has long been known that, in adults, anxious depression, or what the DSM-5 terms a "major depressive episode with anxious distress," is a more serious form of a major depressive disorder (MDD). Recently, scholars have been examining similar patterns in teens. One study found that anxious depressions in children and teens were associated with greater severity, as well as a pattern of depressive symptoms including more severe sleep problems, somatic complaints, more severely depressed mood, and more frequent suicidal ideation. It is important to understand the impact of the anxious depression in order to provide the best care. In addition, social anxiety disorder is a common precursor to depression in teenagers.

Calli is an example of a teen who struggled with both social anxiety and depression. A high school senior, she came to see me because she had been accepted by the college of her choice. This would have been great news for most students and was for Calli, but only to a certain extent. Once all the stress and work of the college admissions process was over, Calli was hit hard by the realization that her best friend would be going to another college in a different part of the country, that she knew no one going to the same college, and that she would be moving far away from home. Calli and Karen (the best friend) had been friends since kindergarten and had attended the same Catholic schools throughout their education. It hadn't really occurred to either of them that going to different colleges would be a major loss. (A similar comedic version of the strength of female friendship during high school is depicted in the delightful movie *Booksmart*.)

Social life in high school had not been easy for Calli, either. She was temperamentally shy as a child, like most people who develop social anxiety disorder. With the exception of Karen and a few male "buddies," she tended to be by herself. She felt like her style did not match that of most of the girls at school. Small in stature and soft-spoken, Calli wore colorful bandanas and T-shirts over black legwarmers. Overall, however, Calli was not unhappy. She had her friend Karen, was an avid cyclist, and loved to read. She spent many contented hours in her room devouring novels and listening to music. This had the added benefit of keeping her from hearing her parents' frequent arguments.

Calli's father was a senior executive at a major corporation who nonetheless worried excessively about money. He was also extremely perfectionistic and critical, and Calli suspected that he, too, might be depressed; he appeared to cope by having a drink or two as soon as he got home. Her mother, a successful self-employed tutor, had always tried to be home with Calli and her brother Tom as much as possible. Her mother was not a shrinking violet; when Calli's father would come home and become critical of her, she would stand up for herself, but this would end in loud and angry mutual recriminations. Calli's mother confided in Calli that, due to her Roman Catholic faith, divorce was not an option. Calli's older brother Tom was now in college, so her "partner in family misery" (said with a rueful smile) was no longer around. Family conflict, like Calli's, poses a risk for teens for developing anxiety and depression.

Upon being accepted to college in March, Calli started to worry. Any question about college (the subject that, according to Calli, "is ALL anyone asks about") would trigger her fears. This would lead to an almost endless series of "what if" questions: "What if I don't like my roommate?" "What if I can't find anyone to sit with at dinner?" "What if my classes are too large?" "What if I need help with an assignment?" "What if I am too afraid to ask questions in class?" "What if I get homesick?" (Even teens from unhappy families become homesick.) The fear of humiliation that she had staved off in high school erupted, and she started to perseverate about the social outfalls of college. Calli was also concerned that the financial cost of college would put additional pressure on her parents and that they would fight even more as a result.

These worries turned into endless and repetitive thoughts. Calli would reach no new conclusions about them, but would find herself losing hours thinking about all these issues. She lapsed into rumination, and her happiness about college faded. She started to have experience symptoms of depression, including trouble sleeping, being less able to concentrate in school, and crying easily. Finally, she confided in her English teacher, who referred her to me.

Normally, Calli would have shared her worries with Karen, but she knew that Karen was struggling financially to afford college and she did not want to add another burden. Calli was experiencing the loneliness and sadness of rumination. Depressive rumination is the repetitive, compulsive focus on thoughts that cause feelings of sadness, anxiety, and distress. Calli did not know that any fear, when shared with another person, loses much of its power. Once the fear is named, you can feel more connected to the person you confided in. That person may have similar concerns or may be able to help brainstorm solutions. A good friend can also help you find ways to distract yourself. It's very difficult to pull yourself out of a ruminative process alone.

We had our work cut out for us. I was happy to be of help to Calli and do what we called a college readiness psychological boot camp or "mood prep." As I got to know her, I discovered that she was a keen observer of social interactions and had a wicked sense of humor. Her parents disapproved of her pointed sense of humor, so Calli had come to devalue it. Some of her social anxiety was based on a fear that friends would disapprove of her as well—back to the "what ifs:" What if she said something that inadvertently insulted someone? What if she made a joke and the other person didn't think it was funny? What if she was humiliated in class for making an unusual observation?

While Calli and I were not able to eliminate her social anxiety, I could help her develop her new skills for dealing with her worries. I asked Calli to create a list of her worries. We then started to brainstorm solutions for each one. For example, if she found herself in a large class, she could focus on one or two people who were sitting near her. People with anxiety disorders often respond well to exposure—that is, facing specific fears. I tend to take a gradual approach, so Calli took a meditation class over the summer and I also encouraged her to start chatting with other people in her favorite bike shop. This is sometimes called "exposure with guided mastery." Calli needed to develop relaxation techniques to quell her anxiety. Fortunately, the meditation class provided one such skill, and we also practiced some breathing exercises. Calli did not have panic attacks, so these were relatively straightforward; we'll explore these techniques in greater depth in Part III of this book. We also talked about her worries about Karen, and Calli realized that Karen would, after all, be able to listen to her concerns, just as Calli wanted to be there for Karen.

By the end of the summer, Calli was feeling supported and more confident. She had developed a growing sense of social self-efficacy, a concept I will discuss more in Chapter 5. In addition, Calli had begun to view herself in light of her skills, not her deficits. For example, I emphasized that she was fortunate to have her "rock-solid" friendship with Karen, as it revealed that she possessed the skills to develop and maintain close relationships and could use these abilities as she got to know new people. We also discussed how she might obtain psychological help on campus, if necessary (see Chapter 17).

Calli continues to stays in touch. When I last heard from her, she was a junior in college, writing for her school newspaper and planning to go to graduate school in public health. She wrote, "You were right: I am not a social butterfly, but now I lead meditation classes and have a 'small band of true friends' [a quote from the novel *Emma*, as Calli was a Jane Austen fan] and I hardly ever ruminate."

WHAT IS SOCIAL ANXIETY DISORDER?

Social anxiety disorder involves persistent, intense, and ongoing fears of social situations that might involve being watched and judged by others. People with social anxiety disorder, like Calli, are especially afraid of behaving in a way that could be embarrassing or humiliating. Their fears are so severe that they interfere with school or other activities. According to the NIMH, over 9% of adolescents suffer from this disorder, which, especially when combined with an MDE, can be debilitating to students and interfere with key elements of development.

The other type of anxiety we will address is generalized anxiety disorder, which is, according to one of my patients, "like worrying on steroids." People with generalized anxiety disorder worry out of proportion to the issues at hand. The worries are persistent and excessive and interfere with daily activities and may be accompanied by restlessness, feeling on edge, being easily startled, difficulty concentrating, or sleep disturbances. The worries may focus on major issues such as job responsibilities or family health or on minor ones such as times of appointments or completing chores. People with generalized anxiety disorder know they are worrying unnecessarily but cannot control their thoughts. We will discuss this topic more in Chapter 13.

When John Mulaney interviewed fellow comedian and actor Bill Hader, they both revealed that they suffered from generalized anxiety, not just performance anxiety or stage fright. In another stand-up routine, Mulaney stated that he had been overly worried since he was a youngster, although he joked that at that time, based on watching cartoons, he was most worried about quicksand. Hader revealed that while he was on *Saturday Night Live*, he was almost always severely anxious and hyperventilated at times. He was helped by therapy and meditation. Both successful men now take antidepressants, prescribed for anxiety, and are open about this fact.

Other anxiety disorders that can appear among teens (and others) include obsessive-compulsive disorder (OCD), phobias, panic disorder and post-traumatic stress disorder (PTSD).

Teen depression or anxiety can strike anyone, independent of social class, ethnicity, or education level. The same negative cognitive distortions affect teens from every background. However, people who live in severe poverty or have suffered abuse are more likely to suffer from depression. There are also some ethnic differences in getting treatment. When Margaret Cho, a Korean-American, was a teenager growing up in Los Angeles, she began to feel depressed, but in her family and culture, expressing such feelings was taboo, as was psychotherapy. As we discussed in the previous chapter, like many girls, Cho also was demoralized because she did not conform to the thin body type that much of culture holds up as an ideal, which led to other problems, including an eating disorder. Ultimately, she learned to cope with depressed feelings by writing, as is evident in her work as a stand-up comedian. She is now also an advocate for the lesbian, gay, transgender, bisexual, queer, and questioning (LGBTQ+) community and for better mental health awareness.

Like depression, anxiety often has its roots in childhood and is sometimes associated with a traumatic event. Kwame Onwuachi, chef and author, describes his first experience with anxiety, at age 3, when his mother left his abusive father for the first time, "In the immediate aftermath of my mother's leaving . . . an unsteadiness crept into my life that hasn't left me yet. That moment introduced a new cast of characters into my world, a new vocabulary of trauma. Worry—that I had done some vague thing wrong but didn't know what it was; confusion as my mother rushed past me . . . an asphyxiating sense of anxiety."[2]

Baron Vaughn, actor, comedian, and co-star of the Netflix series *Grace and Frankie*, has a history of depression. At one time, he was so depressed that he was isolated, staying in bed in his apartment, subsisting on Cheerios, and bathing in dishwashing detergent because he would not venture out to buy basic supplies. Vaughn said that growing up in his small town, the African American community there had little understanding of depression. He saw it as something that "white people do," or for the well-off, "that you have the time to sit there and become depressed."[3] This attitude is not uncommon, and it does the most damage in communities where poverty and stress increase the need for treatment.

These stories also reveal that there are often long delays, sometimes up to a decade or more, between the onset of symptoms and the time when depressed people receive treatment. The vulnerability during adolescence is

2. Onwuachi, K. *Notes from a Young Black Chef: A Memoir*, p. 33.
3. Baron Vaughn, in J. Moe. *The Hilarious World of Depression* [Podcast], Episode #8: Baron Vaughn and His Inadvisable All-Cheerio Diet, January 30, 2017.

seen with other psychiatric disorders as well, with about half of all lifetime mental disorders beginning by age 14 and three-quarters by the mid-20s. Given what we now know about the positive results of early intervention, delays in treatment are tragic.

Journalists contact me periodically for articles about what some call "a smiling depression." This term is often applied to someone, usually a woman, who is struggling to maintain a positive façade while suffering internally. Sydney was a good example of this phenomenon. Sydney's parents had asked her to come see me because she was beginning to skip classes and do poorly on exams. She was still eating and sleeping well but was having difficulty focusing in her classes and felt sad most of the time. However, you wouldn't have known this if you met her. Unlike Jeff, she arrived at my office early, greeted me with a big smile, and was impeccably dressed in fashionable black pants and a matching top, with serious makeup and hair styling. About her appearance, she said, "I'm from the New York area, so of course, it's going to be black!" Sydney continued to smile a lot in our first session, almost as if she didn't want to trouble me with her worries.

After that first session, however, it became clear that Sydney had struggled for many years with feelings of sadness and feeling "less than" because she had been diagnosed with ADD and other learning differences in junior high school and had struggled through high school with the help of numerous tutors. She wanted to work in the fashion industry but wasn't sure in what capacity and didn't actually know how college would fit into that. Her father and stepmother were adamant that she go to a 4-year liberal arts college, so she was giving it her best shot.

Sydney tried to feel better from the "outside in" by always maintaining that forced smile, perfect attendance at school, and stylish clothes, but I could see the fragility just beneath the surface. Although Sydney's college had support services for students with learning differences, she was embarrassed because the center was located in the middle of a larger student services building, so Sydney felt that she would immediately be identified and stigmatized when she walked in. The fact that she had cut herself off from support had caused her academic career to deteriorate significantly. My first step as a therapist was to help Sydney rethink her high school career because in my view, it was an important success that demonstrated her perseverance in overcoming her challenges.

Sydney's story reveals several important issues. One is that despite her attempt to hide her pain, she had symptoms of a persistent depressive disorder (PDD), as she had felt sad for over a year and experienced ongoing hopelessness and pessimism. PDD is a longer-term condition than an MDE. The primary symptom of PDD (also called *dysthymia*) is a depressed mood or loss of interest that lasts for at least 2 years. Compared to the list of MDE symptoms mentioned earlier in this chapter, people with PDD have two rather than five of the other signs and symptoms. A lack of productivity, low self-esteem, and an overall feeling of inadequacy are common symptoms. These feelings last for years and may significantly interfere with relationships, school, work, and daily activities. People with PDD, then, have fewer symptoms, but the symptoms last longer.

Sydney's story also reveals how depression interferes with the educational process. Her learning disabilities were challenging but manageable, but her response of shame and humiliation led to depressed mood and made high school more difficult. Then, in college, the situation worsened because her tutors were gone and she was too embarrassed to get help. While PDD doesn't cripple teens as much as an MDE, it can definitely hinder their ability to develop and to enjoy life. Many areas of life can seem gray—work, school, family, and social activities. Moreover, PDD leads to episodes of major depression 75% of the time, and because of this high risk of MDEs, we need to see it as a major focus of prevention. It can be difficult to identify this disorder at first, because it may seem like a string of bad days or feeling low throughout a season or semester. Using careful, specific questioning, a mental health professional can help make the diagnosis. When people with PDD also suffer from episodes of major depression, the condition is known as a "double depression."

In addition to MDD and PDD, other diagnoses related to mood are disruptive mood dysregulation disorder, premenstrual dysphoric disorder, postpartum depression, stress response syndrome (formerly adjustment disorder), and the bipolar disorders. Intentional self-injurious behavior (SIB), which can involve non-suicidal cutting, scratching, and burning; may be associated with depression; but could also be associated with many other conditions like trauma, emotional dysregulation, anxiety, eating disorders, and alcohol use disorder. Approximately 10–23% of adolescents engage in SIBs. A self-injurious teen merits professional attention to help sort out the stresses and diagnose possible psychiatric conditions.

Sydney was struggling with both depression and ADD. Depression is often accompanied by another condition; this is called "comorbidity." Teens with both ADD and depression tend to suffer more, unless both are addressed. Even with academic support, many teenagers with ADD have a difficult time in school. It is such a struggle for them to maintain their focus and composure during the day that it takes a toll on them psychologically and they can become demoralized. For this reason and others, including family history, there is a correlation between ADD and depression, MDD, and PDD. With appropriate treatment, support, and patience, however, many students with ADD are quite successful. I shared this fact with Sydney in order to help her gain a more optimistic attitude.

The take-home message for parents is that in addition to advocating for their teens at school, it's important to help them find another area where they can thrive, like work or an extracurricular activity that they enjoy. It is also important to monitor symptoms of depression periodically in order to diagnose a depressive episode, should one occur. Sydney's parents were so committed to the idea that a 4-year liberal arts degree was necessary that they did not encourage Sydney's various strengths, interests, and talents. While Sydney wanted to try to finish her degree, I suggested that she also get a part-time job at a nearby women's clothing store where would be able to feel valued.

These formal diagnoses are just the tip of the proverbial iceberg. In addition to major depression, chronic minor depression, and the anxiety disorders, we should also concern ourselves with the young people who have symptoms of depression or anxiety that are not debilitating enough to have a specific psychological disorder. It is difficult to estimate these numbers, but added to the one in five teens having a formal psychiatric diagnosis, it is clear that we are facing an epidemic.

WHY DEPRESSION AND ANXIETY? WHY TEENS?

People can have different vulnerabilities to depression, and different levels of vulnerability as well. A model called the diathesis-stress model presents this formula: High Stress + Effects of Vulnerabilities = Depression. In this model, the word *diathesis* means sensitivity or predisposition and can include biological, psychological, and social factors. Using this formulation, we can examine how to prevent depression and anxiety by identifying what we can and cannot change.

Let's start with stress. Given the numerous changes we delineated in Chapter 2, it is no surprise that adolescents report greater levels of stress than preadolescents. Even the positive changes associated with adolescence can be stressful given the sheer number of them. Think about all of them—the multiple results of puberty, changes in friends and family, more demanding academics, additional responsibilities, and, yes, college planning. Social stress of the last 20 years also plays a role, with increasing concerns about climate change, globalization, school gun violence, and economic uncertainty. Each change requires a response of adaptation so that an individual can return to the previous state of balance, and as a result, stress develops.

Of course, adapting to negative change is more difficult. In addition to academic pressures, teens express concerns relating not only to their personal financial futures but also to the economic and ecological future of the planet. On the individual level, the clear negative relationship between stressful life events (SLEs) and depression has been well documented for over 40 years. In one study, 62% of depressed teens reported at least one severe SLE in the year prior to their depressive episode as compared to 27% of non-depressed teens. Similarly, early exposure to stressful and negative life or environmental events in early childhood is a risk factor for anxiety, as in the case of Kwame Onwuachi. In adults, the loss of an important relationship is often a trigger for a depressive episode. For teens, it may well be worse, because teens are more sensitive to rejection than younger or older people and are still quite vulnerable if they lose a family member. Furthermore, girls are more rejection sensitive than boys, which may be an additional factor in the gender difference in depression and social anxiety disorder.

We cannot protect our teens from experiencing stress; it is part of life. However, given the amount of positive and negative stress, we can and should help teens understand that they do not need to avoid stress but, rather, can learn to cope with it and learn the best techniques for stress management and self-care.

AN OVERVIEW OF VULNERABILITIES TO DEPRESSION AND ANXIETY
Biological Vulnerabilities

Remember that the teenage brain is undergoing a tremendous amount of change. In Chapter 2 we saw that the prefrontal cortex (PFC), the area of the brain behind the forehead that controls the regulation of complex cognitive, behavioral, and emotional functioning, doesn't mature until age 24, while the amygdala––the part of the brain that is associated with emotionality and impulsivity––matures earlier. So, in a way, the PFC needs to catch up. (This is one reason many say the auto insurance companies are justified with their higher insurance rates for those under 25.) Healthy brain development creates new nerve cells; this is called *neurogenesis*. At the same time, the brain engages in "synaptic pruning," which causes other unnecessary connections in the brain to atrophy. This growth process changes the connectivity between and within different regions of the brain. If development goes well, the PFC can communicate better with other parts of the brain. However, while the PFC is developing, it susceptible to being negatively impacted by stress, drugs, and physical or psychological abuse.

At one time, depression was referred to as a "chemical imbalance." This formulation was helpful in that it debunked the idea that depression was merely a failure of willpower. However, in reality, the situation is much more complicated. It's not just that a brain has too much or too little of a particular neurotransmitter, a chemical in the brain that serves as messengers and regulates processes in the body. Some of the neurotransmitters involved in depression are serotonin, dopamine, and norepinephrine. Serotonin is associated with important parts of physiological function, including sleep, eating, and mood. Dopamine creates feelings of satisfaction and influences motivation. Norepinephrine helps the body recognize and respond to stress. It affects blood cells and blood vessels and can raise blood pressure and can also trigger anxiety. You might be saying, "I thought it was all about serotonin." Indeed, at one time, many experts did believe a lack of serotonin was the cause of depression. However, the evidence for this was only that many of the medications that were used to treat depression increased serotonin levels. With respect to anxiety, the same neurotransmitters are involved, which may explain, in part, the overlap between these two types of disorders.

More recent research suggests that depression may be a result of chronic inflammation. Other factors may also be involved. Serotonin does reduce inflammation, and one study found that depressed people had higher levels of a marker of inflammation, C-reactive protein (CRP), in their blood samples. The study was able to establish an association between depression and inflammation, but not clear causality. However, it might account for why many people, including teens, who are medically ill and often suffer from higher overall levels of inflammation become depressed. To keep up to date with see the latest research, I recommend the NIMH website, listed in the Resources section.

Finally, there is a genetic factor involved: Depressed people have more blood relatives who also suffer from depression, and the same pattern is true for people suffering from an anxiety disorder. It is helpful to understand the biological vulnerabilities to depression and anxiety, but at this point in time, we cannot change our genetic predispositions. As for brain development, we cannot make major changes, but we can protect it, as we will see in the chapters on healthy lifestyles (see Chapters 7–9).

Developmental Vulnerabilities

In the psychological domain, teens face a number of changes as well. I view adolescent psychological development as a parallel process to the new brain developments and pruning that we see in the brain. Teens come to see their parents, friends, activities, and values from a new point of view and leave some behind, a type of pruning. Meanwhile, they will move away from their families, seek more autonomy, and create new relationships and goals, a process akin to neurogenesis. This is positive psychological growth and development, but it, too, requires change and adaptation. At the same time, the critical phase of development can be interrupted if a teen suffers a trauma or major psychiatric illness, experiences a parents' high-conflict divorce, or misuses substances. My colleagues and I often used the expression, "She lost time" when we see a young adult who misused substances, usually alcohol, during her teenage years. The building blocks necessary for a successful adulthood may be missing, and as parents and therapists, we need to understand and address these developmental needs.

Cognitive Vulnerabilities

There are numerous cognitive vulnerabilities to depression, including perfectionism, a lack of self-efficacy, body dissatisfaction, and heightened self-criticism. Two other vulnerabilities are "negative attention bias"—that is, a greater sensitivity to unpleasant events and attitudes, and a tendency to ruminate. This repetitive, compulsive focus on negative thoughts is destructive. People who tend to ruminate become depressed at higher rates than people who do not. Those who do have some symptoms of depression and also ruminate tend to go on to have chronic, more long-lasting depressions. People who ruminate also tend to develop anxiety more often and to develop the more complicated psychological disorders, combinations of both anxiety and depression, so rumination is the engine that propels people toward sadness, worry, and depression.

Although there are similarities in the cognitive vulnerabilities between depression and anxiety, there are differences as well. The ruminations of depressed people tend to focus on hopelessness, loss, and self-criticism and are more focused on the past. Anxious people tend to worry more about the future and tend to avoid situations they judge to be dangerous, even though that may not be the case. Anxious individuals usually feel they do not have enough control over the environment.

Social Vulnerabilities

As for social vulnerabilities, we have long known that they have a major impact on teens. One of the most robust findings in psychological and public health literature is that social support is critically important to maintain and support health. When family support is lacking, teens suffer in numerous ways, and intense family conflict can lead to depression. Early adverse life events, especially trauma, are associated with depression and anxiety as well. Divorce and the loss of a close relative also create vulnerabilities. The specifics of family communication can be modified, so Chapter 4 is devoted to the power of a positive family environment.

A lack of social skills and problem-solving create additional vulnerabilities. Isolation and a lack of social support consistently accompany depression. This may explain why students with social anxiety disorder often become depressed, because they avoid social contact for fear of humiliation and thus have less access to social support. Conversely, increased social support is therapeutic. The digital age can lead to greater connection but also has opened up a huge world of social vulnerabilities, including cyberbullying, sexual shaming, fat and appearance shaming, and negative social comparisons. Finally, entrenched gender roles can have a negative impact on all teens' development, especially those who are gender nonconforming. These social forces are detailed in Chapters 9 and 13.

LET'S REDUCE THE PRESSURE

In 1988, the theoretical physicist and educator Freeman Dyson wrote, "We must be careful not to discourage our twelve-year-olds by making them waste the best years of their lives preparing for examinations."[4] Thirty years later, we have not heeded his wisdom. The stress to perform, specifically for college applications, has intensified dramatically. When I talk with high school or college students, they reveal that their mental health is being sacrificed to the pressure of the college application process. I believe that much of the time spent on creating "marketing plans" for teenagers' college applications would be better spent helping these students identify their interests, values, and goals and then finding a college to match. This point of view has been expressed by educators William Damon and William

---

4. Freeman Dyson. *Infinite in All Directions: Gifford Lectures Given at Aberdeen, Scotland, April–November 1985* (1st ed., Gifford lectures; 1985). New York: Harper & Row, 1988, p. 9.

Deresewicz and *New York Times* columnist Frank Bruni and is linked to the issue of sadness among college students. Students who feel that college admission was some sort of "game" or "branding exercise" (two common words in titles of books about the process) are likely to have feelings of self-doubt and lack self-efficacy when they arrive on campus. So why not replace just one AP course with one on identifying psychological strengths and strategies for self-regulation? Some high schools are now offering such courses, but they are variable in quality and not all students take them. Mood management should be a required course for all teens, not only those going away from home to college. Part-time college students often experience even greater stress with the additional burdens of financial concerns, working, and commuting. Their peers who do not attend college have high rates of depression as well. New York State has an excellent model for prevention in that, as of 2016, it requires mental health education in the schools in all grades.

On a public health level, though, most schools and families are not reducing the overall competitive pressure. I've seen several school newsletters publish the names of colleges to which their graduates have been accepted. I know that is part of the mission of "college prep" schools and reflects their marketing plans, but my fantasy is that they would publish the names of students who are exceptionally happy, collaborative, and content, who are taking a gap year, or who are committed to social justice. As parents, we could talk a little less about college admission and more about psychological development and education for its own sake. I realize that it is difficult to go against the dominant culture, but a lot is at stake here. Mood management should become at least as important as academic preparation for college; it really is more important. We teach children how to drive and how to do some basic cooking, but we don't teach them how to deal with the stress, conflict, and temporary sadness that can lead to anxiety and depression.

As a parent, you are the key to making sure that adolescents receive this education. This is a complicated endeavor, and families can provide this foundation for lifelong good health. You must take care of yourself as well. Your family background or your current primary relationship may trigger impulses to over- or under-react to your teen. The specifics of your teen's issues may evoke your own vulnerabilities. The challenge of parenting may be difficult at times, and self-care and self-compassion are important parts of the process. We will pay attention to your psychological health along the way, especially in Chapter 10. This is not only to help you; there is ample evidence that children's mental health is directly affected by the mental health of their parents. You will find ample support here.

Finally, if your student is experiencing symptoms of depression and anxiety and their coping skills and your support are not sufficient, getting help early is critically important and effective. Chapter 14 is devoted to this topic. There have been enormous advances in the treatment of depression, including antidepressant medication and psychotherapy. Evidence-based therapies like CBT have been specifically evaluated and shown to be effective in treating depression and anxiety. Interpersonal therapy (IPT) is another evidence-based treatment.

If we understand that, in addition to everything we have covered in this chapter, depression and anxiety are major barriers to learning, then the need to prevent them makes even more sense. It's a challenging endeavor, but one that is manageable and important to embrace.

PART II

Strong Foundations

CHAPTER 4

Communication Skills

Active Listening, Avoiding the Lecture

Feelings of worth can flourish only in an atmosphere where individual differences are appreciated, mistakes are tolerated, communication is open, and rules are flexible—the kind of atmosphere that is found in a nurturing family.

—Virginia Satir

When I'm working with teenagers or young adults, I usually ask them to describe family dinners because this gives me insight into how their families communicate and how much time they spend together. I saw Kevin, a 16-year-old struggling with sadness, for cognitive behavior therapy (CBT) a few years ago. When we first made eye contact, I could see Kevin's deep need for support. He was carefully dressed in a rugby shirt and khakis, an outfit that somehow made him appear to be even younger. Kevin felt left out—he said that he didn't have "his place" in school because his interests seemed to be different from those of the other kids. He also believed that his father, a successful self- made plumbing contractor, thought he was "stupid." Kevin told me about dinners at home: "Man, it is just awful. My sister and I are sitting there; my mom tends to be a little quiet. My dad asks how our day was, so we say 'fine' and then he launches into a lecture. I can't even tell you what the lectures are about—his views on politics, education, whatever! It is sooo boring." I met with Kevin's parents some months later. Here's how his father, Brendan, described family dinners: "I grew up in a family where my father was a pretty severe alcoholic, but mostly a silent one. But we always knew that during dinner, he could erupt at any moment or that he and my mom would start arguing about his drinking. My brothers and I would pick at our food, really tense, and my stomach was always in knots. It was never a fun time. I vowed then that we would not have silent dinners in my own family. I come from a long line of Irishmen and do not want to people to think that we are all alcoholics but my dad really changed when he drank. Now when I ask the kids questions, they don't say much, so I feel like I should keep the conversation going." Donna, Kevin's mom, said, "I tend to be silent because I know it's so important to Brendan. But it's not working. When the kids were little, it was okay, but now that Kevin is older, it's uncomfortable."

You can see where the communication in Kevin's family broke down despite Brendan's best intentions. He meant well, but he lacked the skills to talk and, more importantly, listen to his family. Perceiving this pattern, Kevin tuned out and didn't really try much. On the plus side, the family did tend to eat dinner together and was committed to making things better. The potential strength of their family foundation was damaged by this lack of skills and, over time, unhealthy habits.

You might wonder how the family dinner is related to the issues of communication and depression. A landmark 10-year study from the National Center on Addiction and Substance Abuse (CASA) at Columbia University revealed the power of the family having dinner together. The family dinner is a "protective factor" for children and teens. Teens from families who eat dinner together tend to do better overall; family dinner can serve as a buffer from the stresses of adolescence. Teens who eat dinner with their families get depressed less often and are less likely to smoke, drink, do drugs, develop eating disorders, or consider suicide. At the same time, they are more likely to do well in school, delay having sex, eat a varied diet, and develop larger vocabularies. *Time* has quoted Robin Fox, an anthropologist at Rutgers University, as follows: "If it were just about food, we would squirt it into their mouths with a tube. A meal is about civilizing children. It's about teaching them to be a member of their culture."[1] It is also a place to share.

A comfortable family dinner allows everyone in the family to share their thoughts, concerns, and feelings and devote time to being together. It can be a daily ritual for connection, support, and enjoyment. Much of modern life creates barriers to this experience, though. Parents are often rushing home from work, and dinner preparation can be hurried. Some mothers are so stressed between the time they get home from work and dinner that

1. Robin Fox, in Gibbs, N. The magic of the family meal, *Time*, June 4, 2006.

they joke that those are "the arsenic hours." Teens, meanwhile, have to interrupt their homework, activities, or athletics. All of these factors can be overcome, but it takes making a family meal a priority, which itself entails reworking schedules and cooperation among family members.

Family dinners also give a snapshot of overall family communication. Let's take stock of the big picture. The goal of communication is connection. Think back a moment to times when you felt understood, accepted, and cared for. These are powerful and foundational experiences that provide security and stability. These are the same experiences we want for our families. Even though teenagers have a push-pull relationship with parents, knowing that their parents are available for connection allows them to grow. The challenge is to figure out how to engage them. A family dinner is but one way to do this.

A PLAN TO IMPROVE PARENT–TEEN COMMUNICATION

The key to improving communication with teens is active listening. It is important for teenagers to be able to share thoughts, feelings, and the events of the day, and to know that they will have an engaged and attentive parent who will not be judgmental. It's not always easy to help them open up or get the conversation started. Here are a few suggestions:

- Ask open-ended rather than closed questions (those that can be answered with "yes" or "no"). Instead of saying, "Did you have that test today in Spanish?" try "Tell me how things went in Spanish class today." Use additional open-ended questions for follow-up. Rather than asking more rapid-fire questions ("Was it this? Was it that?" etc.), try something like "And what about the rest of the day?"
- Try to remember and bring up details from the previous conversations. For example, "I know you were concerned about the try-out for the debate team today. Tell us how it went."
- Ask clarifying questions to indicate that you understand. "It sounds like you were feeling a little worried about time pressures, but you knew that you understood the material. Is that right?" Don't feel bad if you get it wrong and your teen answers, "No that's not it." Usually she will clarify, which keeps the conversation going. And if not, you could say, "Oh, sorry, tell me more about it. I'd like to understand better."
- When expressing yourself, use the word *I*. If you have a disagreement, rather than say, "That was really rude," you can say, "I feel upset when you walk out of the room when I'm trying to have a conversation." The

first sentence is likely to elicit defensiveness, whereas the second might lead to a conversation as to why your teen walked out.

- Similarly, avoid the words *always* or *never*. This is a basic skill used in couples and family therapy. Even if it feels true to you to say, "You never remember to take your dishes to the dishwasher," a simple "Please take your dishes to the dishwasher" will be more effective.

- Don't limit the conversation to school performance. That feels like a lot of pressure. Ask about your teen's favorite interests, activities, or friends. What did they enjoy most and least about the day? Or be creative and encourage conversation on other fronts like current events, movies, books, sports, and music. Although it's more important to listen, sharing your interests and feelings will also create more interaction.

- Choose your time. Ideally, you want undivided attention. Usually that means when your teenager comes to you. Many parents find that the darker, quieter car ride is a good venue, but both parties must unplug first. Once again, you can also learn a lot by listening when you are giving your younger teen and her friends a ride.

- As for disagreements, choose your battles. We will discuss limits in a later chapter, but raising an adolescent requites a lot of limit-setting. Don't waste your time on the small stuff. Suppose Rachel, age 14, comes downstairs wearing a partially backless dress when the family is going to a religious service. You are not thrilled, but she has a shawl that she begrudgingly says she'll also wear "if you're gonna get all mad and stuff." You know that this isn't a bad compromise but are still annoyed that you will have to keep an eye on Rachel during the service. Nonetheless, you could say, "That wouldn't be my first choice about what to wear, but I appreciate that you will bring the shawl." Similarly, if your teen has his own room, let it be. Yes, it's probably messy, but unless you see insects crawling out from under the door, you have more important issues to deal with. If you don't choose your battles, you may end up establishing a "nag-ignore" style of communication.

THE IMPORTANCE OF VALIDATION

Validation is an experience that lets your teen know that you have listened to and heard them and also that you understand. When offering them validation, you are not necessarily agreeing with them, but you are indicating that you can appreciate their situation. Validation shows your teen that you are taking them seriously and grasp the essence of what they are trying to say. It shows both empathy and acceptance and makes people feel safe. A safe and accepting home environment allows teens who may be struggling with depressive symptoms to feel more secure. Following are some suggestions for practicing validation:

- In order to validate an experience, try to name what your teen is feeling. If Marie says, "That coach was so unfair to yell at Laurie that way, what a loser!" and is expressing a lot of body tension, reply, "Wow, looks like you are really angry at her. I can understand why you would be." Notice that you are not agreeing that the coach is a loser—there may be another side to the story and a better way to describe the situation—but you are appreciating Marie's experience.
- Like all skills, active listening and validation require practice and patience. It may sound awkward at first, but you will get the hang of it over time. Even if your teen teases you sometimes about using validating words like "It sounds like," "I get it," "Tell me more," or, my favorite, "Help me understand," if you are demonstrating genuine interest, they are learning what is important to you and what should be important to them.
- Try not to skip over validation and jump right to problem-solving, a tendency shared by most parents. This brings us to an important topic.

What Not to Do

- Don't jump in with problem-solving. Adolescence is a time of increasing independence. Usually, when your teen shares a problem, he wants to be heard and understood. You may want to share how you see the issue, but don't rush in with solutions. Brendan, for example, was worried that Kevin was "too sensitive" so ended up lecturing him about being "tougher." Brendan's concerns, then, led him to give unwanted advice that made Kevin feel worse. That may not be what your teen wants; you may not have all the information and it may close down the conversation.
- Don't forget the power of nonverbal communication. You may be verbalizing acceptance but sending a mixed message by frowning or sighing. This happens especially when you are struggling to understand the situation but are having a negative reaction. In short, it can happen when your teen pushes your buttons. Back to Rachel's dress: It was better to state how you felt rather than agreeing but frowning and otherwise displaying negative nonverbal judgment.

- Similarly, your teenager may feel unable to express anger directly but may be clenching his fist or showing muscle tension in the jaw. For example, back to Marie and the coach: If, at first, she wasn't talking but had tightened her fists in frustration, you could say something like, "You know, you look like you're angry and I'd like to know more about that" to validate her feelings. You may get it wrong, but that's not the important part. The important part is being open and acknowledging that directly expressing anger (or other feelings) is good. You can always listen to clarifications.
- More than anything else, try to avoid invalidating comments. This can happen when your teenager is frustrated and you don't quite understand why. Avoid critical comments like "That doesn't seem that bad" or, especially, "Aren't you overreacting?" It's much more helpful and facilitative to say, "Help me understand." Sometimes you might make an invalidating statement because the material is upsetting to you and you don't want to engage in the conversation. Again, it's better to express yourself rather than trying to brush it off. You may have faced a lot of ostracism as a teen, for example, so when Sally is upset by a minor misunderstanding with a friend, you think it shouldn't be so upsetting compared to your loneliness. But it is important to Sally, so you could ask her to tell you more about her relationship with her friend. We'll look at how understanding your issues can affect communication, in Chapter 10.
- Teens can be harsh critics, so they may even be scornful at first. Don't let the shrug, "Whatever," or classic eye roll push you away! You are the parent and you know your goals. You can ask them to tell you more when they use these responses. Another option is to ignore them, but be persistent, try again another time.

BRING ASSERTIVE COMMUNICATION INTO THE FAMILY

One of the most popular self-help books of all time is *Your Perfect Right,* by Robert Alberti and Michael Emmons. Originally published in 1980 and now in its 10th edition, it has sold well over 1.3 million copies. These numbers and the success of the many subsequent books, some specific to women's issues, reflect the fact that developing an assertive communication style is an ongoing challenge. The title of the book is based on the philosophy that all of us have certain rights, including the right to state our needs and wants, the right to be treated with respect, the right to express personal feelings, values, and opinions, and the right to say yes or no. Assertive communication reduces stress and increases feelings of self-confidence.

Assertive communication stands in contrast to both non-assertive (or passive) and aggressive communication styles. Passive or unassertive communication occurs when people do not speak directly or clearly about what they need. It is self-denying, inhibited, or indirect. It may be that they do not feel that they have the right of self-expression. They may fear retaliation, want to avoid conflict, or lack the verbal skills to engage in a discussion. An example is when your teen wants to disagree but looks down, avoids eye contact, and mumbles. Whatever the reason, in the long term, passive communication results in frustration and a lack of control, and can lead to demoralization and depression. Although a passive person may seem to be apathetic or detached, that is usually not the case, because everyone feels repressed or disappointed when our needs are not met. Another example of passive or indirect communication is reacting to a request, like working late, by shrugging and agreeing in a quiet voice, even though you really want to say no.

Another form of indirect communication is passive aggression. You may ask your partner to clean the pots and pans after you've loaded the dishwasher and your partner agrees quietly. Then you see the sink pile up with pots and pans. Some also call this "guerilla communication." In this example, rather than arguing, the passive-aggressive party first avoids conflict by verbally accepting a request, but they then avoid performing the requested behavior later. In this case, it's usually best to point out the pattern of behavior and try to see what feelings elicited it. It's also okay to express your anger about it.

Aggressive communication occurs at the expense of the other person. Aggressive behavior may include anger and accusations about motivation. Some people who are aggressive also engage in humiliation or ridicule. There are many reasons that people engage in aggressive communication. Some have never seen an assertive communication modeled and have only one way to express themselves. Others lack empathy and are not interested in communication but rather in getting their way or "being right." Still others feel insecure or inferior and therefore let things build up and then explode or defensively attack. Teenagers can be particularly prone to aggressive communication styles because of the powerful combination of intense feelings they experience and having a brain that's not fully developed as far as impulse control is concerned. One example of aggressive communication is when 17-year-old Tom is angry about the consequences of breaking his curfew and throws down his backpack, swears, and walks away.

When *Your Perfect Right* was first published, the authors focused on a straightforward formula for self-assertion. First, determine what you want. You may want to simply express an emotion, as in "I am excited about the game tomorrow," or "I am disappointed that we can't have dinner together tonight." Other times, you might want to express a reaction to a person's behavior. In this case, you need to identify the specific behavior under discussion. When responding to Tom, you could say, "I feel angry that you came in at 2 A.M. last night and did not respect my concerns about coming home late." Then it's important to add your request for the desired change: "In the future, I want you come in on time." You have the right to express how Tom's behavior makes you feel. In this case, you also need to set a limit. As much as teens protest about limits and consequences, if they do not get them, they can feel insecure.

However helpful the assertiveness structure is, effective communication requires more than a simple formula. Sometimes, a person who has not been assertive tries to change and is met with defensiveness or even a counterattack. It is therefore important to plan accordingly. If you were interrupted at a business meeting and said, "When you interrupt me, I feel frustrated. I'd like to finish my thought," a defensive response might be "Why are you making such a big deal about this?" In this situation, it's best to refer back to the behavior rather than to make any generalizations: not "You always interrupt me at meetings," but "As I said, I'd like to finish my thought without being interrupted."

It's also effective to start with an empathetic response and then make the request, and the request needs to be made as a statement, not a question. For example, you could say to your son, "Josh, I know you're really worried about your exams, but I need some of your time to help clean the house and I'm hoping we can do that Thursday afternoon." In this way, assertiveness training has developed into more general social skills and communication strategies.

Cultural differences about valuing and encouraging assertiveness may also affect you and your family. Psychological research confirms that culture influences how people form and maintain relationships and communicate with their families. In *Lab Girl*, Hope Jahren writes about a walk with her father, reflecting on the cultural impact on her own family relationships: "We had long since established the habit of not speaking as we walked the two miles home; silent togetherness is what Scandinavian families do naturally, and it may be what they do best."[2] In a review article

2. Jahren, *Lab Girl*, p. 9.

about these differences, one study found that families from Northern European backgrounds valued individualism, whereas families from East Asian backgrounds emphasized harmony. Latinx families value what the authors term "convivial collectivism," a model of interdependent relationships with the expression of open and frequent positive emotion, regular social get-togethers, and politeness.[3]

In "How to Disobey Your Tiger Parents, in 14 Easy Steps," the Taiwanese-American author Michelle Kuo describes the difficulties of asserting herself with her traditional parents: "I have been moved by young readers asking me how they should talk to their parents about career choices. Their families come from Nigeria, China, Ghana, India, South Korea. These teenagers and college students are at a crossroads in their lives. They want to change the world but fear losing their parents' love."[4] Kuo suggests taking note of parents' worries and showing them stability and persistence. These various cultural attitudes and values affect self-assertion. The differences may not apply to everyone in a cultural or ethnic group—that would be stereotyping—but the important issue is for you as a parent to think about your cultural background and how it may affect your ability to be assertive, how you engage in open communication with your family, and how you might want to change.

In earlier editions of their book, Alberti and Emmons focused a lot on individual assertive exercises. These are still valuable, especially for women and minorities, who continue to face discrimination and microaggressions. In later editions, the authors acknowledge that not every situation requires an assertive response. If you have lots of time, for example, you may not mind if someone jumps ahead of you in line at a coffee shop. You can develop assertive skills but not feel the need to use them all the time.

You can use the skills of assertion in the context of any family discussion. If all members of the family are able to express themselves and be heard, then communication will be improved. With teenagers, it's quite possible that anger will be an issue. Teenagers need to know that it is okay to feel angry and to express it, so long as it's in a direct and constructive way. For example, you could tell Tom, "I get that having no cell phone for two days makes you angry, but please try to say it. It's okay to tell me. What's not okay is doing things like swearing, throwing your backpack

3. Belinda Campos & Kim, H. S. Incorporating the cultural diversity of family and close relationships into the study of health. *American Psychologist*, 72(6), 543–554, 2017, p. 545.

4. Michele Kuo. How to disobey your tiger parents, in 14 easy steps. *The New York Times*, April 14, 2018.

down, and storming off." If Tom sees a direct exchange and resolution of anger modeled at home, he will be more likely to be able to internalize it. Similarly, if you share the work interactions about being interrupted, Tom would see that direct self-assertion can work.

TEENAGE BOYS AND COMMUNICATION

As we discussed in Chapter 2 on adolescent development, one price of traditional masculinity is the repression of emotions and emotional vocabulary. We expect men and boys to be stoic and self-contained. In this time of social change, the view of traditional masculinity is being challenged on many fronts, from the #metoo movement to the economic and social fallout from unemployment. Many social norms have changed, and many young men understand the need for change.

A bit of history: Some of the founders of family systems therapy were able to identify the impact of family dynamics on individual development. However, many of them emphasized, and were blind to the limits of, traditional gender roles. Things changed when four members of the Women's Project in Family Therapy—Marianne Walters, Betty Carter, Peggy Papp, and Olga Silverstein—challenged these enforced gender roles. This took courage, as it always does for people demanding change, and the women were severely criticized by men in the field at that time. They were labeled, among other things, "confrontational." After this reassessment of family therapy, much of the attention was focused on women being able to be freer to be more assertive and show more agency, as we will discuss in the next chapter. At that time, many feminist therapists also acknowledged that flexible gender roles would help men as well.

Today, young men need our help. Esther Perel, a family systems therapist, commented on the stresses on young men, at a conference, "The Masculinity Paradox." She observed, "We behave as if the feminine is natural and unavoidable, while masculinity has to be acquired, often at a high price. Masculinity is hard to develop, easy to lose."[5] My experience is that young men who are not seen as sufficiently "tough" are often bullied and criticized, even within their own families, with comments like, "Man up!" or "Be a man!"

5. Esther Perel in Lauren Dockett & Simon, R. The Masculinity Paradox: What Does It Mean to Be a "Real" Man Today? Psychotherapy Networker, January/February 2019. Retrieved from https://www.psychotherapynetworker.org/magazine/article/23

The high price of masculinity has been borne out by research. The American Psychological Association published new guidelines for working with men and boys in 2019, 12 years after similar guidelines were published about women. In an article introducing the guidelines, the following research was cited: "traditional masculinity—marked by stoicism, competitiveness, dominance and aggression—is, on the whole, harmful."[6] Traditional masculinity is associated with considering risky behaviors normal and engaging in them more often, compared to men with less traditional attitudes. Omar Yousaf and colleagues found that men who accepted traditional notions of masculinity were more negative about getting mental health care than those with more flexible gender attitudes, which is especially relevant to the psychological development of teenage boys. Taken together, it is clear that we have an opportunity and a duty to help young men develop a language of emotions, to communicate with their family and friends more directly, and not to fear vulnerability, as vulnerability can ultimately lead to better health.

COMMUNICATING ABOUT YOUR TEEN'S DECISIONS: WHAT WE CAN LEARN FROM MOTIVATIONAL INTERVIEWING

Decision-making is an important part of adolescent development. We want our teens to learn to make safe and healthy choices, despite peer pressure and a media environment that glamorizes most unhealthy choices. Motivational interviewing (MI) can provide us with some helpful tips. I teach at the medical school at Brown University and my students are primary care physicians. They are committed to both the treatment and prevention of illness. Therefore, they spend time trying to change their patients' lifestyle choices (like being overweight and sedentary, abusing alcohol and drugs, and smoking). These can be frustrating interactions. For many years, doctors tended to lecture their patients. Yet the vast majority of people who are overweight or smoke already know these conditions are bad for their health and still have trouble making changes. Hearing your doctor go over the material in greater depth is not helpful and usually does not lead to change.

In contrast, MI is a style of interaction where it is assumed that a person is ambivalent about change. A woman who drinks too much alcohol might

6. American Psychological Association, in Pappas, S. APA issues first-ever guidelines for practice with men and boys. *Monitor on Psychology, 50*(1), 34, 2019.

want to cut back but knows that it is relaxing for her to drink. Or a smoker knows that it is bad for his health but has had such a long-term addiction that he feels helpless to change. There is ample evidence that MI is much more effective than giving advice or lecturing in helping people change. A systematic review of the evidence concluded that "motivational interviewing appears to be most effective for stopping or preventing unhealthy behaviors such as binge drinking, reducing the quantity and frequency of drinking, smoking and substance abuse."[7]

What can parents learn from the research? Many of the skills in MI have been derived from the general communication skills we've explored so far, especially active listening, empathy, reflecting, and clarifying. MI can be valuable when your teen is trying to make a decision. Although it might be tempting to say, "Of course, the logical answer is x or y," MI will be much more engaging and useful to your teenager in helping her come to a decision. With MI you can assist your teen with their ambivalence by eliciting the pros and cons of each option. Let's say your son wants to quit smoking. After you've gone through the pros of quitting (health, appearance, better stamina for sports, money) and cons (needs nicotine to relax, his friends all smoke, helps him concentrate), you can ask questions like "What helped you when you tried to quit last year?" "What got in the way of quitting?" "What concerns you most about smoking?" "What do you think would be the biggest benefit of quitting?" Hearing the list of reasons to change will increase his motivation. Only when he says he wants to quit can you ask, "How can we help?" "Do you want to take a step now to quit?" When MI goes well, it feels like a comfortable dance. When you lecture someone, they become defensive and it feels like a tug of war.

WHY YOU ARE STILL TEMPTED TO PROBLEM-SOLVE AND LECTURE

Ever since you became a parent, you have probably spent a good deal of your life helping your child grow. When they were very young, they needed you to protect them and keep them safe. As they reached school age, they needed your advice, guidance, and problem-solving skills. However, as a teenager, a key coping skill is for them to learn their own problem-solving methods and

7. Helen Frost, Campbell, P., Maxwell, M., O'Carroll, R. E., Dombrowski, S. U., Williams, B., . . . Pollock, A. Effectiveness of motivational interviewing on adult behavior change in health and social care settings: A systematic review of reviews. *PLoS ONE*, *13*(10), E0204890, 2018.

skills. This developmental change is a process that affects you, as well as your child. Of course you still want to give your best advice and solutions; you've probably gotten pretty good at all that. I know I often felt that I had just mastered parenting in one stage of development when my son was on to the next one. Problem-solving is just not what most teenagers need. It's better to support them in creating their own process of decision-making, and this will be much more meaningful and important in the long run. It will give them self-confidence and competence, described in the next chapter.

As for lectures, they seem to be the go-to mode, especially when other people are not responding. That is what was happening to Kevin's father, Brendan. Brendan couldn't understand why Kevin and his sister didn't want his advice; he was so much more stable and successful than his own father, so he kept trying, but lectured more and more. However, the process of lecturing keeps other people from getting involved in the conversation, so it can be counterproductive, especially with teenagers.

If you absolutely cannot contain yourself because you have an idea you feel you must share with your teen, it's best to start with something like "Hey, I have an idea about dealing with that coach, would you like to hear it?" If she says no, you are better off pulling back and trying another time. If she says yes, she has now agreed and is more likely to engage with you.

BACK TO THE FAMILY DINNER

Kevin responded to a short course of CBT, targeting his negative self-image and sadness. As for fitting in, Kevin was interested in the statistics involved in the creation of sports teams. This was before the publication of Michael Lewis' book (and the subsequent movie), *Moneyball*. Once Kevin realized that being a sports agent or sports writer were actual, respectable careers, he began to feel better about his interests. I encouraged him to meet people outside of school who were involved in those careers. Kevin's parents were very concerned about him as well. When they confirmed that their family dinners and lack of communication were upsetting to them as well, I met with them once and then referred them to a family psychotherapist. The idea of therapy was difficult for Brendan to accept at first, but he was motivated to make things better at home so he and Donna ultimately followed through.

You and your spouse or partner may want to discuss the concept of the family dinner as a tool for communication. If you agree on its importance, then you want everyone to feel comfortable so they can be mindful of their time together. All too often, one parent, usually the mother, rushes home from work and tries to get a healthy meal on the table, and then after dinner, everybody's rushing to get chores and schoolwork done. This puts everybody in a state of stress and tension.

In a two-parent home, there is no reason that preparing dinner needs to be the ongoing responsibility of one parent. It's possible that given the family division of labor it is a logical choice, and it may feel like the only option in a single-parent family. Either way, it's important to simplify meal preparation as much is possible. Children can help starting at an early age, from a 4-year-old setting the table to a 15-year-old ultimately cooking better than you do.

Remember that it is a family dinner. You don't want one person to dominate, neither a parent nor a child. It's easy to lapse into a dialogue—with the parent who feels closest to one child taking over rather than creating a general conversation with all members engaged and involved. Be sure to facilitate the conversation and encourage everyone.

A flexible approach will help. According to a study of families that had frequent family meals compared to those that didn't, being flexible as to the types of food and having less pressure on children to eat everything were associated with more frequent family meals. In other words, food and eating don't need to be a big production. In addition, it doesn't have to be dinner, and it doesn't always have to take a lot of time. Ideally, gathering once a day is a comfortable ritual, but life is not always ideal. Given teens' and parents' busy school and work schedules, you may only eat together a few times a week or you may not have a lot of time. But you could add a weekend lunch, pizza night, or another option you'd all enjoy. The actor and comedian Bill Hader remembers watching a movie together and discussing it every Friday night as his important family event.

WHEN COMMUNICATION BREAKS DOWN: THE IMPACT OF DIVORCE

Divorce can be seen as the ultimate breakdown in family communication. The divorce rate in the United States has been declining since the 1980s. However, there are many children who are still exposed to family separations because their parents lived together but never legally married. Thus, the impact of divorce on children remains a significant public health issue, with 30 to 50% of the children in the United States expected to experience parental divorce or family disruption. Many children do well after divorce, but 25 to 35% experience significant problems. Some of the negative consequences include problematic substance use, tobacco use, and mental health problems. For a smaller group, the impact of divorce continues throughout adulthood. Some researchers believe that divorce disrupts development and therefore makes children more susceptible to psychiatric conditions like depression.

The New Beginnings Program (NBP) at Arizona State University, led by Sharlene Wolchik, co-director of the REACH Institute and professor of psychology, is an excellent model of a preventive program for a group of children who are at risk for depression and other negative consequences. We will look at it in some detail because of its implications for parents. NBP reviewed the data to identify and target important preventive factors, including increased parental warmth, effective discipline, and decreased interparental conflict. The program includes custodial parents, mostly mothers, of children ages 3–18 and consists of 10 sessions of parent-focused, structured groups that include both educational and experiential components. Parents are assigned weekly skills practice with their children. Specifically, the program involves a clarification of the children's problems after divorce and emphasizes the importance of positive reinforcement, listening, taking time to think before responding, and shielding children from interparental conflict. Parents are also taught effective strategies for discipline and about setting clear and realistic expectations and developing and evaluating change plans.

The program has been was very successful in many ways and has been evaluated rigorously at both 6-year and 15-year follow-up. After 6 years, there was a 37% lower rate of mental health problems, including aggression, anxiety, and depressive symptoms, and less use of alcohol, marijuana, and other drugs. At the 15-year follow-up, the researchers were able to locate 89.6% of the families. Some of the benefits experienced by these emerging adults were lower rates of internalizing disorders, such as major depression, lower rates of substance-related disorders and problems in the past 9 years for men, and more positive attitudes toward their own parenting when the children or teens from the program reached adulthood.

We can learn a lot about preventing depression in children of divorce from these impressive results. The authors concluded that, by using new skills, parents played a central role in helping children adapt to the period following divorce: "Children had more positive outcomes based on the quality of their relationship with the custodial parent, the amount of time shared with the noncustodial parent, and lack of parental conflict."[8]

---

8. Irwin Sandler, Schoenfelder, E., Wolchik, S., & MacKinnon, D. Long-term impact of prevention programs to promote effective parenting: Lasting effects but uncertain processes. *Annual Review of Psychology*, 62(1), 299–329, 2011, p. 299.

The content of the program is similar to the communications skills we have addressed in this chapter and the skills you will learn in Chapter 11, on CBT. When I asked Dr. Wolchik what advice she would give to parents of high school and college students, she responded, "Teenagers still need reassurance when their parents are going through a divorce. It's important for them to know you'll be there for them and will communicate in an engaged, responsive, non-defensive manner. Also, allowing them to love both parents, even during times of major disagreement, is one of the biggest gifts you can give children. You cannot control your ex-spouse's behavior and criticizing her or him will only serve to make your teenager feel conflicted."[9]

As for interparental conflict, the teens I have seen who were upset by high-conflict divorces, not only was family life disrupted, but they were still having to deal with clashes between their parents. They feel like they are getting the worst of both worlds. For all these reasons, I recommend that custodial parents get as much support as they can, communicate often and positively with their children, and, despite their at times justified anger, avoid conflict with the other parent in front of children of all ages.

Fortunately, the NBP has now adapted the program for delivery to African Americans, Latinx Americans, and Asian-Pacific Islander families, and is collaborating with the court system in Arizona. They are also developing Internet material to help parents with this challenging transition.

Whether it is the family dinner or general communication skills, whether you are currently in a relationship or not, or whether you are recovering from a divorce, please understand and accept that all of these skills take time to develop. They may not work at first. It's best to practice them in a non-stressful situation. Over time, you will find that these skills will take the conversation to wider-ranging and deeper levels, help you and your teen feel more closely connected, reduce family conflicts, and provide the foundation for other conversations.

9. Sharlene Wolchik, Personal communication, February 20, 2019.

CHAPTER 5

"I Got This!"

The Joy of Competence and Self-Efficacy

A major building block for teen psychological health is the sense of competence and self-confidence. If a teen believes she can affect her world in a positive way, she will be prepared to learn and use coping skills that can be used to deal with stress, mood management, and life in general.

SOCIAL LEARNING THEORIES AND DEPRESSION

During the mid-1970s and 1980s, Albert Bandura developed the concept of self-efficacy, referring to an individual's belief in their ability to control their behavior in order to affect outcomes of the behavior. Bandura proposed that self-efficacy determines how people feel, think, motivate themselves, and behave. He also suggested that a person's "self-worth" could be defined as the total sum of individual competencies. Bandura's ideas built on the earlier work of Erik and Joan Erikson. Erikson, in the *Eight Stages of Man* and other works, suggested that children ages 5–12 who are industrious or hard-working and diligent will become competent and self-confident, especially with respect to their peers. Robert White, writing in the 1950s and 1960s, emphasized the importance of competence and confidence and related the desire for mastery to the excitement of exploration and the reduction of fear and anxiety.

I have always believed in the validity and relevance of these theories. I love watching babies with their "busy boxes" when they realize, in delight, that if they pound a little rubber ball, it will squeak. I'm a big fan of kids learning new games, absorbing the rules and figuring out how to proceed. I enjoy listening to the pleasure that high school and college students derive from sharing what they have learned and accomplished. Mastery does indeed bring a sense of joy. On the flip side, lack of competence and confidence are consistent with some of the symptoms of depression, including hopelessness, an inability to concentrate, and lethargy.

I see *competence, self-efficacy,* and *agency* as similar terms; they all refer to the belief in one's own ability to take positive action. For the purposes of this chapter I will use the term *self-efficacy* because it has been a major focus of psychological research for over forty years.

One consistent result of this research is that teens with high self-efficacy acquire the skills and motivation to succeed, whereas those with low self-efficacy may give up early because they do not believe they can make a difference or be successful. Therefore, perceived self-efficacy gives teens the motivation and persistence to proceed in difficult times. They can visualize success when they think about a challenge, whereas those with low in self-efficacy will visualize failure.

Bandura suggested that there are four ways to learn self-efficacy. The most obvious way is to practice, to have experiences of mastery in overcoming obstacles. Observing social models is a second way. Persuasion is a third option that can encourage self-efficacy, and, finally, eliminating anxiety or other physiological states that interfere with development will also facilitate more self-efficacy. Parents can use all of these strategies.

Social learning theory proposes that we learn skills and our self-concept from observing and imitating others. As you have probably noticed by now, given my emphasis on parents as role models, I am a believer in the tenets of social learning theory; they are extremely powerful in raising children. Bandura's work, now renamed *social cognitive theory,* is viewed as a bridge between behavioral and cognitive theories owing to its emphasis on the way we learn and think, with interactive influences between the person's thinking, behavior, and environment. The way children interact with their environment is a result of what they have observed and learned from their parents and others, including extended family and teachers, characters in the media, peers, and friends. Their ability to affect the environment can lead to rewards and impact the way they see themselves.

If children become competent in several areas of life, they will then feel confident to move forward and challenge themselves. However, it is not only a question of feeling confident but also the actual attaining of skills and knowledge. Therefore, assisting and allowing the child to learn how to solve problems on their own is critically important in creating self-efficacy.

Self-efficacy is developed throughout childhood; as stated earlier, Erikson emphasized ages 5–12 years. For the next stage, adolescence, Erikson pointed to the importance of developing an identity; teens need to develop a sense of self. As with all of Erikson's stages, the development of identity builds on the previous stage's sense of competence and ultimately involves learning the many roles of adulthood. Erikson focused primarily on occupational and sexual identity, but self-efficacy affects virtually every area of life.

Bandura suggests that a lack of self-efficacy could lead to depression in several ways. Unattainable standards may lead to low self-efficacy; they may leave a teen to experience multiple failures and cause disappointment and pessimism. The similar learned helplessness theory, proposed by Martin Seligman, asserts that people become depressed when they believe that they cannot make effective change in their world. Thus, they give up and become hopeless. Hopelessness can lead to psychological paralysis and depression.

As for anxiety, Bandura wrote, "People who believe they can exercise control over potential threats do not engage in apprehensive thinking and are not perturbed by them. But those who believe they cannot manage threatening events that might occur experience high levels of anxiety arousal."[1] He added that when people feel their coping skills are inadequate, they have increased autonomic responses and experience distress. This theory has been supported by research for many years. Thus teens with high self-efficacy, when faced with sadness or anxiety, believe that they can deal with those mood states. They may utilize distraction, relaxation procedures, and other calming techniques and find a way to gain social support. Those low in self-efficacy will have neither the skills nor the confidence to manage moods.

In summary, encouraging the development of self-efficacy is an important strategy to support your teen's ability to manage sadness, anxiety, and all forms of adversity and these abilities are fundamental for a good adjustment to college life. We will explore other cognitive theories of depression put forth by Aaron Beck and Albert Ellis in Chapter 11, on cognitive behavior therapy (CBT).

1. Alfred Bandura. Self-efficacy conception of anxiety. *Anxiety Research*, 1(2), 77–98, 1988.

Self-efficacy is not one global characteristic. We all have different types and levels of competencies—academic, emotional, physical, sexual, and social, just to name a few. A lack of academic self-efficacy be can problematic with respect to depressed mood in students; academics are an important part of their lives, so a low level of academic self-efficacy can leave students with a general feeling of disappointment.

I saw Elyse, for example, who had come East from a large Midwestern high school where she had done very well, focusing on English and language arts. Her parents, both high school teachers, were very proud of her high school performance; she had obtained excellent grades and gained admission to a competitive college. They were very supportive and assumed that Elyse, with her good grades, would choose her courses wisely. Once in college, Elyse limited herself to the same areas of study, English and history, not because she liked them so much but because she shied away from areas of study like the math and the sciences, where she felt less competent. She feared that she would not be able to "do well," by which she meant "receive an A."

Elyse's attitude is, in part, a reflection of our culture's emphasis on performance rather than true education. Despite her high school grades, Elyse did not have general academic self-efficacy, although she knew she excelled in English and the language arts. She did not believe in her abilities to explore and challenge herself with new material, so she had a limited view of her competence. The idea of new areas of study unsettled her.

Elyse had originally come to see me because of a roommate problem, which we resolved relatively quickly. She was a very serious young woman. She was a bit rigid in her posture, wore large black glasses in the style of the time, and her blue eyes seemed a little wary at first. As she shared more, she also talked about feelings of malaise, being disappointed in herself, and becoming slightly bored. Like too many students, Elyse saw herself as climbing the next rung of a ladder to get into a competitive graduate school or to obtain a high-status job. Education was less a process and more a vehicle.

When we talked about high school, I discovered that, unfortunately, Elyse also had a history that is all too common in girls. She had limited herself to only the basic college prep courses in math and science. She believed that she "was not good enough at math" even though her SAT scores indicated that her aptitudes for math and science were above average. It appeared that she had fallen into a common trap. Research suggests that teenage boys and girls have similar abilities in math. Girls, however, have greater skills in the language arts and so, based on their internal comparisons, they may believe they are not talented in math even when they may be average or above average. Most boys assume that this same level of math ability is fine.

The result was that Elyse had had little exposure to math; therefore, she had not practiced studying it. This, in turn, led to avoidance of the subject, due to her low perceived self-efficacy in the area. And over time, this lack of self-efficacy generalized to many courses outside English and the language arts. So even though Elyse originally had some academic self-efficacy, her anxiety about grades limited her choices despite her desire to branch out.

We explored the pros and cons of her trying at least one course in an area outside her usual area of study, and Elyse decided she would "risk it" once, because she knew that her diminishing interest in her current studies was a bad trend. Elyse discovered that she could master an introductory sociology course that included some basic scientific concepts. She also learned that although she could perform well in the class, she didn't really enjoy it. This was a much better result than avoiding the subject because she was anxious. Elyse's confidence boosted; she next challenged herself by tackling another new subject and over time, she developed a more flexible approach. Among her important discoveries were that she was a quick study and that she could ask for help if she needed it. Elyse finally surprised herself by developing a passionate interest in environmental sciences that had some elements of math and science.

Some students have clear differences in aptitude and interests and have an accurate read of their strengths and weaknesses. They are content to do well in those areas. Elyse's problem was that she had a wider range of aptitudes, but her fear had limited her. She had been about to prematurely close off options. For most students, academic self-efficacy and a history of competence form a core experience of college life and can give them a solid foundation. But the college experience involves much more than academics.

PHYSICAL AND SOCIAL COMPETENCE

Some studies have found that, during adolescence, boys have higher levels of self-competence in physical appearance and athletics, whereas girls have higher levels of social self-competence. It is easy to see how these differences can develop, based on socialization. One researcher emphasized that is it extremely difficult for a teenage girl to have high self-competence in physical appearance because of the "unattainable thin ideal." For this reason,

I encourage teenagers, especially girls, to identify any physical activity that they enjoy, rather than focusing so much on appearance. We will explore this issue in greater detail in Chapter 6, on healthy bodies.

As for boys and social competence, let's look at the vicious cycle of low social competence from Bandura's social cognitive perspective. Alexandros was a brilliant and hard-working first-year physics student from Greece. Although he was an excellent student, he lacked social skills. His mother was devoted to Alex but tended to try to solve problems for him; his father was a somewhat detached professor, and Alexandros was an only child. He had always been awkward with peers, and his challenges multiplied when he came to college in the United States. Alexandros felt unable to attain his goal of initiating a friendship or joining the competitive national physics challenge, where he could have met students from other colleges. As a result, he felt less competent and confident overall and he was not be able to receive the necessary social support and feedback we all need. Alexandros lapsed into isolation and would often bring his food back to his dorm room rather than face the sea of new faces in the cafeteria. Alone, Alexandros was less likely to fend off negative thoughts and worries.

Alexandros could have joined a social skills group offered by the college's counseling center or visited a meeting of the international students' society, but he was too shy to attend either. Fortunately, one of his professors referred him to me at the end of his first semester, so Alexandros' worries and loneliness did not develop into a depressive episode. A depressed person feels that he is not at all the master of his fate; quite the contrary, he is buffeted by many factors in the environment.

With his bleached white blonde hair and European style clothes, I thought that Alexandros' shyness might appear to other students as being aloof or snobbish. I shared this feedback with him and he was surprised, and he slowly began to understand that he would need to overcome his involuntary nonverbal messages. In therapy and through his additional reading about shyness and social skills, we were able to create a set of small problem-solving steps that Alexandros mastered over time. He started by accompanying his roommate to a meal. Next, he went to class and chatted with a classmate about the next assignment. Then he introduced himself to a young woman in his dorm. We had created a set of small-talk questions and answers and these steps went well. After one semester, while Alexandros was not the life of the party, he had a few friends, lived in a "science house," and felt quite comfortable. I emphasized that this type of slow but steady approach to problem-solving could be used in any number of situations. Alexandros' social self-efficacy continued to grow over time, and this improved his overall mood.

The relationship between confidence or self-efficacy and depressive symptoms may be a two-way street. Bandura suggested that feelings of depression interfere with beliefs about competence. A large 2016 study that followed 1,700 teens between the ages of 14 and 16 for 2.5 years found that, in contrast to earlier studies, self-efficacy did not predict depressive symptoms but, to the contrary, that depressive symptoms led to decreased feelings of self-efficacy. The authors suggested that depressive symptoms had "a contaminating effect" in that they inhibited the growth of self-efficacy. Similarly, anxiety interferes with academic, physical, and social development because teens are not confronting new challenges but, rather, avoiding them. The growth of diligence, building on the earlier stage of industry, is a key element of adolescent development but can be disrupted by symptoms of depression or anxiety. Thus we need to pay attention to depression and anxiety at an early age to prevent the disruption of development and learning.

However, I disagree slightly with the authors' conclusion that self-efficacy should not be a focus in programs that have the goal of preventing depression, just because this study produced results that have yet to be replicated. It is not an either-or proposition. Remember that one aspect of preventing major depression is early detection. Assessing self-efficacy as well as symptoms of depression may lead to improved care. For example, a teen who does not admit to symptoms of depression may reveal low self-efficacy, which could lead to further inquiry about depressive symptoms. Each person has individual needs. Some teens may need attention directed toward their depressive symptoms, and others may benefit from learning greater self-efficacy. Many will need both. In addition, teaching self-efficacy is in some ways quite similar to elements of CBT, a validated, effective treatment for depression.

I believe that we need to give teens a good foundation by helping to instill in them self-efficacy along the way. This is especially important during adolescence, when teens like Elyse and Alexandros prepare to face the multiple demands of college life. Although we may need to help our teens develop skills, we should try not to take over. We should avoid too much problem-solving; parental over-involvement reduces self-efficacy and autonomy. It is a question of balance, though some teens, like Alexandros, could use some direct help and feedback. Elyse might have felt more empowered if her parents had encouraged her to spread her academic wings a bit. As Barbara Oakley, a professor of engineering, wrote, "Do your daughter a favor—give her a little extra math practice each day, even if she finds it painful."[2] I would additionally suggest that you do your son

2. Barbara Oakley. Make your daughter practice math. She'll thank you later. *The New York Times*, August 7, 2018.

the same favor in whatever areas he avoids. We may need to help our children develop skills that they can then use on their own. We can do this directly (by listening and sharing ideas) or indirectly (by making them aware of opportunities outside the home). Ultimately, we want them to be able to say, "I've got this."

The question then becomes, how do we instill feelings of self-efficacy in our teenagers? Earlier chapters emphasized the overall belief in each child's unique value. Now we are emphasizing that belief in each child's unique capabilities. Remember Bandura's suggestion that to promote self-efficacy we can use persuasion, modeling, encouragement, and practice, and we need to help reduce children's negative moods. Here are some ideas on how to carry this out:

- Help identify your teen's strengths and weaknesses. Consider all areas—social, altruistic, physical, and creative. Don't limit your thoughts to academic pursuits or the resume building for college applications. That is a separate endeavor.
- Give them feedback and encourage them to further develop their skills and identify any weaknesses. They may want to work on the weaknesses, but they also need to be aware of any special strengths. They need to appreciate and internalize their strengths and generalize from their islands of competence, whatever they may be.
- Constructive, specific, and loving feedback is a gift. Praise needs to be genuine and based on specific behaviors. Remember that teens are keen lie detectors. Erikson wrote, "Children cannot be fooled by empty praise and condescending encouragement. They may have to accept artificial bolstering of their self-esteem in lieu of something better, but what I call their accruing ego identity gains real strength only from wholehearted and consistent recognition of real accomplishment, that is, achievement that has meaning in their culture."[3] I would expand the sentence to include persistent effort as well as accomplishment. An example of constructive feedback might be, "I know how much you and your friends enjoy debating one another, but I noticed that you and Orin were pretty loud and that Sam was silent. I wonder if he felt left out because he is not as verbal as you are."
- The previous example can also lead to the distinction between arrogance and confidence. Confidence is a sense that one can do something but not at the expense of others. Arrogance shows a need to make the other

3. Erik Erikson, *Identity and the Life Cycle*. New York: Norton, (1959/1980), p. 95.

person feel inferior. The boys debating may have felt they had verbal debating self-efficacy. However, if they knowingly talked loudly in order to silence Sam and make him feel left out, they were being arrogant.

- As for pointing out weaknesses, it is important to do so also in a specific and constructive fashion. Negative feedback only works if there is also a history of positive feedback; otherwise you will be communicating a global attitude that your teen is "always messing up." For example, I saw a young woman who periodically asked her father to read her research papers during high school. She finally gave up after she realized that they were always returned, covered with red pencil marks. Even if she had made a number of grammatical errors, more effective feedback would have included a conversation about how most of the content was engaging and challenging but that the grammar needed some work.

- Praise your teen's efforts, not only their abilities. If they attempt new challenges, have only partial success, and learn from their efforts, they will benefit. Practicing any skill and learning from the results will reduce anxiety about potential failure. If your son or daughter decides to start cooking, for example, and bakes a chocolate cake that tastes good but has fallen you can say, "This tastes great. I admire that you're taking on this new skill. It may take more time to improve, as baking can be difficult, but I think you'll enjoy it!"

- Provide examples and opportunities for challenges. Robert Bjork has identified the concept of "desirable difficulties," which suggests that we encourage behaviors that are somewhat challenging. Such activities are not too easy, nor are they merely an extension of previous accomplishments; at the same time, they are not so difficult as to prove demoralizing. They may involve some frustration at first, but attempting to do them is better in the long run. The task must be reasonably attainable, though. I would have done Elyse a disservice had I encouraged her to take a college math course first—that would have been too much of a jump. On the other hand, she could have sailed through college with English and language classes but missed the opportunity to stretch herself and discover something she felt passionate about.

- Classes and other opportunities do not have to cost a lot of money. Many libraries and community organizations are available and can be good resources. Part-time jobs usually boost self-efficacy in teens. Challenges in the home, whether building a bookcase or reorganizing the kitchen, or other opportunities can produce positive growth.

- Foster a variety of problem-solving techniques. On an interpersonal level, these might include communication, acceptance, or negotiation. Greater flexibility in problem-solving can provide more general feelings of self-efficacy. If your daughter has had an argument with a friend about a trip they want to take and the conflict continues despite the fact that she has been assertive about her interests, you might say, "I'm glad that you can state you mind. In this case, though, maybe try brainstorming a place that neither of you is committed to now and see if there is a third option."

- Don't be overprotective or controlling. Although I think the huge negative attention given to the issue of "helicopter parents" is overblown in comparison to all the other problems teenagers face, it is necessary to give your teen autonomy to learn their own style of problem-solving. I have seen parents, like Alex's mother, who tried to intervene with teachers even when their teen was a senior in high school. What does a teen learn from that parental takeover, compared to helping her brainstorm ways to approach the problem herself? What will she do the next year on her own at college or at a job?

- Encourage brainstorming in general. When tackling or discussing any problem or issue, don't settle for the tried-and-true solutions. Many of our children are more creative than we are and it's important to foster that trait. Some teens prefer to brainstorm alone and jot down ideas, while others enjoy the give-and-take of discussion.

- Encourage your teen to push back against stereotypes about competence. I have seen women physicians, especially African Americans or Latinas, who were informed during high school by counselors or teachers that medicine would not be a realistic career choice. What a blow to academic self-efficacy! I have also talked with young men who were taunted because they played the violin or another musical instrument that was deemed "unmanly"—another cruel attack on creativity and musical competence. These negative messages are especially damaging as research suggests it is easier to discourage self-efficacy than to verbally reward it. Self-advocacy is a key life skill, and your support of your teen can be the major force for their developing it.

- Self-reflect: Do you limit yourself to a small area of activities out of fear or performance anxiety? It's okay to be honest and admit that some areas are not your area of strength. You, too, might benefit from taking small risks to explore areas of interest that you fear. I saw one mother, who believed she was "an athletic disaster," ultimately take up running at the age of 41 in order to be a better model for her daughters. In modeling such risk-taking, you hope your child will be more confident to explore a wide range of interests and abilities. You can also point out other positive role models.

If we value college education, I believe it should be for the love of the process of learning, not only the desired outcome. I understand the need for our children to attain financial self-sufficiency or career success, but not to the exclusion of everything else. We would do well to remember the words of the educational philosopher John Dewey. Over a hundred years ago he wrote, "Education, therefore, is a process of living and not a preparation for future living.[4]" He also wrote, "Failure is instructive. The person who really thinks learns quite as much from his failures as from his successes."[5]

4. John Dewey (1897). My Pedagogic Creed. *School Journal*, 54(3), p. 78.

5. Dewey, J. (1998). Analysis of reflective thinking. In L. A. Hickman & Analysis of reflective thinking. In L. A. Hickman & T. M. Alexander (Eds.), *The Essential Dewey: Vol. 2. Ethics, Logic, Psychology*. Bloomington: Indiana University Press, p. 144.

CHAPTER 6

Self-Regulation

Healthy Sleep, Nutrition, and Physical Activity

At one time, lifestyle factors such as physical activity, nutrition, and sleep were seen as foundations only of physical health. But over time, it has become clear that they are major factors in mental health as well. In short, maintaining a healthy body is one of the best ways to maintain a healthy mind. Today, it is not unusual for a psychiatrist treating depressed patients to ask about their diet and physical activity. I have a colleague who works with refugees and who encourages walking and other forms of exercise to help them with their symptoms of depression and ongoing posttraumatic stress disorder. In addition, the whole field of sleep medicine has now become a primary focus in psychiatry and internal medicine alike. These issues are all particularly relevant to the prevention of depression.

The adjustment to college involves numerous changes in diet, sleep, and physical activity. Self-regulation is therefore a major issue for students. The term *self-regulation* refers to the ability to manage your behaviors in a way that is consistent with your values and your long-term self-interest. Another way of describing self-regulation is the ability to control yourself, by yourself. The sheer number of changes associated with the transition to college can be overwhelming for students on their own for the first time. While we will discuss emotional self-regulation in greater depth in Chapter 8, on distress tolerance, in this chapter we will examine the issues of self-regulation as they relate to health-promoting behaviors like sleep, physical activity, and nutrition. In the next chapter we will consider self-regulation and risk reduction as they relate to alcohol, tobacco, and drug use and to sex.

Let's take a look at the general concept of self-regulation before examining the specifics of nutrition, sleep, and physical activity. Contrast the life of a high school junior and a first-year college student: High school students organize their day around the school schedule. Their days have a predictable and routinized start-and-stop time with structured classes, study periods, and lunch periods. After school, they often have sports, another activity, or a job. When they get home, they usually want to eat and then must do homework. At night, there may be more homework, and probably some social media. Some parents restrict their teens' use of social media and screen time; others do not. Many students find this type of a schedule to be restrictive, but it does provide them with a clear structure for food, physical activity, and academics.

Sleep is a major problem in the high-schooler's schedule, however. Most high school students are sleep deprived, mainly because most schools start so early. The biological clock of many teens directly clashes with typical school day with its early start time. In addition, many students stay up late to use social media or watch television or movies online. A study by the Pew Research Council revealed that 45% of teens are online almost *constantly*. Another 44% were online several times a day. This amount of online time clearly disrupts sleep schedules and may limit physical activity level as well. The survey of teens aged 13–17 also found that 95% of teens had smartphones, with few differences based on race or income. The most common social media sites were Snapchat, Instagram, and Facebook. (The study was done before Tik Tok became so popular.)

By contrast, the organization of a first-year college student's day and week can start from scratch. In many colleges, even first-year students create their own class schedule. The school may provide food in a cafeteria or the student may not have a meal plan and need to purchase and cook their own food. There are usually facilities for physical activity, but no requirements. Students need to organize all of these activities into a schedule while simultaneously maintaining their academic performance, making new friends, and exploring new ideas.

Once again, there is the issue of getting enough sleep and of sleep disruption. Despite the fact that most college classes start later than those in high school, college students still tend to be sleep deprived, but for other reasons. Some required courses start early. There are also many distractions from the ideal bedtime that allows 8 hours of sleep. The location of the student's room and having roommates might interfere with sleep. External limits on social media are totally removed. Overall, college can be a resource-rich environment, but the individual student is suddenly totally responsible for self-regulation. Many parents and students are unaware of these challenges and are therefore unprepared for the stress of these changes and the subsequent need to develop self-regulation skills.

As parents, one of our first experiences of teaching self-regulation is with the sleep of infants and toddlers. The idea of sleep training is based on the belief that the baby or toddler must learn the skill of self-soothing. Therefore, the baby may need to cry for a few minutes before going to sleep or gradually learn to fall asleep, becoming less dependent on a consoling parent. In the 1980s, Richard Ferber, Director of the Center for Pediatric Sleep Disorders at Children's Hospital Boston popularized a program that suggested babies should be allowed to cry for increasing amounts of time.

As a child grows, we add the skills of healthy eating and, ideally, physical activity. We hope that our teens will have internalized these overall skills of self-regulation before they move on to be on their own. But self-regulation is a more complicated process than it may seem to be. There are many barriers to establishing and maintaining healthy behaviors. Still, the general ability to self-regulate is more important than any one specific area of regulation.

In order to regulate healthy behaviors, teenagers first need the cognitive skills to see the value of basic health—that physical activity, adequate sleep, and good nutrition are important not only for a healthy body but also to maintain psychological health and to achieve many of their personal goals. In addition to understanding the value of healthy behavior, teens need to feel competent and develop the skills to eat well, get adequate sleep, and get enough physical activity. The specific skills needed for self-regulation include paying attention, setting goals, taking action, and monitoring ongoing behavior. In addition, developing delayed gratification or engaging in a health behavior because it is better in the long run is critically important. For example, it might be alluring to text friends all night, but getting enough sleep is a healthier choice and will lead to a better next day. Finally, teens need to feel confident that they can maintain the skill set even when stressful situations or environmental barriers occur. We all understand how a healthy diet can be disrupted by a sudden loss or stressful situation leading to a desire for comfort food. The same is true for getting enough sleep and physical activity. So self-regulation is a process of education, competence, confidence, and learning to overcome barriers so that healthy behaviors can be maintained.

Maintaining self-regulation also involves self-compassion, a combination of kindness, mindfulness, and a sense of universality. A self-compassionate attitude has been shown to be associated with more favorable long-term self-regulation. When there are slips in self-regulation, whether it is not exercising or eating unhealthy foods, some teenagers, especially girls, are judgmental and harsh. This reduces feelings of competence and increases guilt and self-criticism and usually leads to overeating. In general, many people are overly self-critical about their slips in self-regulation, which is counterproductive. In contrast, a self-compassionate approach involves accepting that some errors are part of the human condition (universality), that each of us deserves understanding (self-kindness), and that we do not need to be plunged into guilt and shame (mindfulness).

Nutrition, physical activity, and sleep are three components that work in harmony to create a healthy lifestyle; if one is disrupted, the others often follow. In the next sections I will provide suggestions or tips for promoting each component, but my first overarching suggestion is this: Limit the smartphone use! As parents, many of us are abdicating the responsibility to limit screen time. They disrupt every aspect of self- regulation. With respect to food, smartphones at dinner interfere with conversation and can lead to distracted eating, which can itself lead to overeating. With respect to physical activity, if teens are on their smartphones or laptops for a large portion of the day and night, they have less time for exercise and become more sedentary. As for sleep, not only do smartphones (and computers, televisions, and video game consoles) displace sleep time, the light they emit disrupts circadian rhythms. In addition, the content of texts or images on social media can create arousal and, often, upset.

With 84% of teens having smartphones and many of them staying in their bedrooms with their phones, it's clear that something is wrong. Most likely, the reason that parents are not setting limits is that many of us are also addicted to smartphones. Some have referred to this as "distracted parenting." Parents may feel that by the teen years, children are pretty much safe and can use smartphones on their own. That flies in the face of the evidence that social media is damaging to mood, sleep, physical activity, time for other activities, and, especially for girls, body image. Many parents try to limit drinking, drug use, and smoking; I suggest we add social media to the list. Unless we become better role models and break the smartphone habit, not much will change and our teens will suffer the consequences. This is an example of how our love affair with new technology has interfered with our best judgment; technology can be used for good or harm. As we shall see, another type of technology that has harmed teens is the introduction and marketing of vaping products.

We will now examine the ways in which nutrition, physical activity, and sleep can protect students from depression or precipitate the development of depression. In addition, we will examine the interactions between the three factors.

NUTRITION

There have been major advances in studying the impact of nutrition on depression. In general, what we eat for optimal health has been controversial. Nutrition fads have misled American parents for generations. Low-fat diets that ended up replacing fat with sugar and other carbohydrates caused weight gain. The high-protein diet was associated with kidney damage. Emphasizing the importance of dairy products, especially milk, may have led to consuming too many calories. Now, common sense and science both show us that a diet of lots of vegetables and fruits, whole grains, and fish, with less fried food or fatty meats, is ideal for optimal health and preventing depression. Michael Pollan has summarized it: "Eat food. Mostly plants. Not too much."[1] There are studies that show that this food plan may also help depressed people recover.

In contrast, the standard American diet (SAD), with fast food, processed food, sugar, additives, and preservatives, can lead to chronic inflammation that in turn leads to depression. The research that a modified Mediterranean diet can decrease the risk for depression is clear. A meta-analysis, or survey of a number of studies that are statistically similar and can be combined, concluded, "The Western (similar to the SAD) dietary pattern is associated with an increased risk of depression and the healthy (similar to the Mediterranean) diet plan is associated with a decreased risk of depression."[2]

We have known for some time that depression is associated with poor eating habits. However, the reason for this correlation was unclear. Was it that people who are depressed choose unhealthy foods? An Australian study answered this question. They selected people who were already depressed and being treated with psychotherapy and/or medication. Then they randomly assigned people to one of two conditions. One group was to meet with a nutritionist and follow a modified Mediterranean diet, with lots of olive oil and vegetables, nuts, and only low-fat protein like chicken and fish. They were discouraged from eating red meat or processed foods

1. Michael Pollan. *Food Rules: An Eater's Manual*. New York: Penguin, 2009, p. xv.
2. Rachelle Opie, O'Neil, A., Jacka, F., Pizzinga, J., & Itsiopoulos, C. A modified Mediterranean dietary intervention for adults with major depression: Dietary protocol and feasibility data from the SMILES trial. *Nutritional Neuroscience*, 21(7), 487–501, 2018.

and were to limit their alcohol intake to two drinks per day, preferably red wine, and to limit sugar-sweetened beverages to two per week. The other group was to follow their normal diet but meet in a social support group. After 12 weeks, the authors, led by psychologist Felice Jacka, found that the group on the Mediterranean diet improved their depression scores by 11 out of 60 points, an improvement of over 30%. The authors found that the people on the routine diet also improved, but only by about 4%. And there was more good news: people on the Mediterranean diet did not restrict calories and the cost of the healthier food plan was about 20% less than that of the normal diet. Now we know that the best nutrition we can provide for our families for general health is also the best nutrition for psychological health.

If we try to provide and model a common-sense healthy food plan at home, our teens will usually follow over time. Yet the negative food environments at many colleges, especially late-night snacking and lack of portion control, can be tempting. Despite advances in nutritional education, and although first-year college students no longer gain the "freshman 15" pounds, they still gain an average of 7 or 8 pounds. In addition to the negative impact on mood from dietary inflammation, weight gain can also hurt body image and create depressed mood as well.

When we eat is also relevant. Most teens know that eating breakfast is healthy and that eating late at night can pile on extra calories, but about 25% of teens skip breakfast. Teens who eat breakfast tend to have a lower body mass index (BMI) and can concentrate better on academics. As for weight gain, Dr. Marcie Beth Schneider of the American Academy of Pediatrics Committee on Nutrition states, "We know that the biggest predictor of overeating is undereating, Many of these kids skip breakfast and lunch, but then go home and don't stop eating."[3] Therefore, the "late-night snacking/no breakfast" food plan of many students may account for some of the weight gain in the first year of college. Eating a lot at night also interferes with sleep.

Finally, we have the key element of how we eat. As we discussed with respect to the family dinner, mindful eating benefits the whole family. Too often, we rush through a meal, barely tasting the food or multitasking during a meal by looking at smartphones, reading, or watching television. Dr. Susan Albers of the Cleveland Clinic suggests practicing the five S's of mindful eating. Like all mindful behaviors, the first step is to sit and focus

3. Schneider, M., cited in https://www.healthychildren.org/English/healthy-living/nutrition/Pages/The-Case-for-Eating-Breakfast.aspx

all your attention on the meal. Next, proceed slowly. Simplify foods so that the healthier foods are prominent. Savoring involves being aware of the food's taste and texture. Be sure to swallow before taking another bite and try to avoid the food-shoveling habit. Albers adds smiling after each bite, but I can't imagine that helps the social life of teens, so perhaps it should be an internal smile! Mindful eating is neither about following any particular diet nor restricting foods. It is about slowing down, developing awareness, and being grateful for the opportunity to eat in a meaningful way.

H_2O

We can all benefit from drinking more water. About 60% of the body is composed of water, and drinking enough water helps with elimination, lubricating joints, and maintaining body temperature. You may have heard of the advice to drink eight 8-ounce glasses of water each day, which is easy to remember, but is likely an overestimate. According to the Mayo Clinic, drinking when you are thirsty is the best plan. A person may need more or less water based on their health, medical conditions, exercise level, and the environment. As a general health habit, it is advisable to drink water before meals and before, during, and after exercise. Contrary to popular opinion, caffeinated coffee and tea are not dehydrating but may cause headaches, jitteriness, and insomnia. In contrast, alcoholic beverages are dehydrating. Sports drinks that replenish electrolytes are only necessary after more than an hour of intense exercise. In contrast, "energy drinks" are more likely to contain sugar and caffeine and have little to no nutritional value. Another excellent strategy is to drink water when you feel hungry, as this will increase your water intake and limit calories as well. Although water is ideal, fluids can be gained from other beverages as well.

Nutrition Tips

In addition to providing the healthy foods as described earlier, here are some specific ways to help your teen self-regulate their eating so they have skills to take with them:

- Teach your teen how to read food labels. This will heighten their awareness of protein, fat, vitamins, and additives as well as calories. Look at the portion size. A label may read "100 calories" but that may be for ¼ cup of food.

- Have water available at every meal.
- Avoid drinking caffeinated beverages and drinks that may be high in caffeine and sugar. One regular 12- ounce soda contains as many as 11 teaspoons (46.2 grams) of added sugar, several teaspoons more than is recommended for an entire day.
- Try to avoid food struggles. Yes, your teen may become vegetarian or prefer another food plan, but all the more reason to listen, discuss nutrition, and not become adversaries.
- Slow down! Eat mindfully.
- Instill a common-sense approach. Recently I read an article about what college students eat, and one young woman said that she had a dinner of popcorn and seltzer because she wanted to eat one thing "that was healthy." The article did not reveal which "thing" she thought was healthy.
- Help teens plan to eat breakfast. Show them how to organize the night before, make healthy smoothies, or pack a protein and fruit or vegetable in a zip-lock bag.
- Be careful about some protein or "power" bars that are really candy bars in disguise. This goes back to reading food labels.
- Remember compassion and self-compassion. If your teen is self-critical—"I ate too much. I hate myself"—ignore her, or speak with kindness about that not being true or not being the most important part of her. If, in your opinion, she did overeat, ask her if she'd like your help with portion control or another issue in the future. Model that same compassion with respect to your eating as well.

PHYSICAL ACTIVITY

Recently, a dean referred Nick to me during his second semester of college. By then, Nick was sad and felt tired all the time. Nick's black, curly hair was unruly and his brown eyes were wary. Although not overweight, he described himself as "flabby" and wore an oversize sweatshirt and sweat pants to our first visits. He said he had withdrawn from the few friends he'd made during his first semester and wanted help, but was not feeling hopeful. He added, "and besides, my family is not the therapy type." As it turned out, Nick was suffering in part from a lack of physical activity and its after-effects. He came to college to be on the wrestling team, having been a star on his high school team, which had placed well in the state finals. Nick was a first-generation college student from a working-class Italian-American family and was a little bit nervous about making friends in college. He had been looking forward to the wrestling team as a big part of his college social life.

As is often the case, things didn't turn out quite as planned. The first problem was that Nick, who wanted to be premed, needed to study much more than he had thought. He had found high school to be easy, so he had not studied a lot and had not counted on needing to devote so much time to labs and reading assignments. With the wrestling team's grueling schedule of practices and matches, Nick felt overwhelmed. Ultimately, Nick decided that it would be best for him to quit wrestling. This was a reasonable decision for his academic career. Unfortunately, there were quite a few unexpected consequences. The first was that his physical activity level plummeted and he had not yet found another sport or activity that he enjoyed. Like many high-performance athletes, he no longer wanted to wrestle at all, even intramurally, if he could not be among the best. This led to some weight gain, as Nick's previous level of intensive activity had burned many calories and he had not adjusted his intake accordingly. In addition, he had started to drink beer again, which had been forbidden during training.

Nick had also lost most of his social life. It wasn't that the wrestling team rejected him, although some of the team members were very disappointed when he quit the team. Rather, their social life was structured around their practice hours, the actual meets, and going out when they could. After leaving the team, Nick no longer shared the team's schedule. Nick had, moreover, started to feel less confident overall, because being an athlete had been a large part of his identity. By the time he came to see me he felt "alone, sloppy, and sad." Nick's story exemplifies how physical activity is one the most powerful factors in preventing depression. Wrestling gave Nick feelings of autonomy and competence. His high level of physical activity structured his week and made him feel good overall, and the team provided him with a built-in friend group within a large university. His training had allowed him to eat more, which he enjoyed, and sleep well. Nick had lost much of that by the time he came to see me.

Research supports this analysis of Nick's situation. A Canadian review of studies involving a total of almost 90,000 healthy children from ages 8 to 19 found that those who were physically active more often experienced fewer signs of depression. This was especially true for those who engaged in vigorous exercise. A review in the *American Journal of Preventative Medicine* revealed that even moderate exercise could prevent episodes of depression over the long term. The study analyzed 26 years of research findings and found that even low levels of physical activity, such as walking 20–30 minutes per day, can have some positive effect on preventing depression.

Students who are physically active also tend to have better grades and cognitive performance.

However, the United States has one of the lowest levels of physical activity in the world. If we accept the US Centers for Disease Control and Prevention (CDC) recommendation that teens get 60 minutes of physical activity in a given day, then only 27.1% attain that goal 7 days a week, and only 21.6% get vigorous exercise 5 days per week. Physical activity in teens, especially in girls, decreases as they go through adolescence. This is in part because, despite social changes (for example, Title IX in the United States), boys have the advantage of being expected to engage in team sports; this is less true for girls. It's imperative to change this trend because there is a large body of research suggesting that a lack of physical activity is associated with depression in adulthood as well as adolescence, and physical activity level during adolescence predicts physical activity of adults.

Given that physical activity is crucial for teen mental health, we need to look at the factors that maintain it. A study of teenage girls and physical activity found that they were more likely to continue with an exercise program if it was related to connecting with others rather than to weight loss. This is not surprising, because weight loss is an extremely external and illusive motivator, as we have discussed in other chapters. In this study, as it was for Nick, the positive outcomes associated with physical activity included autonomy, a sense of confidence, and relatedness.

What to Do about Nick and the Rest of Our Teens

Sometimes, psychotherapy is a collaboration in which the patient and the psychologist create a story together from a new point of view. Nick's narrative was clouded by the symptoms of depression. He believed that he was stupid, that his college career had gotten off to a bad start, and that he had made some "dumb decisions." He regretted joining the wrestling team, then regretted quitting it. Overwhelmed, he had started to believe that he might not make it through college and have to return home as a failure. This would be disappointing not only to him but also to his parents because they had financially sacrificed to send him to a private college.

Initially, Nick could not see other options, but over time, Nick and I created a different narrative together to correct his negative attributions and predictions. Our story emphasized that he had been successful at almost everything he had tried previously and was a hard worker. Nick had good social skills and was comfortable reaching out to people. It seemed reasonable that he would be able to make friends in his labs, in his dorm, and perhaps, over time, his old friends from the wrestling team. Nick also began to see that that he had allowed himself to lose his love of physical activity when he quit the wrestling team.

I believe that enjoyment is the strongest motivator for maintaining any physical activity. It's possible to structure the environment so that you will continue doing any exercise, but it's a lot better if you look forward to it and enjoy it. Nick had been a wrestler for so many years because it was the high point of his day. If students can manage it, I usually suggest that they try to stay in organized athletics if they enjoy it, because athletic teams also provide a needed structure for many students. However, Nick's decision was right for him at the time. He did need the time to stay in the premed program after all. He was a good athlete overall, so I encouraged him to try every sort of physical activity that he could. With some encouragement, he did and ultimately decided that the best plan for him would be to work out at the gym around his class schedule. Over time, he looked forward to the gym and he made friends who were there on the same schedule. By creating this new structure of classes, working out, and studying, Nick began to regain his self-confidence. And, he added, "It is good to feel strong again."

As for food, once his physical activity was back to its original level, Nick could eat what he enjoyed without weight gain. Unbeknownst to Nick, alcohol is a depressant, so we talked about his beer consumption, to avoid a new problem. When we last met, Nick was doing very well. He felt "almost back to his old self and this therapy stuff wasn't so bad," he said with a grin.

As parents and as a society, we have a long way to go toward encouraging more physical activity. The data on the lack of activity of high school students are alarming; and rates are even worse for older teenage girls from racial minority groups. We can only assume activity levels will get worse as the digital age increases and the use of social media impacts almost every realm of adolescent life.

Here are some ideas for increasing and maintaining physical activity:

- Start early! Continue or incorporate some physical activity into your life and into your conversation about its importance to you.
- If there are options for your teens to join you, take every opportunity for hiking, walking, running, cycling, or doing other activities together.
- Family support matters, so any help you can provide will help your teen develop a healthy lifestyle. Whether it's giving them a ride, attending sport events, helping them join a gym or community center, or praising them, all of this will benefit them.
- Encourage your teen to experiment with a wide variety of physical activities.

- Pay special attention that girls are exposed to opportunities for activities that are enjoyable and not about weight loss alone. One of my patients was surprised that her daughter chose kickboxing, but it is the love or passion for the sport or activity that matters.
- If your teen is overweight, activity level becomes even more important. Healthy food choices are necessary, of course, but participation in sport or activity will help give your teen physical self-confidence and better overall fitness and may lead to weight loss.
- Limit screen and smartphone time.

Don't Forget to Breathe!

"Don't forget to breathe!" I often hear these words when I'm in a class at the gym, and it's true: Many times, when we're working out or just having a busy day, we really forget to breathe, certainly to breathe properly. For increased mindfulness, the first step is to become *aware* of breathing. By slowing down and noticing your breath, you can have increased awareness. This will also increase your sense of calm. I find that when people are stressed, the biggest breathing problem is forgetting to exhale completely.

Breathing deeply is also a good habit for overall health. One type of deep breathing is belly breathing. It involves the following technique: Lie down on the floor on your back and place a hand on your belly. Breathe deeply so that you feel your hand rise and fall. If your chest is moving instead of your belly, you're not breathing deeply enough. By focusing on your hand on your belly, you can make sure that you are taking a deep breath. Breathing can also be helpful when you're in pain. A deep, slow breathing technique has helped people cope with pain. It will not make the pain go away, but it can be useful in terms of distraction and relaxation. Another deep breathing exercise, Dr. Andrew Weil's 4-7-8 breathing, is an easy exercise (and one of my favorites!): Breathe in slowly for 4 seconds. Hold your breath for 7 seconds. Then breathe out slowly, for 8 seconds. You'll probably find that at about second 5, you'll begin to feel more relaxed.

SLEEP BASICS

And then there's sleep—a problem associated with depression before, during, and many times after college. Sleep restores our immune, nervous, and muscular-skeletal systems. Adequate sleep also improves mood, memory, learning, attention, and emotional regulation. Given these effects, you probably won't be surprised to learn that healthy sleep is also associated with academic success. It's no wonder that we feel really revived when waking up after getting enough sleep. In contrast, chronic sleep deprivation is associated with accidents, poor concentration and cognitive functioning, irritability, impaired memory and judgment, and numerous medical conditions.

We all have a 24-hour internal circadian rhythm that promotes sleep at night and wakefulness during the day. The word circadian is derived from the Latin words circa, "about," and diem, "day." Light and dark are the primary drivers, with darkness being a signal for sleep. The sleep cycle is composed of alternating REM (rapid eye movement) stage sleep and non-REM. REM sleep also involves dreams, and in this stage, the body is temporarily paralyzed while the mind is awake. REM predominates later in the night, non-REM sleep, earlier. For non REM sleep, Stage 1 is transitional sleep, relaxed wakefulness. During Stage 2, moderate sleep, one can be easily awakened. Stage 3 is slow wave sleep (SWS) composed of deep sleep. Increasingly longer, deeper, REM sleep occurs toward the morning. The stages of non-REM and REM sleep cycle several times during the typical night.

The American Medical Association and the American Academy of Pediatrics have indicated that insufficient sleep is a serious health risk and a threat to academic success for teenagers. Ideally, adolescents should get 9 hours of sleep per night. However, adolescence is also associated with circadian evening time preference, meaning that their circadian rhythms make it preferable to stay up later, putting teens at odds with the typical school start time. Therefore, according to the National Sleep Foundation, 75% of high school seniors reported sleeping less than 8 hours per night, compared with 16% of sixth graders. As for college, a large study of college students (over 7,600) revealed that 27% of them reported poor sleep quality, 36% got less than 7 hours of sleep a night, and 43% took 30 minutes or more to fall asleep. In another study, those with sleep disorders were in academic jeopardy more often than others.

Sleep disruption, sleep deprivation, and insomnia are closely related to depression in many ways. *Sleep disruption* occurs when factors interfere with sleep, including noise, light, temperature, substance use, or withdrawal from substances. *Sleep deprivation* is the result of getting less sleep than you need and may be voluntary or a result of poor planning, as it is for many teens. *Insomnia* refers specifically to an involuntary inability to fall or stay asleep.

Non-REM sleep is necessary for turning off the neurotransmitters and for resting receptors. This allows for restoration of all the systems of the body and better regulation of mood and cognition. It's easy to see how being deprived of these necessary functions can trigger depression. At the same time, depression and its treatment interfere with sleep. Depression increases the percentage of REM sleep and many antidepressants reduce REM sleep, so the effects occur in both directions.

A small study of students during the first 9 weeks of college found that male students who gained weight reported more variability in their sleep. There was a trend toward students who slept less gaining more weight. The authors suggested that the weight gain may also have been a result of poor planning and less time for exercise. As for insomnia, a 2001 Brown University Health Promotion study revealed that only 11% of students reported good sleep quality, and 18% of men and 30% of women reported insomnia. In the previous 3 months, half of the students were sleepy in the morning.

Arthur Spielman has suggested that we look at insomnia using the three-factor model—predisposing, precipitating, and perpetuating factors. A predisposition to insomnia might be an anxious temperament. Insomnia can be triggered or precipitated by stress, a change in environment, loss, or substance use. Then worry about sleep can take over, perpetuating insomnia. Taking naps and using high-energy, caffeinated beverages will also perpetuate the vicious cycle of insomnia.

Given the prevalence and serious nature of sleep problems, what can we do as parents to help our teenagers?

- Education: we can talk with our teens about the importance of sleep in general.
- Smartphones: back to role modeling. In addition to the "no smartphones at dinner" rule, many families have a "phone in the charger after 9 o'clock" rule.
- We cannot control our teens, but we can control the pace and atmosphere of the home. And let's face it, many of us are feeling harried, with too much to do. Unfortunately, most people cannot rush through the evening, then hop into bed and go right to sleep. It could help to slow down the pace of household activity earlier in the evening.
- You can also talk with your teen about establishing a sleep ritual, perhaps listening to a podcast, then reading, then relaxing more with meditation or calm music before trying to sleep.
- If your teen has insomnia, start with sleep hygiene:
  - Reduce caffeine intake overall and especially after 4 o'clock in the afternoon.
  - Get enough physical activity, but not right before bedtime.

- Use the bed only for sleeping. Use a desk or a chair (preferably one outside the bedroom) to do homework and other activities.
- Try to maintain a consistent bedtime ritual to slow down.
- Don't eat a lot close to bedtime, and make a particular effort to avoid fatty foods and carbonated drinks.
- Get exposure to natural light during the day.
- If you cannot sleep for a certain amount of time, say 20 minutes, get out of bed and do something else before returning to bed to try to sleep again.
- Become a sleep advocate. Studies examining later school start times are clear: They lead to more sleep because teens are able to sleep later, up to 1 hour more on school nights.
- If your teenager continues to have problems with insomnia, it's important to seek treatment as soon as possible. Cognitive therapy of insomnia, or CBTI, is extremely effective and generally covered by insurance. It's critically important for your teen's physical and psychological health.

BODY DISSATISFACTION: A MAJOR DISRUPTION IN GIRLS' SELF-REGULATION

Body dissatisfaction is so common among women in the Western world that it's considered "normative discontent" in psychological circles. A 2011 *Glamour* magazine survey found that 97% of young women felt body hatred at least once a day. The 2014 version of the same *Glamour* survey found that 80% feel bad just looking in the mirror. Body dissatisfaction can have a profound effect on physical and emotional health, triggering the release of stress hormones, hidden inflammation, problematic eating patterns, mood changes, irregular menstrual cycles, social anxiety, and depression. Thus, body dissatisfaction has pernicious effects on a teenage girl's physical and psychological health, behavior, and quality of life.

The extremely self-critical thoughts about bodies, an internal phenomenon, is worsened by the external phenomenon of "fat talk." College-age women try to use fat talk as a way to connect, commiserate, and bond, to fit in socially. A 2014 study from Northwestern University found that contrary to popular belief, fat talk is common to young and older women, and women who engage in the practice frequently report higher levels of body dissatisfaction and guilt. And it becomes a contagious, self-perpetuating phenomenon. Through fat talk, women essentially reinforce the notion that it's acceptable to loathe their bodies. While half the women in the Northwestern study "believe fat talk makes them feel better about their bodies," those who engage in it more often tend to feel worse. Co-rumination about body dissatisfaction as well as other problems is associated with anxiety and depression in teenage girls.

Meanwhile, behavioral body bashing occurs when girls develop disordered eating habits or punish their bodies with extreme exercise. Severe dieting immediately puts teens on a path of dysregulation, the last thing we want to see. They restrict food, then become hungry and may binge or over-exercise. They lose weight, then regain it. This early pattern can develop into lifelong weight fluctuation, rumination, and self-criticism. Another powerful negative result of this pattern and the emphasis on women's bodies causes teens to become disembodied: By separating themselves from their bodies, they lose a deep sense of connection to them and compassion for them.

A variety of social factors combine to make teenage girls feel bad about their bodies, including unrealistic images and messages in the media, marketing and advertising campaigns that glamourize an extremely thin ideal, harsh comments from parents or other influential people during childhood, and comparisons on social media. Individually and collectively, these influences cause teens to judge themselves harshly in ways that detract from our other attributes and accomplishments. All of this hits girls even at a young age but becomes very powerful at the onset of puberty.

If a teen's family focuses excessively on appearances—how she looks, what she wears, and how others see her—this can lead to heightened body criticism or dissatisfaction. In fact, how family and friends talk about her appearance as a teenager can affect how she feels about her body as an adult. Research has found that college women who grew up in households where parents made lots of comments about family members' weight or size tend to have more negative views of their own bodies and more disordered eating habits. This makes perfect sense if you think about it: If a girl was teased or criticized about her developing body or size as a teenager, there's a good chance she internalized those negative messages, which would leave her feeling uncomfortable about her body. These familial effects have become so widely accepted that researchers in Toronto developed a Family Fat Talk Questionnaire.[4]

Meanwhile, when people feel weight-related devaluation, rejection, or discrimination (what's often referred to as "weight stigma"), they

4. Danielle Macdonald, Dimitropoulos G., Royal S., Polanco A., & Dionne, M. The Family Fat Talk Questionnaire: Development and psychometric properties of a measure of fat talk behaviors within the family context. *Body Image*, 12(1), 44–52, 2015.

experience a decrease in motivation to exercise, an increase in calorie consumption and patterns of disordered eating, a drop in their perception of their overall health, and higher levels of cortisol, certainly a vicious cycle of dysregulation.

When it comes to body dissatisfaction, there's a two-way street: Just as psychological and emotional factors—such as low self-esteem, shame, depression, anxiety, perfectionism, and a history of sexual abuse—can set the stage for body dissatisfaction, body dissatisfaction can lead to depression, anxiety, shame, self-consciousness, and low self-esteem. It can also fuel the rumination habit, which, in turn, can trigger depression, anxiety, binge eating, or binge drinking. Feeling bad about her body can also make a teen feel disempowered, and it can take a toll on her self-efficacy, which can have harmful ripple effects in every aspect of her life.

Intensely negative body image also creates social anxiety, including fears of rejection. Several years ago, I worked with a multiracial woman named Sofia, who was born in the Cape Verde Islands off the coast of Africa (she said, "My real name is Maria Sofia, but all the girls in Cape Verde are named Maria"). A part-time community college student and single mother, Sofia, at age 20, had such severe social anxiety and depressed mood that she would stay home with her 2-year-old daughter most of the time when she wasn't working. The fears stemmed largely from her childhood: Growing up with seven older siblings who teased her relentlessly and told her she was ugly, Sofia had always been shy and had a very poor physical self-image. With her father working two jobs and her mother overwhelmed with childcare, Sofia was left to suffer the mocking and often mean-spirited behavior of her siblings. When she was 12, her family moved to the United States and she was thrown into a middle-class high school that was oriented toward sports, cheerleaders, and parties.

There, she felt extremely sad and isolated. Even after leaving home, Sofia continued to hear her brothers' voices in her head, saying, "You're ugly, you're fat!" She always wanted to be more like the tall, thin, fair-skinned girls at her high school. I can still remember this woman of average height and weight, with beautiful eyes and long, curly dark hair—attractive in her own right but unable to appreciate it or have a full life, owing to her social anxiety and depressed moods that stemmed from internalized harassment. It was many years ago, but I can still see and hear how Sofia described her depressed mood: "I am so tired of feeling sick and tired." Sofia is not unusual. Teenagers who have the most negative feelings about their bodies tend to suffer from low self-esteem and depressed mood and experience more physical problems, such as pain.

- Reduce or eliminate negative commentary about people's appearances, in reality and on media.
- Emphasize fitness, not being thin.
- Point out that we should try not to see our bodies as detached objects for improvement but as integrated parts of the self that can provide us with the abilities to move, lift, and stretch and to enjoy life.
- If your son or daughter starts to become extremely self-critical about body image, reassure them of your love and admiration of them as a person. Usually reassuring them that they look fine to you will be brushed off.
- If reassurance is not successful, be direct and try distraction. "Let's talk about something else," or "Let's take a walk."
- Create a rule of no cruel teasing in the home.
- Reduce or eliminate your own preoccupation with body image.

THE PRACTICE OF GRADUAL SELF-REGULATION

Given the contrast between high school and college we described at the beginning of this chapter, it makes sense to approach the transition gradually. We all understand the excitement as a teen is getting ready to attend college. Some parents are uncomfortable bringing up a topic that is not totally positive about the upcoming college experience. As one parent told me, "I really would rather talk about dorms and roommates." Most parents hope it will be a happy time, but, as we reviewed in Chapter 1, the conversation about self-regulation doesn't need to be negative. You can remind your teen about what she does really well, whether it is exercise, nutrition, or sleep habits. You can also let her know about the changes and challenges that are likely to occur. Self-regulation skills are essential for success in college, so start early. This will make it more likely that the transition is a positive one.

CHAPTER 7

Healthy Boundaries

Growing Up Safe

In the Cameron Crowe movie *Almost Famous*, Frances McDormand plays the mother of a 15-year-old boy who takes the opportunity to leave home and write for *Rolling Stone* magazine. As her son gets on the bus to leave, she shouts, "Don't do drugs!" When I saw the movie with my extended family, the scene got a big laugh in the theater. The teenagers shared in the son's embarrassment and the parents understood the mother's fears. And it's true: the "Don't do it" approach is not enough, nor is it the right strategy to help keep our teens safe, no matter how sophisticated its phrasing may be.

As much as we want our teens to adopt healthy behaviors, we also want them to avoid harmful ones. This chapter addresses alcohol, tobacco, and marijuana use and unsafe sex. Are you scared yet? Don't be. It is part of adolescence to take risks. As Chapter 2 detailed, the prefrontal cortex that helps us with decision-making is still developing in teens. At the same time, peer pressure is prominent and powerful. Some brain imaging studies show that several areas of brain make adolescents more sensitive to the reinforcement of peer relationships. Therefore, decisions about risk-taking are heavily affected by friends. At the same time, one study found that 60% of teens listed their parents as the most important influences on their decisions, compared to 40% who listed friends. This chapter will empower you to use that influence as best you can. We will explore ways to talk about risk-taking behaviors. We will also review some facts about each subject. The facts shouldn't be ammunition for lecturing your teen, but they will be helpful; knowing them, you will better understand your teen's situation and you can use them if they ask questions.

We cannot cover all the forms of substance use in this chapter, but we can look at strategies for reducing the likelihood of substance misuse and unprotected sex within the context of maintaining healthy boundaries. Teens need to know that knowing what not to do is just as important as knowing what to do to preserve their health. Learning to set boundaries on possible high-risk behaviors is one key to adult health and wellness.

These topics are especially important for those suffering from depression or bipolar disorder. High school students who have had a major depressive episode have higher rates of underage drinking, marijuana use, and tobacco consumption. This is likely a result of teens attempting to self-medicate, manage a stressful environment, or cope with a traumatic history. Therefore, even if you find exploring these issues with your teen a bit uncomfortable, it's more than worth the effort.

RELATIONSHIPS AND COMMUNICATION

Here is the most important fact: Teens who have a positive relationship with their parents are less likely to engage in risk-taking behaviors. The communication skills from Chapter 4—listening, validating, and using motivational interviewing—are useful here. However, it can be challenging to maintain your composure when you are talking about potentially addictive or risky behaviors because they can be dangerous, and our tendency as parents is to protect our children from harm, so you may have strong emotional reactions. You can acknowledge to your daughter that you think the stakes are high while at the same time try not to lose your temper or blurt out statements like "Who doesn't know that you should leave a party where alcohol is served?" (she may not know how to negotiate this); "You're crazy to eat a pot brownie" (she may lack information about edibles); or "It's just stupid to smoke cigarettes" (she may be responding to peer pressure or trying to lose weight). Even though these comments may make sense to you, they will shut down communication. It's better to discover what your teen thinks are reasonable choices, and then you can share yours. You also want to know what gets in the way of your teen making healthy choices and whether she has the refusal skills to deal with peer pressure.

Ideally, the conversation about risk-taking behaviors needs to start early, even before middle school, so your child can understand your values and so you can push back against messages on social media that underage drinking and using tobacco and marijuana are glamorous. Remember, if you don't start the conversation, another source will fill the vacuum. If you're reading this book to understand and communicate with your 16-year-old, there is a lot to learn, but also be sure to consider younger siblings. If you have any doubts about this, check out the powerful 2018 movie *Eighth Grade*, which follows the story of Kayla, a 13-year-old struggling with social anxiety, parties, and her attempt at reinvention.

A good time to talk about substances is when the subject comes up naturally, as when you and your teen see something on television, in a movie, or on social media, or when one of you shares an anecdote that deals with alcohol, drugs, or tobacco. Since these are not directly related to your child's behavior, the conversation can have a bit of emotional distance. It can also provide an opportunity for you to use the motivational interviewing skills with "pro and con" underage drinking and tobacco and marijuana use. Here's an example:

"So, Eve [a character on TV] wants to start smoking cigarettes to lose weight. What do you think about that?"

"Well, it could reduce her appetite."

"Sure. Do you see other pros to smoking?"

"Yeah, it might make her look and feel cool."

"Ok, How about the cons?"

"Well, it's pretty expensive."

"Any others?"

"I hear you can get addicted."

"Yes, and girls get addicted to tobacco more quickly than boys do, too. It sounds like a major reason for Eve to smoke is her appearance."

"Yeah, I get that."

" She might lose weight if she smokes but will also get yellowed teeth, finger stains, and early wrinkles."

"But mom, of course she could just vape."

Uh, oops, full stop. Mom is not up to date. Vaporizing tobacco rose more quickly than any other substance use in a recent long-term study, "Monitoring the Future," conducted at the University of Michigan Institute for Social Research. The study included a nationally representative sample of almost 50,000 students in 8th, 10th, and 12th grades. The headline of the press release regarding changes between 2017 and 2018 says it all: "Largest Year-to-Year Increase in Substance Use Ever Recorded in the U.S. for 10th and 12th Grade Students." The results are even more striking when you take into account that the research has been ongoing for 44 years and has examined 1,000 year-to-year changes during that time.

Vaping is inhaling nicotine delivered through an aerosol by heating it until it is vaporized (hence *vaping*). Marijuana can also be vaped, and in the survey, vaping marijuana also increased, but not to the same degree as vaping tobacco. There is no doubt that flavored e-cigarettes and those designed to look like a small flash drive were meant to target teens, and now we know this strategy was successful. In 2015, Juul (the leading brand of vaporizers and flavored tobacco cartridges) created a new market for teens, by using bright colors and flavors, although e-cigarettes were originally supposed to be a form of harm reduction for adult smokers. Garry Trudeau satirized this situation in *Doonesbury* when he created two characters in dialogue, Buttsie, the tobacco cigarette, and Juuly, the e-cigarette. Juuly: "Ironic, right? I was developed to help your generation, but ended up hooking a generation of my own!" Buttsie: "Tell me about it! That's why big cig is buying you up and pushing me out. . . .The truth is . . . I'm over." Juul spent more than one million dollars on marketing and advertising and sponsored teen events and music festivals. Meanwhile, few of us were aware that one Juul pod contains as much nicotine as about 20 regular cigarettes. The U.S. Food and Drug Administration (FDA) announced that it would ban most flavored e-cigarettes in 2018. Several state attorneys general are suing the company to impose limits on youth access to e-cigarettes, and Juul reversed course by advertising that e-cigarettes should not be used by those under 18 years old. However, we are late in protecting our teens. The use of all other addictive substances dropped between 2017 and 2018, but vaping nicotine skyrocketed, with about 21% of high school seniors reporting vaping nicotine in the past 30 days. When I was searching for vaping manufacturers other than Juul, I found over 120 of them. Many teens believe that vaping tobacco is harmless when we have long known that withdrawal from nicotine is extremely difficult.

Then the situation became deadly, with over 2711 cases of respiratory illness as a result of vaping reported as of January, 2020, including 60 deaths. While the precise causes are not clear, the illnesses affect healthy young people and are related primarily to vaping marijuana but also, in some cases, vaping nicotine. The illness now has the acronym EVALI for "e-cigarette-or-vaping associated lung injury."

"Pediatricians are warning that they are seeing alarming symptoms in teens who became addicted to nicotine from e-cigarettes. Dr. David Cristiani, of the Harvard T. H. Chan School of Public Health, commented, "There is clearly an epidemic that begs for an urgent response."[1] Several

1. Matt Richter & Grady, D. Cases of vaping related illnesses surge, health officials say. *The New York Times,* September 6, 2019.

states have prohibited the sale of flavored e-cigarettes, some school districts are suing Juul, and after the FDA announced a plan to ban all flavored e-cigarettes. Juul finally agreed to pull all flavored e-cigarettes from stores. The Centers for Disease Control and Prevention (CDC) recommends that everyone stop vaping. However, we now have a generation of young people who have been vaping nicotine for several years. Over five million minors, mostly high school students, report using e-cigarettes, with 25% of high school students reporting use in the previous month, up from 20% the previous year. Among high school seniors, 1 in 9 vape on a near-daily basis and many are now addicted to nicotine. Nicotine interferes with adolescent brain development so this is dangerous, long-term crisis.

Ultimately, the proposed ban on flavored e-cigarettes was watered down, with menthol, one of the most popular flavors, being excluded. In addition, now many teens are turning to disposable vaping products that are not covered by the federal ban. The vaping nicotine epidemic is a tragic turn of events, following years of a decline in teenage cigarette smoking.

UNDERAGE DRINKING

The Columbia Addictions Center reports that "adolescent substance abuse is America's number one health problem." Notice that it considers substance abuse the number one "health," not "mental health," problem. Although I have concerns about marijuana use, alcohol continues to be the dangerous substance of choice, which is easily obtained, for teenagers. Michael Stein and Sandro Galea, of the Boston University School of Public Health, clarify the situation: "Even though the opioid epidemic is growing, alcohol kills more Americans than heroin, fentanyl, and prescription pills combined. During the past decade, death as a result of alcohol of increased by 35%. Men make up 3/4 of these deaths but young women are experiencing the greatest rise."[2] Stein and Galea suggest that five factors account for the increase: advertising (to the tune of two billion dollars annually), individuals drinking more, Americans having more disposable income to spend on drinking, cultural complacency about alcohol, and drinking while driving. Although people with higher incomes drink more than poorer people, the latter group has suffered more negative health effects due to the combination of alcohol with higher rates of cigarette smoking and mental health problems.

2. Michael Stein & Galea, S. The public's health. *Boston University School of Public Health Newsletter*, December 19, 2018.

As for binge drinking, although the "Monitoring the Future" study found that underage drinking has declined since the 1970s, there is still cause for concern: Another study of underage drinkers found that 40% would get drunk, 37% would drink 5 drinks in a row, and 13% would drink 10 in a row. Technically, binge drinking is an episode that creates a blood alcohol concentration level of 0.08 grams percent or higher, which would typically be after four drinks for women and five drinks for men over a 2-hour period. Although the overall number of teens drinking may be down, binge drinking is still a significant problem. Young women are binge drinking more often now, which is problematic because women experience negative health effects at lower doses of alcohol than men. According to the excellent website College Parents Matter, even the 21st birthday deserves more attention, since more than 80% of students report drinking to celebrate. There is no problem with this until you realize that one study suggests that almost half of 21-year olds drink more during that celebration than they ever have before and that 35% of females and 49% of males drank enough to reach a blood alcohol concentration of .26 or higher while celebrating their 21st birthday, certainly raising the possibility of alcohol poisoning.

Underage drinking is especially problematic for teens who have had a bout of depression, because they are twice as likely to start drinking (girls are in fact more than twice as likely). Unbeknownst to many, alcohol is a depressant. Many teens, especially those who have some social anxiety, like the initial effects of disinhibition and relaxation, but alcohol depresses mood, disrupts sleep, and slows reaction time. The earlier a teen starts drinking, the higher the likelihood they may be diagnosed later with an alcohol use disorder. Here are some other facts that you and your teen may not know about alcohol and underage drinking.

- It takes 2–3 hours for alcohol to leave the system. So, a quick cup of coffee is not enough for sobering up.
- Beer and wine are not necessarily safer than hard liquor; they just contain different amounts of alcohol per ounce. In the United States a "standard" drink contains roughly 14 grams of alcohol. A 12-ounce beer with 5% alcohol, 5 ounces of wine with 12%, or 1.5 ounces of distilled spirits with 40% all contain that amount. Many craft beers have higher amounts of alcohol, with an average of 5.9% by volume and some with 10% or more.
- Teens who drink alcohol are more likely to become victims of violent crime and sexual assault or be involved in motor vehicle accidents.
- The website collegedrinkingprevention.gov features a very informative graphic that allows the user to click on the organs of the body to find out

alcohol's effect on them. Some of the facts it includes are as follows: only recently have we discovered that alcohol abuse increases the risk of lung injury; binge drinking as well as long-term drinking affects how quickly the heart beats and therefore can cause heart arrhythmias; and two million Americans suffer from liver disease caused by alcohol. The site also shows that the liver is more complicated than we may realize as it performs more than 500 different functions.

MARIJUANA

Marijuana is the second most commonly used intoxicant in adolescence and is increasing in prevalence, with 38% of high school students using it at least once in the past year and 21% in the previous month. Teens are coming to perceive fewer risks of marijuana use. What teens don't understand is that even if marijuana is legal, that doesn't mean it's a good idea for a teenager or emerging adult to use it much. Research suggests that regular use may negatively affect attention and memory, and further investigation is needed to assess its effect on the developing brain. One fact we should communicate to our teens is that, with respect to marijuana and other illegal drugs, the margin for error is slim. Here are some marijuana facts:

- The chemicals, or cannabinoids, in marijuana are THC (tetrahydrocannabinol), the main psychoactive component, and CBD (cannabidiol).
- Today's marijuana is roughly nine times more potent than it was 20 years ago.
- There are ongoing studies of the use of THC and CBD for the management of pain, but there is much more work to be done.
- Although I am in favor of legalization of marijuana, I am very concerned that it will become even more available to teenagers. Some legalization advocates reply to my concerns by saying that alcohol is already available, but I'm not sure we want to increase the amount and types of potentially harmful substances available to teens.
- We do not know enough about the effects of marijuana on teenagers, because the federal government severely limited funds for such research. Most studies are based on people who are already using marijuana, not controlled clinical trials of the direct effects.
- Although marijuana is being legalized in many states, that doesn't mean it is safe for *teenage* use. With the adolescent brain still under construction, marijuana can interfere with development.

- As marijuana becomes legal, some drug dealers have taken to "enhancing" their products in order to stave off competition from legal dispensaries. In some communities, unfortunately, the enhancement can be cocaine, heroin, and, rarely, even fentanyl, a powerful synthetic opiate. Fentanyl is more often found in heroin and is responsible for more fatal overdoses in the United States than any other substance. Other contaminants can be bacteria, PCP (phencyclidine, a dissociative also known as angel dust), embalming fluid, and even laundry detergent.
- It takes edible marijuana over an hour to take effect and hours more to leave the system, so if a teen eats a marijuana gummy bear and does not immediately feel any effect, she might consume another one, not understanding that the first simply hasn't yet started affecting her and that if she experiences negative effects like extreme anxiety, they could last for 6 hours.
- As described earlier, vaping THC can cause pulmonary illnesses and, in some cases, death.
- Forty percent of teens report that they can get marijuana in a day or less and almost 25% report that they can get it within an hour. Availability will only increase as marijuana is legalized.

MDMA

- MDMA, ecstasy, or Molly (short for molecule) quickly increases levels of serotonin, norepinephrine, and dopamine, with the result of emotional closeness, elevated mood, and increased empathy. These effects last from 3 to 6 hours, and some people take a second dose once the first starts to fade. I have seen many students who, the following week, experience the negative effects documented by research—irritability, sleep problems, depressed mood, and anxiety. Other reported adverse effects are decreased appetite, loss of interest in sex, and memory and attention problems—in other words, an experience very similar to depression.

OTHER SUBSTANCES

Stimulants (Adderall, Ritalin, Vyvanse, etc.) are extremely effective when used as prescribed for students with ADD. However, some students share their prescriptions for these "study drugs," and some others sell their medication. Students believe that these stimulants enhance academic performance, which may help explain why studies estimate that between 5 and

35% of college students in the United States and Western Europe without ADD take them illegally. Lisa Weyandt of the University of Rhode Island and Tara White at Brown University conducted a small pilot study of students without ADD who took stimulants. The researchers found that although students report enhanced mood, "the standard 30 mg dose of Adderall did improve attention and focus—a typical result from a stimulant—but that effect failed to translate to better performance on a battery of neurocognitive tasks that measured short-term memory, reading comprehension and fluency."[3] This study will need to be replicated with large numbers, but it is possible that students are taking medication that they think enhances performance but is really a placebo effect, or that the physiological effects are activating overall.

There are numerous other substances that teens use, including the depressants GHB (gamma hydroxybutyrate), flunitrazepam, or Rohypnol, also known as "the rape drug;" hallucinogens (most prominently LSD and psychedelic mushrooms); dissociatives like PCP and ketamine; sedatives (Xanax, Ambien); and opiates. The National Institute on Drug Abuse maintains an excellent reference of potentially abused substances and their effects, at https://www.drugabuse.gov/drugs-abuse/commonly-abused-drugs-charts.

If you want to help your teen who is using a substance, you can ask them exactly how the drug makes them feel better. Less socially anxious? Elevated mood? Less bored? Numb? This will help you understand their attraction to the substance and perhaps help them find another way to manage that problem. A substance use disorder is diagnosed when there is problematic, recurrent use of drugs or alcohol that causes significant distress or impairment in a person's life.

PARENTAL MONITORING

Many studies have documented the relationship between depressed mood and underage drinking. One study found that high levels of parental monitoring reduced the likelihood of alcohol-related problems by 50% in teens who had high levels of depressed mood. The results of this study emphasize that we need to monitor underage drinking and depressed mood in teens. But how, you may ask, do we monitor? You can start by asking

3. Lisa L. Weyandt, White, T. L., Gudmundsdottir, B. G., Nitenson, A. Z., Rathkey, E. S., De Leon, K. A., & Bjorn, S. A. Neurocognitive, autonomic, and mood effects of Adderall: A pilot study of healthy college students. *Pharmacy*, 6(3), 58, 2018.

where your teen is going, with whom, by what means of transport, and for how long. Cell phones now make it easy to call and be called, but be sure the phone is fully charged or ask that your teen take a charger with her. Outside of parties, most substance use occurs between the hours of 3:00 and 6:00 P.M., after school and before most parents get home from work. I am not suggesting that we all quit our jobs and stay home, but once again, phone calls, structure, and interest can let your teens know you care about where they are. Too little monitoring and too much free time can be problems. If a teen doesn't have after-school activities, I recommend leaving a list of family chores.

TEEN SEX

And then there is the whole issue of teen sex. As uncomfortable as you may be talking about underage drinking and marijuana, you may be even more uncomfortable talking about sexual health. Nonetheless, sexuality is simply part of life, and communicating with your child about sex makes them more likely to have healthy relationships, avoid unplanned pregnancies, and prevent disease. Try to overcome your embarrassment, because this is another area where open communication and sharing information can be vitally important. You *can* make a difference, because teens who talk with their parents about sexual issues, in general, are more likely to defer sex until they are older and more likely to use protection. And, good news: Planned Parenthood has a resource for talking with your teen about sex, at https://www.plannedparenthood.org/learn/parents.

Sex as a Safety Issue

One reason to talk about sex is the issue of safety. This is another area of health where times have changed significantly. For example, in 1960, we knew of 3 sexually transmitted diseases (STDs); we now know of 35. Teens make up 33% of the population but account for 50% of STD cases. One in five teens has an STD and 80% of the time the diseases are "silent"—that is, they present no symptoms, which can present serious harm for a teen's future. For example, pelvic inflammatory disease, an infection of women's reproductive organs, can result from an untreated STD and interferes with fertility.

You might be wondering, "What does safe sex have to do with depression?" As it turns out, quite a bit. Just as with alcohol and marijuana, healthy sexual relationships are all about maintaining respect for the body. Depressed teens, especially young women, are less likely to use protection than those who are not depressed.

You'll probably need to take some time to think through your own feelings about sex and especially sexual behavior among teenagers. These include when you think it would be acceptable for your daughter or son to have sex and whether you think they should be out of high school or should be in a committed relationship first. In addition to participating in an ongoing conversation, the attitude you take toward sex will determine how open your teen can be with you. All too often we only emphasize the dangers of sex rather than putting sex into the larger context of healthy relationships. And these relationships may be heterosexual or gay or lesbian.

A few facts about teenagers and sex:

- By age 18, 93% of boys and 62% of girls have been exposed to online pornography.
- Although parents would like their teens to abstain from sex until they are at least in college, research shows that 44% of females and 49% of males report having had sexual intercourse between the ages of 15 and 19.
- Drinking is associated with unprotected sex.

Sex as an Issue of Respect in Relationships

There are divergent paths about sexual behavior with teenage boys and girls, but for both girls and boys, we need to emphasize the importance of consent, healthy relationships, enjoyment, and protection. Young men and women alike are pressured to behave according to specific roles. Young men are sometimes encouraged to have as much sex as possible to bolster an image of masculinity. For young women, it's more complicated. The message from many non-parental sources is to dress and act in an extremely sexualized manner. Yet, at the same time, a young woman can be shamed at a moment's notice if she has engaged in sexual behavior and made someone else angry or jealous.

In *Untangled*, Psychologist Lisa Damour's excellent book about teenage girls, she points out that we need to encourage girls to be assertive and to discuss sexuality with their partners. Young women need to identify what they enjoy sexually rather than react to what young men ask of them. Since many boys learn about sexuality from pornography, unfortunately, many of them expect girls to engage in similar sexual behavior, without any discussion. Damour points out that a young man may not be an appropriately mature partner if he does not seem able to discuss a sexual relationship. At the same time, there can be misunderstandings as to what sexual intercourse means in the context of a relationship. I have talked with both young men and women who have been disappointed when they assumed that their partner was serious about them because they were having intercourse. This issue is explored in greater detail more in Chapter Nineteen.

One of the reasons that sex and alcohol do not make a good combination is that consent needs to be mutual and thought through, and being drunk reduces one's ability to think anything through. Young men and women alike need to know that having sex when both people are drunk or high can be seen as sexual assault.

HOUSE RULES

You want to have ongoing, open communication with your teen, no matter what the topic, but especially regarding risk-taking behaviors and safety. It is not contradictory, though, to have clear house rules that are consistent and have consequences. Even if your teen sometimes breaks the rules, they will know where you stand and what you value. I suggest the following rules, which are based on my clinical experience:

- No one drinks alcohol or uses marijuana until age 21.
- Teens will leave parties where alcohol is consumed or where there is non-consensual sexual activity.
- No one drives in a car with anyone who has been drinking at all.
- Older siblings will not obtain or share alcohol or encourage younger ones to drink.
- No smoking in the house, near the house, or in family cars. (That also means you; teens whose parents smoke cigarettes are three times more likely to do so.)
- No exposure to secondhand smoke.
- No parties in houses without adults. If your daughter or son goes to a party where the parents are supposed to be home, confirm it.
- Most important, you can jointly agree on the "safe pick-up" rule. Your teen can call you at any time for a ride and you will pick them up, without any judgmental remarks.

Consequences

It's best to clarify the consequences of breaking the rules before they are broken. These can range from time limits on cell phones or other screen time limits to grounding. It's not a good idea to cut your teen off from all social contact for a long period of time; they may then lose hope and break more rules, and escalation is the last thing you want. I similarly advise against taking away sports or valued extracurricular activities; these are important for providing structure and maintaining connections to larger communities. These are all examples of deprivation as a consequence. I like the idea of adding rather than subtracting, by having the teen who breaks rules perform more household chores or community service in a time period and with standards set by parents. After the consequences have been completed, try to move on. If you bring up your teen's missteps a lot, it will just lead to a cycle of anger. A clear consequence fully paid should be enough. Your teen knows you disapprove; that's why the rules exist. Additional verbal criticism will not be effective.

REFUSAL SKILLS

Suppose your child wants to live by house rules and really doesn't want to drink, smoke cigarettes, or use marijuana and other drugs but is not verbally skilled or is shy or is desperate to be accepted. You can be an enormous help by exploring the precise elements of her social world and help her develop refusal skills. These are similar to the assertiveness skills discussed in Chapter 4. Refusal skills are an example of setting limits with friends or having healthy boundaries. Refusal skills are direct verbal expressions of turning down an offer to smoke, drink, or use marijuana. The first step is to be clear with a "No, thanks" spoken in a firm voice with good eye contact and upright posture, but it's best to keep it casual at first. If the person persists, she can ask them to stop. To reduce the chance of the other person feeling rejected, your teen can suggest an alternative activity or change the subject. She should also know that she doesn't have to justify her preferences but can say, "I'm just not into that right now." When all else fails, it is best to leave the scene. Yes, there is a risk that your teen will be rejected socially, but it's usually not only because she refused risky behavior. Moreover, engaging in them does not guarantee inclusion, either. In fact, getting drunk or high when she doesn't want to increases the likelihood of more social discomfort and potential dangers.

If your teen wants to delay sex until she is older or wants to refuse a partner, you can brainstorm what to say, especially if the potential partner is persistent. Some possibilities include "I don't want that responsibility right now" and "That 'no' I said before was a complete sentence." If a young woman is told to prove her love to a young man, she can say, "I guess we'll have to find another way." It's important to rehearse these comments because your teen could be taken by surprise, and it is difficult to be assertive in sexual situations.

In addition, to the extent you have influence, know that any teen dating someone more than 2 years older is at greater risk for an unwanted sexual experience. I have seen young teens date older ones and then feel overwhelmed by the sexual demands of the relationship. At the same time, they may have lost contact with their peers, so they feel isolated and unable to share any concerns.

Here are some suggestions about communicating and setting limits on sexual behavior in teens:

- Listen first; try to understand and help your teen clarify their views.
- State your views clearly without imposing them on your teen.
- Emphasize that your interest in their sexual behavior is one of safety and respect.
- If your teen wants information, be sure to go slowly and ask if they have any questions.
- Young men and women need to understand that the bodies displayed in pornography don't look like the average person's body. Early exposure to pornography tends to warp young men's views about sexual behavior. Most actors in pornography have been surgically and cosmetically enhanced. Pornography also takes sex out of the realm of communication and relationships and therefore is inherently dehumanizing.
- Young women and men need to know that masturbation is healthy. As Planned Parenthood maintains, "It is the safest sex there is." For this reason and others, teens may need more privacy and the ability to close their doors to the bedrooms. Masturbation is also a way for teens to begin to understand their sexual needs.
- Young men and women need to know that businesses use sexuality as a lure to sell their products––cigarettes, clothes, cosmetics, and alcohol, just to name a few. Media literacy also includes the fact that increasing "sexuality" is a product they are trying to sell you.

SENSATION-SEEKING TEENS

Many limit-setting strategies are effective in general, but less so with particularly sensation-seeking, impulsive teens. Even within one family, house rules may work quite well with one teen but not another. Impulsivity and sensation-seeking are recognized as key factors in adolescent risk-taking. In addition, adolescents tend to underestimate the probability of certain risks, such as fast driving, alcohol use, and so on. High-risk–taking teens tend to be popular and have more friends in high school, so their behavior is initially rewarded in a powerful way.

So what to do? As parents, you can continue to do be consistent about rules and consequences and try to keep lines of communication open. Even though you don't want to tell your teen that certain friends are bad influences and should be avoided, you can demonstrate your knowledge and suggest that you know bad things can happen and that if your teen is uncomfortable, he can call you. Sometimes sensation-seeking teens also have ADD with hyperactivity or a mood disorder, or a history of trauma, so you should have a low threshold for seeking mental health consultation. Similarly, if a teen is showing signs of drinking too much or using too much marijuana, it is often better to get help early. If your teen refuses, you can seek professional consultation for yourself first, to help you manage the situation and practice self-compassion.

SEXUAL ASSAULT

Another reason you want to establish trust and open communication is if sexual assault occurs. The data about sexual assault continue to be horrifying. The National Sexual Violence Research Center reports that 1 in 5 women and 1 in 71 men will be raped at some point during their lifetime. The victim knows the perpetrator the majority of the time. By age 17, 18% of young women and 30% of young men report that they have been assaulted or abused by another teen. Most of them did not tell a parent and only 19% reported the assault to police. Your teen needs to know that not only will you be open to talking with them if an assault occurs but that you want them to involve you. The aftermath of assault includes increased rates of anxiety and depression, PTSD, and an increased risk of being assaulted in the future. Most communities have sexual assault and intimate partner violence centers (see Resources) that can provide support and will even have people accompany victims to hospitals and help them talk to the police.

Finally, a critically important skill you can give your teen is the ability to self-assess. This involves taking a step back, when sober, to think about the results of behavior and how it fits into current values and future plans. It's a bit like going through the pros and cons of motivational interviewing. For example, every day we learn that there is no privacy on social media, so that funny, drunk photo on Instagram will not be very funny when a teen later applies for a scholarship or a job. A hangover may be harmless now and then, but if a teen is hung over every weekend, with grades slipping and exercise plans abandoned, a re-evaluation is in order. If the hook-up she felt pressured into led to feeling hurt and rejected, she might want to reconsider for the future. Self-assessment may not be utilized at first but is worth discussing early on. It can be developed over time.

Here is a successful example of parental monitoring and developing self-assessment: Susan and her husband Manny have a son, Pete, who has a serious major depressive disorder that was exacerbated by drinking alcohol. For many months, Pete was put off by their monitoring and asking him questions about his mood and drinking. Then, one day, after months of sobriety and improved mood, he came to his mother and said, "I'm feeling the urge the drink. Not sure what to do." He not only went to his mother for advice and support, he had learned to *internalize the questions* his parents had been asking him. If you help your teen establish healthy boundaries, with knowledge, communication, self-assertion, and refusal skills, and the ability to self-assess, they will be better able to stay safe and avoid harm during their college years. We will look at how these skills come into play, in Chapter 16, College as a Land of Challenges.

CHAPTER 8

Distress Tolerance, Distraction, and Mindfulness Matters

THE PARADOX OF DISTRESS TOLERANCE

It may seem paradoxical to encourage your teen to experience more discomfort if you want to prevent depression, but that is precisely the topic of this chapter. It is based on the evidence-based conclusion that teaching our children and teens how to tolerate, manage, and sometimes accept distress will help them in many ways, including to prevent depression.

As parents, we have a natural tendency to protect our children and help them avoid pain. We try to listen, comfort, and give advice—especially give advice. But as children reach adolescence, they need to develop their own skills of distress tolerance and self-soothing. After all, within a few years, they will be away from home. As a parent of teenagers, you know that they experience intense emotions. In my experience, parents find distress tolerance to be more difficult than some of the other skills we've covered so far.

WHAT IS DISTRESS TOLERANCE?

Simply put, *distress tolerance* is the ability to experience and withstand negative emotions, including anger, shame, sadness, and disappointment. Distress tolerance is a critically important part of healthy adult development; a lack of distress tolerance puts teenagers at risk for substance abuse, destructive impulsive behaviors, and depression. In fact, a full 50% of the acute diagnoses in the list of psychiatric diagnoses included in the fifth edition of the *Diagnostic and Statistical Manual* (DSM-5) involve a lack of distress tolerance. In addition, distress tolerance helps people avoid the long-term behaviors that harm health and interfere with close relationships, including substance abuse, smoking, and inability to control anger.

Before teens can manage and regulate their emotions, they need the ability to identify and label them. We can think of these abilities as developmental "prerequisites" to self-regulation and distress tolerance. One strategy I suggest when a teen seems to be upset emotionally but not able to identify the precise feeling is to ask, "What does this feeling remind you of?" or to suggest some common sayings, like "down in the dumps" or "riding a roller coaster." Some teens might balk at this at first; I then invoke the importance of identifying the feeling, by quoting the Yale Center for Emotional Intelligence: You have to "name it to tame it." Another approach is to have a student use two scales, mild to intense, and pleasant to unpleasant. That is one reason I like the Mood Meter app, described in the Resources section, because it uses visual cues of colors to help identify emotional states.

At the same time, it is natural for teenagers to use their adolescent behaviors—avoidance, withdrawal, excessive engagement in social media, and impulsive behaviors—to try to relieve distress. Unfortunately, all of these add an additional layer of problems to the original distressing emotions. And stresses on today's teens—academic achievement, homework, social life and social pressure, sexuality, competition, college applications, financial problems, divorce and marital separation—are more numerous and more intense than in previous generations. So, too, is the prevalence of depression, and these two facts are linked. The impact of stress and the inability to manage negative emotions are contributing factors to the development of depression. It is clear that our teenagers need our help.

I have learned a lot about distress tolerance from working with depressed teens and young adults. Gisele, 19, was an example of the tangled web of emotional factors tied to distress tolerance. A sophomore in college, Gisele was struggling in her classes, had gained about 20 pounds, was smoking marijuana daily, and believed herself to be an utter failure. Her parents were threatening to pull her out of school because her grades were marginal, something that was out of character for Gisele, who had previously earned A's and B's in high school in Los Angeles. Back then, she had some close friends and was always energetic, but by the time she came to psychotherapy she was struggling with depression and anxiety. Her parents could not understand the situation. Previously, they had always encouraged her but also protected her from sad feelings by taking her shopping, engaging tutors, and hoping she would avoid any sadness. I was originally part of their quick-fix plan, along with a tutor, for Gisele to bounce back.

Like many students, during her freshman year, Gisele felt overwhelmed by the academic competition with other students and the new social demands of a large university. She became increasingly sad and worried and started drinking a lot and smoking marijuana daily to numb her feelings of inadequacy. After being passed over for a sorority, Gisele plunged into self-doubt and firmly believed that other students would reject her. Constantly engaged in social media, she began feeling "disgusting and fat" and compared herself negatively to other, especially thinner, women. To lose weight, she tried skipping meals, but then became hungry and felt even more alienated, which resulted in her overeating and drinking and smoking more marijuana. By the time I met her, she was wearing a hoodie that almost entirely covered her face, her long hair shielding the rest of it, and she curled on the sofa in my office, unable to make eye contact, tearful and ashamed. I also thought she looked a bit hungover.

My sessions with Gisele helped her name and directly experience such emotions as loneliness and disappointment. We used the strategies described in the following sections. It took some time for her to understand that, in the long run, expressing her feelings was preferable to her usual patterns of behavior. Gradually, Gisele developed the ability to identify, withstand, and share these "unacceptable feelings." She came to believe that she was strong enough to learn to tolerate her distress rather than turn to substance abuse, overeating, and avoidance. With her permission, I would periodically speak to Gisele's parents to reassure them that Gisele's recovery would take time and to help them understand that protecting her from negative emotions was not only impossible but that she would be happier in the long run if she learned to tolerate, experience, and grow from the whole range of emotions. This was difficult for them to understand at first; they meant well in trying to protect her. But they also knew that now that Gisele was far away from home, she needed to learn how to manage her moods without them.

HELPING TEENS LEARN TO TOLERATE DISTRESS

There is a lot that parents can do to help their teenagers learn and use distress tolerance skills before college, the subject of this chapter. But first, be sure to review the all-important communication skills presented in Chapter 4. Then, in the following pages you can read about a wide range of distress tolerance skills and how to teach and model them. I have used them in my clinical practice for many years. But you know your child, so you are in the best position to sort out which ones may be effective and to choose a time and place to communicate this information. If one technique doesn't work, notice that and try another. You are not a failure; you are learning. A clue that it's not working is when your teen responds with a "Yeah, yeah, are we done yet?" or the powerful nonverbal shrug combined with the infamously dismissive, "Whatever." You'll be able to tell by his tone if the interaction has essentially ended. These are signs that you may have lapsed into lecture territory—it's the wrong time or not the best approach. Learn, and move on.

Following are some techniques, values, and attitudes that can help you, your teen, and the whole family. As a therapist, I needed to learn the skills before I could effectively share them with my patients. Similarly, as a parent, you'll benefit from doing the same. Practice some of the skills in this chapter first and remember to keep a flexible and responsive approach as to what works. These skills are based on the communications skills discussed in Chapter 4 but are specific to dealing with distress.

The Strength of the Family during Times of Distress

As discussed in Chapter 1, despite their focus on friends, teens still need to know that they can count on a secure family foundation. Part of psychological health is also the ability to express all emotions without serious conflict. In many families there is either too much expressed emotion, which quickly leads to conflict, or emotions get repressed (the "stiff upper lip" or "man up" attitude). It never hurts to say something like "We will always be hear for you" or "I've got your back" or some expression of rock-solid commitment. Even if your teen may scoff at the time, they'll remember during times of stress or change.

Be an Empathic Listener

Empathic listening is a key step in any effective communication, especially if a teen is upset. It may be difficult to listen quietly to intense negative emotions but by listening carefully to your teens, you will be able to help them name their emotions with clarifying questions, restatements, and synonyms. "Sounds like that was really disappointing, upsetting?" Then the two of you will be more in sync.

For example, you may know that Beth did not do as well as she had hoped on her SATs. Then you notice that she has become withdrawn, so her nonverbal behavior is telling you that something is wrong. But what is it? Too often, there is a tendency to rush and console her by saying something like "I know you must be feeling disappointed about your SATs. Maybe we can get you a tutor." This sounds helpful, but by saying this you are trying to solve a problem prematurely; if you clarified it with Beth first, she might respond, "No. I actually ran into my ex at school and that made me sad and anxious during the test." In a case like that, Beth doesn't need a tutor; she needs a chance to talk about her ex.

Model Healthy Expressions of Emotion

Demonstrate the attitude that the expression and experience of difficult emotions are not only acceptable but also healthy. This is a challenge to distress-intolerance beliefs like "Talking about it won't help" or "I can't handle feeling this way." If your teenagers come in expressing a lot of anger or upset, rather than pulling back or trying to prematurely fix the situation, consider saying something like "Wow, tell me more about that," or use a synonym to name the emotion to let them know you understand. If your daughter was fat-shamed during a physical education class and says she is upset, you could try to clarify the emotion by saying something like "Wow that sounds tough. Maybe you are feeling humiliated?" Let her respond so you can make sure you understand. And then just sit with the emotion for a while. This lets your daughter know that you care and can accept her emotions.

Let Them Know You Understand How They're Feeling

Validation has been shown to defuse intense emotions, improve self-esteem in teens, improve parent–child communication, strengthen overall family functioning, and lead to other productive interactions, an impressive list of positive outcomes that can help prevent depression. A study by a team of Harvard psychologists led by Perry Hoffman and Alan Fruzzetti also found that learning validation skills lessened depression in mothers and increased their satisfaction with relationships with their children. This makes sense, because a validating conversation can lead to stronger emotional engagement. For example, if your son was just rejected by another teen and says something like "I am *done* with trying!" it might be tempting to rush in with "But don't give up." Instead, a validating response would be "That sounds like a frustrating situation. I can understand why you might be aggravated."

Are You Practicing What You Preach?

Teenagers still look up to their parents as role models. It may not always feel that way, but teens list their parents as the best resources for talking about mental health issues. However, teens are also brutally able to sense and point out any sniff of hypocrisy, so the next step is to reflect on your own level of distress tolerance. No matter what you say to your teenager, if you explode or quickly shut down when something makes you angry, then whatever you say is meaningless. Being a parent increases feelings of vulnerability. Parents can feel alone and overwhelmed at times, especially during the storms of adolescence. If your teen's emotions trigger unresolved emotions in you, you will not be able to communicate effectively, and this cycle of emotions can create a negative communication cycle, the exact opposite of your goal.

For example, I discovered that Gisele's mother had an extremely deprived and traumatic background and so he desperately wanted to protect his daughter from similar experiences. In addition to self-reflection, an important part of learning and sharing distress tolerance skills is taking care of yourself, both physically and psychologically. Gisele's mother had never shared his history in depth before, and that sad legacy interfered with his daughter's growth, the opposite of his goal.

ACCEPTANCE STRATEGIES

Acceptance of distress as a part of life has deep historical roots, but for many years, therapists focused on change alone, not unlike Gisele's well-meaning mother. When I attended an Alcoholics Anonymous (AA) meeting for a graduate school seminar, I first listened to the Serenity Prayer. Originally created by the theologian Reinhold Niebuhr in the 1940s, the Serenity Prayer has been adapted by 12-step programs:

> God grant me the serenity to accept the things I cannot change,
> The courage to change the things I can,
> And the wisdom to know the difference.

Although many people resist the religious overtones of AA and do not identify with the Christian emphasis in some 12-step groups, acceptance is not a value unique to these programs; similar ideas can also be attributed to many other sources, including the stoic Epictetus, most Buddhist teachers, Jewish and secular philosophers, and even a Mother Goose nursery rhyme:

> For every evil under the sun,
> There is a remedy, or there is none.
> If there be one, try and find it;
> If there be none, never mind it.

I tried to remember the focus on acceptance, but the rest of graduate training ignored this issue completely. Fortunately, times have changed. As you will see in Chapter 11, more recent schools of therapy, like dialectical behavior therapy (DBT) and acceptance and commitment therapy (ACT), have a strong focus on the value of accepting some distress.

MINDFULNESS MATTERS

I would urge you to bring mindfulness into your family. Acceptance is a major tenet of mindfulness and meditation practice, both of which can improve distress tolerance. Mindfulness is an approach to life that aims to cultivate attention to the present moment, which usually employs meditation as a support to that attention. In this context, "present moment" means the most basic perceptions you have, not your thoughts and judgments. Much distress results from our analysis of or reactions to stimuli, which therefore leads to inattention to the initial perception. Through mindfulness you can develop habits of the mind that reduce distress by refocusing on a perception itself, rather than on the reactions to it. This is one reason many meditation trainings begin with a focus on a particular physical sensation, as it is "closer" to the present moment.

Mindfulness has been shown to be effective in treating numerous conditions and helps prevent relapse of depression. It is being tested as a treatment for depression as well. Another issue important to adolescent development is that mindfulness has been shown to increase brain functioning in the areas of the brain that control focus and emotional regulation.

Many of the mindfulness concepts I describe here have been adapted from the mindfulness-based stress reduction program (MBSR) originally created by Jon Kabat-Zinn, at the University of Massachusetts Medical

School. The program has now graduated over 24,000 participants. Once again, you can use these concepts and strategies and bring them into the family, rather than lecture to them. Your teen may not want to join you for a mindfulness meditation class, but if he does, all the better. There are also courses that have been adapted to the needs of emerging adults, like Koru, developed at Duke University by Holly Rogers and Margaret Maytan. At the same time, I am delighted to see that mindfulness seminars are being included in some high schools, so perhaps your teen will be able to teach you! In the meantime, we can follow the same processes we used in other chapters—learning, communicating, modeling, and advocating.

Mindfulness helps a person to manage negative emotions and create a more meaningful way of life. According to Kabat-Zinn, mindfulness has three primary elements:

- Paying attention to the moment
- with purpose
- and without judgment.

Paying attention to the moment is increasingly important because our "moments" are usually lost in a sea of multitasking, digital media, and overcommitted families and teens. It is also specifically relevant to depression because paying attention to the present means that a teen is not judging themselves or thinking about potentially negative self-assessments and pessimistic thoughts. Observing emotions without judgment allows us to experience them and to accept them. Mindfulness takes effort at first, so you need to be intentional in your practice, especially when you're just starting out.

It Will Pass

Another foundation of mindfulness is recognition of impermanence as a fact of life, which can help a person with symptoms of depression. Everything passes; time goes on; change is constant. When you are experiencing a negative emotion, if you attend to it, observe it, and name it, it will almost always pass. So if we feel intense sadness, rather than immediately concluding, "I can't stand this," Kabat-Zinn suggests looking at the emotions from a neurological perspective. Tell yourself, "That is an emotion, just a set of firing neurons." It has no inherent power over you; it will pass. He also uses the metaphor of emotions as waves on an ocean: "They come and go and yet the ocean remains." Other metaphors for the impermanence of emotional states include watching the cars on a train pass by, seeing the objects in a river flow away, and watching light clouds drift away.

Awareness of Breathing

Most of the time, we are not aware of our breathing, but mindfulness requires that we pay attention. You are breathing in, you are breathing out. Notice: Does your breathing change when you're under stress? When you're in a blue mood? Many mindfulness programs begin their sessions with an anchoring breathing exercise, as it brings focus and stability to the body as we prepare for the next step.

Some mindfulness programs also begin with a "body scan," in which participants become aware of the various feelings in their body. Are you comfortable? Can your body feel the support of the chair or the floor? What else can you feel?

Mindful Observation

The hospital where I teach twice week is part of a large complex located in an impoverished part of the city—not very pretty. I walk through a large parking lot that is surrounded by other parking lots to get to the correct entrance. I am often very focused on the workday ahead as I walk in. Then, one day, I decided to try to observe mindfully. I took the same route but focused on what I was seeing, the details, the colors, not that the parking lot was crowded, or that the door would jam as it often did or that I was late or in a hurry. Suddenly I noticed two beautiful trees—one an old maple, tall and changing colors with the seasons, another a smaller ginkgo, with its distinctive leaves. For over a decade I had not really seen them because my mind was cluttered. This is one example of mindful observation.

To behave mindfully, I first needed to stop and escape from my preoccupation with the day ahead. Mindful observation requires adapting a "beginner's mind." I took my walk as if I had never done it before. When walking, I needed to pay attention to walking in the environment, not my inner monologue. I needed to notice the temperature, the sun, or clouds. Breathe the air. Then pay attention and look carefully. Are there additional trees? What is on the old patio outside another door? Look up. Are there patients or staff looking out the windows? Listen: Are people talking? Are there sirens on ambulances headed to the emergency department?

Here is a mindful observation exercise to try: Look out a window. Try only to observe; don't categorize, judge, or evaluate. Notice the glass, the sill, the street, the leaves, nearby buildings, and the people or vehicles going by. Notice any changes. What is the light like? Is it cloudy? Listen closely to the wind or other sounds. Try to stay in the moment without judgment. If you see your lawn and think, "The lawn's a mess, it needs raking," or if your mind drifts away, gently bring it back to the present scene. Use your sense of smell. Can you smell food, grass, leaves, exhaust fumes? Remember, attend and label, no judgment! Breathe the air. This mindfulness exercise takes only 5–10 minutes.

SELF-SOOTHING SKILLS

Self-soothing skills can also be helpful for withstanding negative emotions. They are not distraction skills; they don't necessarily turn you away from the negative, but they can help you go from a negative state to a neutral one. Some of the skills are similar to elements of mindfulness. One type of self-soothing skill involves using your five senses to help you feel calmer and be better able to tolerate distressing emotions.

Visualization

Visualization enables people to use their histories to create a safe and calm scene. An old family room, a hike, a warm beach, or fireside scene can be used to elicit the scene—the more details, the better. Sometimes a specific color can also provide a visual sense of calm.

Taste

Mindfully eat a small amount of something you love or slowly sip your favorite beverage. Some mindfulness groups suggest eating a raisin to challenge you to take your time eating, but a tiny bit of anything will do. Take your time; many people take a second bite before they even swallow the first. Feel the texture of the food.

Touch

Experience all sorts of textures. Rub your hands on various materials: cotton, a smooth piece of wood, or a rough sponge. Walk barefoot and feel the wooden floor, the cold tiles, the fresh grass. Add smell; bury your face in a lavender-scented pillow. Get a massage, exchange massages with your partner or spouse, or give yourself a massage.

Deep Breathing

As discussed in Chapter 6, one of my favorite exercises comes from Dr. Andrew Weil and is called the 4-7-8 technique. Again, here's how it works: Breathe in slowly for 4 seconds. Then hold your breath for 7 seconds. Finally, very slowly breathe out for 8 seconds. This technique is quick, easy to learn, and easy to share. Knowing that you can breathe deeply at any moment can help create the confidence that negative emotions will pass. Some families take a quick time-out for deep breathing during times of high stress. Deep breathing can also be similar to saying grace before a meal. It allows everyone in the family to take a minute, relax, clear their minds, letting go of the day's stresses, and then be able to focus on the moment.

Stretching

When a person is struggling with symptoms of depression, physical activity can be daunting or feel like too much effort. In that case, they can start slowly by stretching mindfully. Stretching poses can be very simple. For example, you can stand with your feet hip-width apart and raise your hands to the ceiling, reaching gently. If you're feeling tension in your neck at the end of the day, you can do some gentle neck rolls. Any simple stretching exercise will do, as long as it has these elements of mindfulness: practicing with attention, avoiding judgment by moving slowly, and trying to feel the motion, rather than narrating or interpreting the experience. You're not competing, not even with yourself, or striving to be better. You are simply stretching.

Yoga

If you appreciate stretching and focusing on bodily awareness, yoga is another alternative. In addition to our sessions, Gisele joined a yoga group and shared what she learned with me. Many of us immediately think about the difficult poses, with names like downward-facing dog, but in reality, yoga is an ancient tradition with the goal of bringing the body and mind together. The word *yoga* is derived from a Sanskrit root for "union" and is related to the English word *yoke*, the wooden structure that keeps horses and oxen walking in a straight line. The various yoga exercises are aimed at taming the mind by focusing on disciplining the body. Yoga can also improve flexibility, balance, and strength. Gisele became skilled in yoga and her entire appearance changed, standing up to her full height with poise and grace. She also described a time when her boyfriend disappointed her, and instead of turning to marijuana or blaming herself, she took some time to step away and do some breathing and stretching with yoga poses until she felt able to express herself constructively. Gisele then became a yoga advocate and encouraged her younger siblings and all her friends to try it.

If you are not attending yoga classes regularly but enjoy it, you might find it helpful to buy a pack of yoga pose cards. These are both fun and easy to keep on hand.

Progressive Muscle Relaxation

At the end of a long day, many of us don't even notice that the muscles in our shoulders and neck are tightly coiled. That's how intense work, family, or school stress can be. Muscle relaxation is a straightforward technique to counteract the stress and tension of the day. The first step is to get into a comfortable position and take some slow breaths. Try to let your thoughts drift away, and breathe gently. Sometimes we don't know how to relax our muscles unless we tense them first. Next, breathe in and make a fist with one hand. Make it tight so that you can feel the tension. Notice that tension for about 10 seconds. Then, breathe out, and let your fist and arm relax and feel the tension dissipate. Try it again. The next step is to bring your arm up and tense your bicep muscle. Again, feel the tension and pause. Then release your arm and feel the tension go away. You will repeat each movement. You can then move on to your forehead, eye muscles, chin, neck, shoulders, back, chest, thighs, calves, ankles, and toes. Although this seems like a long list, you can complete it in about 20 minutes, but don't rush! Remember: Breathe in to tense, breathe out to release. End the session by breathing and noticing your relaxed body. If a certain part has tensed back up, repeat the process. Then slowly count to five before returning to your more relaxed day. You'll find links to videos and suggested apps on muscle relaxation at the end of this chapter and in the Resources section.

DISTRACTION SKILLS

Distraction skills are called into play after emotions have been identified and experienced. Using distraction skills, you interrupt your negative mood state by engaging something that takes your attention elsewhere. These are important skills to learn, especially when it feels like negative moods are taking over. They are not problem-solving skills, but rather strategies to take the mind away from distressing emotions, which might make problem-solving easier in the long run, as decision-making may improve without the interference of distressing emotions.

Distraction skills are especially relevant to those who may be prone to depression because of the tendency to ruminate. As described in Chapter 3, a large body of literature has documented the destructive effects of rumination. In *Great Expectations*, Dickens describes this scenario with his famous character, Miss Havisham: "She had secluded herself from a thousand natural and healing influences; that, her mind, brooding solitary, had grown diseased." This extreme outcome of rumination illustrates the importance of practicing distraction.

- To begin, you can ask your teenager what distraction activity would be helpful. If he begins with unhealthy behaviors like using alcohol or marijuana or refusing to go to school, don't forget to validate the impulse, desire, and even short-term appeal of these options, but point out that there are other methods they probably know or can learn.
- Don't choose social media; avoid or limit it. Recent studies suggest that increased time on social media can be detrimental to teens, especially girls. It makes sense that during a time of social anxiety and fear of potential rejection the comparisons of the "ideal selves" displayed on social media can lead to lower feelings of self-esteem.
- If your teen asks for your ideas, use your knowledge of the activities they love and enjoy. An athlete? Go running or practice. An artist? Get out the easel or other materials. A writer? Think about a journal entry. Are there family activities, even from the past, that they preferred? Puzzles, games?
- Suggest turning to the power of friendship. If your teen can identify a trusted friend, encourage him to reach out. For most teens, friends are the strongest allies and most powerful influences. As we have seen earlier, good friends are much more than distracting. Learning to listen and empathize, to share and be vulnerable, are lifelong tools for growth, stability, and connection. Spending time may well be enough; he doesn't have to plunge into an intense discussion. If he doesn't have close friends

at school, help him identify others in the community—music or theater groups, sports, youth groups, or other activities.

- Is your teen an advocate or passionate about a cause? Encourage some political or community involvement. Contributing to a productive endeavor can distract from distress and, perhaps more importantly, can emphasize meaningful ideals. In addition, this will help your teen connect with others who share his values.
- Think about becoming a mindfulness advocate. Mindfulness training is now available in educational programs for younger children and teens. Recently, I saw a poignant "to-do list" written by a child in a mindfulness class. It reads: "1. Breathe in. 2. Breathe out. 3. Breathe in. 4. Breathe out," and so on. If you can't find a class, encourage your children's school, religious school, or community center to start one. Volunteer to help organize it if you can and ask other family members if they'd like to help.
- Want additional ideas? Turn to Peter Lewinsohn's list, the Pleasant Events Schedule (PES), a list of 347 activities, available online. See the Resources section for more information.

Remember that all of these skills require flexibility and practice. Some of them will come easily whereas others may require more practice. Still others may not be right for you or your teen. Try to have fun and create some new ones. Just take a moment to evaluate them after you've tried them and adjust accordingly.

It's important to remember what not to do, so here is a review:

- Don't lecture.
- Don't minimize. For example, you might try to make your teen feel better by saying, "That's not such a big deal." It is to them at the moment.
- Don't joke, tease, or humiliate. This is among the most hurtful responses. Boys in particular are often subject to these comments. The response "Oh yeah, Joe is a real ladies' man" may make light of a rejection Joe has shared with you, but will usually make him feel worse.
- Don't compare your teen to siblings, cousins, or family friends; for example: "Yes, that happened to cousin Carrie and she moved on." Instead, if your teen asks for help later on, you can suggest Carrie, but not right away.
- Never assume you understand before clarifying with your teen. Remember communication and validation. You may be tempted to make "Oh yes, I felt the same way in high school and . . . " your first comment. However, it might not have been the same way then as it is now. Find out by asking for more details.

- Avoid blaming or taking a harsh stance against the other people in your teen's narrative of negative emotions. Of course you're angry at that kid who hurt your son, but social situations change, especially among teens—they may come back!

THE LIMITS OF DISTRESS TOLERANCE AND DISTRACTION

Some distress tolerance and distraction skills may not work or may prove unsustainable. The situation may move from a specific emotion to more prolonged negative mood states and sadness. If your teen has been consistently sad and withdrawn for over 2 weeks and 5 other symptoms of depression, including sleep and appetite changes, loss of interest, feelings of guilt and lack of self-worth, extreme fatigue, a decrease in concentration, or thoughts of suicide, then it's time to consult a mental health professional because these are symptoms of a major depressive episode. This may also be true if your child has suffered a trauma, reports symptoms of panic disorder, or shows evidence of substance abuse. Remember that early intervention is another form of prevention of more serious conditions. We will expand this discussion in Chapter 14, No Shame, No Stigma.

Similarly, if distress tolerance skills are extremely difficult for you, think about whether you have a history of depression, are currently depressed, or have another psychological condition. In this case, you could first try spending more time on developing these skills yourself. If you find them difficult to do on your own, consider joining a mindfulness meditation group, or if you experience extreme distress, consult a mental health professional.

On the other hand, if these skills have been helpful, keep them as part of your family's routine. Don't forget to practice periodically. Keep them close at hand; you don't need to wait for a crisis. As Jon Kabat-Zinn suggests, "You don't want to start weaving the parachute when you are about to jump out of the plane. You want to have been weaving your parachute every morning, noon and night, day in, day out, so that when you need it, it will actually hold you."[1]

1. Jon Kabat-Zinn, in Moyers, B. *Healing and the Mind*. New York: Knopf, 2012, p. 143.

CHAPTER 9

Social Power

The Good, the Bad, and the Ugly

I have been presenting papers on depression, behavioral medicine, and women's health for most of my career. I realized early on that social support is extremely powerful and one of the most well-documented, positive factors for improving and maintaining health and well-being. Social connection is critically important to both psychological and physical health. Research confirms the power of social healing: "When considering the umbrella term social connection, there are perhaps no other factors that can have such a huge impact on both length and quality of life—from the cradle to the grave."[1] Social support is so significant that public health advocates have called for social connection to be a priority in public policy. I conclude most of my presentations by emphasizing the healing power of social support. People who are vulnerable to or suffering from depression, an isolating condition, can experience an enormous benefit from social support of all kinds.

In the 1970s, a study of women who were at risk to become clinically depressed, based on their social and economic situations, found that the one factor that differentiated the women who fell victim to depression from those who did not was the presence of an intimate confidant. The trust, sharing, and connection that come from having even one close friend

---

1. Julianne Holt-Lunstad, Robles, T., Sbarra, D., Kazak, A. E., & Smith, T. W. Advancing social connection as a public health priority in the United States. *American Psychologist*, 72(6), 517–530, 2017, p. 527.

helped these women overcome the odds. This study is one of many that revealed the enormous benefits of more social connection.

Social connection is a key element in preventing depression in adolescents. Children who have strong emotional bonds with others have better health overall and better psychological adjustment. The presence of social support in the life of an adolescent—whether within or outside the family——can delay the onset of depression. Conversely, family conflict predicts relapses of depression.

Family relationships can have a powerful, long-lasting effect on psychological and medical conditions. In a long-term follow-up study by psychologists Linda Russek and Gary Schwartz, college students were first questioned about their relationships with their parents and their chronic conditions were then monitored over time. Those students who reported having a caring parent had a lower risk of conditions like ulcers and heart disease even 35 years later.

The biological reasons for social support being critical to health promotion are not completely clear. However, researchers generally believe that close family and other relationships lead to higher levels of oxytocin, a neurochemical that is sometimes termed the "love hormone." It plays a role in maternal bonding and enhances positive feelings more generally. Oxytocin can also reduce blood pressure and levels of anxiety and depression. Positive relationships also lead to lower levels of cortisol, the stress hormone that can lead to inflammation that has been implicated in the development of depression.

Yet the influence of social factors is more complicated, especially in the digital age. We know that relationships and social power can also be negative. Involvement in social media can lead to health or harm. Although most teenagers enjoy using social media, there are pernicious effects as well. I recently reviewed peer-reviewed articles on body image in teenage girls. The negative effects of social media, especially Instagram, are troubling. The amount of time teenage girls spend on social media is directly proportional to their negative feelings about their bodies.

Then there are the ugly effects of social power. These include bullying, body shaming, and the invasion of privacy. Included in this latter category are the dangers posed by sexting, the exchange of sexually explicit texts or photographs. Adolescents can be impulsive and often experiment with their sexual boundaries, so sexting can at first appear to be a private but exciting exchange. Few teenagers understand the potential hazard, that in an instant their impulsive, personal exchange can turn into public humiliation. One of my patients, a quiet 25-year-old, still remembers with tears her shame when, 10 years earlier, her then-boyfriend circulated a relatively modest (bra and panties on) photo of her torso to all his friends. It is one thing to lose trust in a romantic relationship; it is quite another to be publicly humiliated.

Cyberbullying is another ugly and cruel act. Teenagers who are vulnerable to depression make an appealing target for bullies. In the past, a teen could feel safe at home or with a close friend, but in the digital age, cyberbullying can be literally a 24-hour-a-day phenomenon. Overall, then, it's important to understand the three different types of social power.

THE GOOD

Social support begins at home. The strength of a supportive family foundation is essential for a teenager to move from childhood into adulthood. As long as teens feel that they can rely on a loving and encouraging family foundation, they feel secure to move ahead with their own goals and take steps toward independence. A strong and accepting family provides a "safe haven." In addition, as demonstrated in Chapter 4, if teens have learned active listening and assertive rather than aggressive or passive communication, they will be well prepared to face the social challenges ahead.

Relationships with other family members are also significant. Despite the attention usually paid to sibling rivalry, siblings can provide emotional and practical assistance. In loving families, even the most competitive teens will come to the aid of their brother or sister when they need it. It's important to facilitate rather than disrupt this bond. You can do this by ignoring siblings teasing or hassling one another and encouraging their positive interactions. Try not to label or pigeonhole each child. I have seen some very accomplished teens who see themselves as "less than" because their sibling was labeled as "the smart one" or the "social one." In one example from my practice, the parents of a high school junior who had four siblings discouraged her from developing her considerable skills in soccer because she was "the academic one" and her younger sister needed to be "the athletic one."

This power of perceived support has been documented in families with teenagers from many different backgrounds. In study by Mayra Bámaca-Colbert, Mexican-American adolescent girls who felt supported by their mothers had higher levels of self-esteem and fewer depressive episodes compared to those with less support. Notably, she found these results across the different stages of adolescence, again illustrating the power of family as a secure foundation. Support from friends became more powerful in later rather than early adolescence.

Social support from adults includes more than just the nuclear family. Extended family relationships and friends can provide both emotional and practical support to parents and teenagers. I have treated many young people who can identify a helpful grandparent, aunt, or uncle in their lives who played a vital role in boosting their moods and fostering self-esteem. Studies of resilience in children have shown that teenagers need two things: a spark of something that engages and inspires them, and a relationship with at least one caring adult. These two factors can help children and teens overcome even trauma and neglect.

Teenagers will appreciate the value of close friendships and ties with extended family members if they experience them at home. In addition, you can explicitly discuss the importance of friendship and family with your teen. In contrast, sadly, I have seen quite a few families where arguments have led relatives to stop speaking to one another for many years. This type of rift leads to family isolation and causes intergenerational harm. If parents are alienated from their siblings, it will be difficult for cousins to maintain close relationships. I asked one young woman why her father did not speak to her uncle and she replied, "I have no idea; it's just always been that way."

Although the family continues to be the basis of security for teenagers, one of the major changes of adolescence is that social influence shifts from parents to peers. Don't be surprised if your friendly 11-year-old daughter who likes to go to the movies with you morphs into a 13-year-old critic who wants to be dropped off a block from wherever you're going, asks you to be quiet so you don't embarrass her in front of her friends, and criticizes most of what you wear. Young men who once confided in you may become withdrawn as they move toward their friends and adopt what they see as a male model of self-containment. These changes may be difficult to tolerate but are completely normal and predictable. In fact, as we start to look at the impact of emotional expressivity in adolescent males, their selectivity in expressing emotion may well be adaptive. We know that expressing emotion promotes social adjustment and that suppression of negative emotion causes harm. However, another study of teenagers found that boys who expressed emotions only to their friends but *not* to strangers had better social adjustment.

An example of the move from parental to peer approval is revealed in the fascinating British documentary series 7 *Up*. British director Michael Apted has followed a group of 20 people from different social classes, starting at age 7, interviewing and filming them every 7 years, most recently at age 63. At age 7, one of the boys brags that he reads the newspaper to see the information about the stock market. By age 14, sitting with two friends, he sheepishly confesses that he only said that to please his parents, realizing how his earlier comments were very uncool and pretentious.

THE BAD
Divorce and Family Conflict

At one point, mental health professionals debated the psychological impact of divorce on children. Ultimately, it became clear that, when income and resources are stable, the impact on children is not so much related to divorce but rather to exposure to family conflict. This suggests that reducing family conflict is critically important for preventing or mitigating depressive symptoms. Coming home to an angry or bitter parent or family is upsetting and harms the natural development of independence. It also appears that family conflict may lead to cognitive styles associated with depression—pessimism and dependence—that also interfere with peer relationships. A study of Latina teens found that conflict with their parents over gender roles was associated with depression.

Social Isolation

Just as social support is a positive force, social isolation is a negative one. This is especially true with respect to adolescent depression. Social rejection is extremely painful, given teenagers' desire to be included. Social isolation can be a cause or a result of depression. Teens who are becoming depressed tend to withdraw. This detachment from others leads to isolation and makes negative mood or depression much worse. Depression becomes a disorder of disconnection. If you can encourage your teen to confide in you or another adult, you can help identify whether he is being rejected by others or is pulling away from people.

If you are concerned that your teenagers are not part of a social group at school, the first step is to talk with them about it. For some teens, having one or two friends is enough, so it is important not to project your needs onto them. If they are feeling lonely and want your help, you can suggest the many other options for socializing or meeting people—classes outside of school, a job, volunteer groups, religious youth groups, and camps. I have seen many students who did not fit in at school but felt support and validation from their long-term camp friends.

More of the Bad—Does Social Media Cause Depression?

Today's teens are referred to as "digital natives" because they have no memory of a time before smartphones or the Internet. The impact of social media on them is enormous, for several reasons. First is the sheer amount of time spent: The average American teens spend between 6 and 9 hours a day on non-homework media-related activities. This amounts to an entire work or school day. The implications are numerous and substantial.

It is usually difficult to sort out the effect of social media on body image or other issues. However, consider what happened in Fiji. For generations, the South Pacific culture, which was primarily agrarian, was oriented around food because it was impossible to predict each year's harvest or supply of fish. Meals were important, lavish events that were associated with prosperity, and the comment "You've gained weight" was considered a compliment, as the culture cherished a fuller female figure. Then, in 1995, television was introduced to this archipelago of islands, and things began to change. Between 1995 and 1998, Anne Becker, now a professor of global health and social medicine at Harvard Medical School, studied the effects of TV on teenage girls in Fiji. The study included two groups of girls, with an average age of 17, who were matched for age, body mass index (BMI), and other factors. Those studied in 1995 had viewed less than 1 month of television, whereas the 1998 group had been exposed to it for 3 years. During that 3-year period, the Western thin ideal of feminine beauty was introduced with shows at the time, like *Beverly Hills 90210*. The percentage of teenagers who were preoccupied with calories and who engaged in disordered eating behavior more than doubled. Those who watched television three or more times per week in the 1998 survey were 50% more likely to describe themselves as "too big or fat" and 30% were more likely to diet than girls who viewed television less often. Before 1995, the concept of calories was foreign to this culture; by 1998, 69% of the teenage girls in Fiji reported that they had dieted. Based on what they'd seen on television, many of them said they wished they could be taller and slimmer or that being thin was the key to getting a good job and becoming successful— notions that had previously been unheard of in their culture. The Fiji study examined the effects of watching *television three times a week*; now we are dealing with the effect of online media *many hours per day*.

It's been clear for at least 10 years that the use of Facebook and Instagram (which Facebook purchased for one billion dollars in 2012) can be dangerous for some teenagers. There has been a debate in the psychological literature as to whether social media sites actually cause depression. This is somewhat simplistic, as a major depressive episode is clearly affected by numerous factors. Nonetheless, there are aspects of social media that can decrease feelings of well-being. This occurs primarily because of negative social comparisons. The social media profile allows an individual to create an online persona. A newsfeed and posts about events or photos, a "status update," can become a measure of popularity as a teen observes how many "likes" a post receives. Jean Twenge, of San Diego State University, was one of the first to sound the alarm about the dangers of social media. In 2013, she concluded that social media builds shallow, "weak" ties, and increased self-focus, including narcissism. Twenge has examined different theories of why depression and anxiety are increasing so rapidly and has concluded that social media is a major cause, calling it "the worm in the core of the apple."[2] The more dramatic rise in depression among teenage girls, she contends, is a result of their greater use of social media. In addition to the exposure to negative social comparisons, girls have increased anxiety when a text or message is not answered, and the resulting anxiety can be a precursor to depression.

A 2013 study by educational psychologist Tracy Cross revealed that teens spending a larger amount of time on Facebook experienced a decline in subjective well-being. In contrast, direct, face-to-face interaction improved well-being. This is problematic for today's teens because they are communicating through social media more and seeing one another less.

In addition, the impact of social media has become more sophisticated over time. An article published by UNICEF reveals, "It is no secret that social media platforms were deliberately designed to hold users' attention as long as possible, tapping into psychological biases and vulnerabilities relating to our desire for validation and fear of rejection. Too much passive use of social media—just browsing posts—can be unhealthy and has been linked to feelings of envy, inadequacy and less satisfaction with life."[3] Teens are especially vulnerable to feelings of vulnerability and social media feeds into their fears.

The Facebook studies seem quaint, now that teens have moved on to Instagram and Snapchat. Instagram, now with 1 billion active monthly users, added a feature called Instagram stories, which incorporates videos. Teens can measure their digital popularity or lack of popularity in new ways every day, by focusing on likes, comments and emojis, all part of the

2. Jean Twenge. *iGen: Why Today's Super-Connected Kids Are Growing Up Less Rebellious, More Tolerant, Less Happy—and Completely Unprepared for Adulthood—and What That Means for the Rest of Us.* New York: Atria, 2017 p. 112.
3. Fersko, H. Is social media bad for teens? https://www.unicef.org/stories/social-media-bad-teens-mental-health, October 9, 2018.

ever-expanding methods that developers employ to reward increased time on their webpages.

Teens are in the process of creating new identities but still desire connection and approval from their peers. Teens and young adults develop more meaningful identities by talking with close friends. Even though some teens may be looking for this type of interaction on social networks, it is more likely that they will be exposed to self-aggrandizing updates from others rather than a genuine exchange. It's easy for teens to overlook the fact that when people create a profile or post photos on social media it is a curated process. Only the best versions of who they are and what their lives are like, and the most attractive edited photographs and videos will do. If a teen has any tendency toward negative self-appraisal, as teens vulnerable to depression do, it is likely that social media will worsen their self-assessments.

The rise of social media has bombarded all of us with even more body-related messages to contend with on a daily basis. With some effort, it's possible to sidestep exposure to picture-perfect images of women in magazines, but those on Instagram and other sites are almost impossible to avoid, especially for teens who often use social media as their primary mode of communicating with each other. A desire to message a friend can be sidetracked by looking at your most recent number of likes, comparing your photos to a young woman you see as prettier or to an ad for jeans. Let's follow a possible internal dialogue: "I want to message my friend Gail. . . . Oh, I only have a couple more likes of my photo from Jeannie's party. . . . Oh, Jeannie looks so cool. . . . There's an ad for those new tight jeans. . . . Wow, that model is skinny. . . . Too bad that my butt is too big." A wish to connect becomes harsh self-criticism in a matter of seconds.

A few researchers have criticized the social media–depression hypothesis. They suggest that more vulnerable teenagers may be drawn to the negative social comparisons. That may or may not be an accurate critique in general, but for our purpose––the prevention of depression—the impact on more vulnerable teens is precisely the point. For those of us concerned with harm reduction, the dangers of social media should be a major focus.

THE UGLY

Body Shaming

If a teenage girl has the bad luck to be overweight or even weigh slightly more than the thin "ideal," the situation is even worse and leads to body shaming. When people feel weight-related devaluation, rejection, or discrimination (often referred to as "weight stigma"), they experience a decrease in their motivation to exercise, an increase in their calorie consumption and patterns of disordered eating, a drop in their perception of their overall health, and higher levels of cortisol. In a 2015 study involving 110 female undergraduates, researchers at Rutgers University conducted a fascinating (but troubling) experiment in which the women were made to experience weight stigma during a staged group shopping activity involving designer clothing. Researchers measured BMI and self-perceived body weight beforehand and measured cortisol levels before and after the session. During the experiment, those in the control group were told by a thin female moderator that they couldn't participate because the group was full. By contrast, those in the stigmatized group were told by a thin organizer, "Unfortunately, your size and shape just aren't ideal for this style of clothing and we really do want everyone to have fun and feel good. Plus, we want to return the clothing to the designer in good condition."[4] These are cruel words for anyone to hear, but especially for a young woman. Here's the surprising part: Participants who perceived themselves as heavy, even if they weren't overweight based on their BMI, experienced significant cortisol increases after the weight-stigmatizing interaction, but those who perceived their weight as normal did not experience a cortisol spike. This suggests that internal body criticism may be even more harmful than hearing hurtful comments. Conversely, self-perception of "being normal" served as a buffer to negative comments.

Lesbian teens are less likely to be dissatisfied with their bodies. It is thought that they feel this way because they experience less pressure to achieve the thin, ideal feminine image. Some studies that compared lesbian to heterosexual women revealed that lesbians were less dissatisfied with their bodies and expressed an ideal body that was larger.

As for young men, they have similar but less frequent and less intense exposure to an ideal male type—tall and muscular. On dating sites, for example, the one compromise that most women refuse to make is to date someone shorter than they are. For numerous reasons, the negative effect is not as severe, but there is damage. The exception here is gay men. A study of the media influence on body image found that gay men had significantly more vulnerability to media pressures and had greater levels of appearance-related anxiety than heterosexual men. As I've watched the social changes

4. Mary Himmelstein, Incollingo Belsky, A., & Tomiyama, A. The weight of stigma: Cortisol reactivity to manipulated weight stigma. *Obesity*, 23(2), 368–374, 2015.

over the past 30 years, I am horrified to see that the pressure on women to attain some unrealistic thin ideal has not subsided, and pressure on young men to be more muscular is getting worse. This is certainly not what anyone had in mind when we said had a goal of equality.

Bullying and Cyberbullying

Just a few individuals can wreak havoc in other people's lives. This is especially true with respect to cyberbullying. You may remember Kevin, the 16-year-old boy who didn't fit in and who hated family dinners, from the Chapter 4. Today, Kevin is a young and energetic businessman, but a dozen years ago, times were tough. When Kevin was 13, Jamie, a new student, transferred to his school from out of state. Jamie was a bit more mature than the others because he was a year older. With his awkward style and lack of social skills, Kevin was drawn to Jamie because they both seemed to be outsiders at first and had common interests in math, music, and video games. Kevin was unaware that Jamie had been bullied in his previous school and had seen that he had a chance to start over, now as a bully himself. This pattern is not uncommon: Numerous studies suggest that victims of bullying become bullies as a coping strategy. After a brief period of friendship, Jamie became friends with other teenagers in the class and quickly ostracized Kevin. At first this wasn't so bad because Kevin was frankly used to being "on the outs." Over time, though, he was quite hurt and told me it had become even more difficult now to trust other potential friends. Then things got worse. Jamie organized several online war games, where players could engage one another in tournaments. Kevin enjoyed these games a lot because they were an alternative to athletics, which exposed that he was physically uncoordinated. However, over time Jamie blocked Kevin from his games and also began to humiliate and scapegoat his former friend in their smaller social network. Jamie also bullied other teens on the playground by taunting, pushing, and tripping, all out of sight of the teachers.

Kevin is not alone in experiencing bullying. One in three teenagers report being bullied at one time or another. The three factors involved in bullying are intent to hurt, repeated behavior, and a power differential. Jamie was older and more socially sophisticated, and he persisted in deliberately hurting Kevin. Teenagers have always had to cope with aggressive behavior from others, but the facelessness of the digital age and the absence of adults exacerbate the situation. It's partly a result of the fact that there are few social consequences; Jamie became a popular kid at school, after all. And neurologically, the orbitofrontal cortex, the part of the brain that receives and interprets visual and social cues and emotional reactions, is not activated online. People express more aggression and other uncensored thoughts online because they do not see the reactions of their victims.

The effects of bullying can be indirectly and physically harmful as well. In one study examining bullying, heterosexual boys who had been bullied and taunted by being called "gay" or "faggot" turned to steroids in order to change their bodies. Interestingly, this was not true for gay teens. The long-term consequences of steroid use—kidney problems, liver damage, enlarged heart, high blood pressure, and negative changes in blood cholesterol—are well known and can even increase the risk of stroke and heart attack in young people.

Sexual Shaming

Teenage girls can be bullied, too, with ostracism and mockery, as Kevin experienced. In fact, some studies suggest that girls engage in more cyber- (as opposed to in-person, physical) bullying than boys do. They can be sexually shamed as well. Sexuality is still considered less acceptable for teenage girls than it is for teenage boys. A boy cannot be "slut shamed." As we examined earlier, sexting can easily become public, go viral, and destroy a girl's social life. Girls who are not as developed as their peers can be taunted, and girls who are more developed can be body shamed. It is painful to read stories about teenage girls who were shamed to the extent that they attempted suicide.

Bias and Stereotyping

Social media, Internet sites, and television can inflict societal as well as individual harm, and we all need to examine implicit and explicit bias. In Chapter 1, we examined poverty and racism as stresses that contribute to the development of depression. Teens who are poor or from sexual minority groups often lack social support. Numerous studies and books have also documented the harmful effects of stereotyping. Mass media and social networks can spread bias exponentially. We've seen how Facebook has been used to promote racism and hate speech against immigrants and people of color. It often takes a member of the targeted group to increase consciousness and challenge long-standing, "acceptable" bias. The character of Apu on the animated hit television series *The Simpsons* is an example of this. For 28 years, the white actor Hank Azaria played a convenience store owner who was extremely stingy, had an extremely long last name—Nahasapeemapetilon—and spoke with a broad Indian accent, all while generations of fans laughed. Only after Hari Kondabolu's 2017 documentary *The Problem with Apu* raised consciousness and exposed the harm of this stereotyped character on Indian people and Indian Americans did a real examination of this specific bias begin.

DEVELOPING SOCIAL CONNECTIONS AND PREVENTING HARM OF SOCIAL POWER

Social power, then, has enormous power to create support or inflict harm. As parents we must increase positive support and help mitigate the negative effects of social power. Here are some ideas about how you can help your child develop and maintain social connections and reduce the bad and ugly effects of social power:

- Explicitly state and model the value of relationships in your family life.
- Above all, try to reduce family conflict. If there are no programs available to you in your community and family therapy is not available, consider some of the books and online materials in the Resources section at the end of the book.
- If you are going through a divorce or separation, do your best to reduce continued conflict in front of your teens.
- Encourage communication and support among siblings and cousins.
- Pay attention! As revealed in Chapter 4, it's more important to listen than to talk. Sometimes driving younger teenagers and observing other activities will provide you with the opportunities to listen, observe, and learn a lot about the quality of their friendships. Even if you hear the tapping of texting, they sometimes still make comments to one another about the texts!
- If your younger teen is on the shy side and wants your help, you can act as a social skills coach. She may want to hear about strategies of reaching out to other teens or suggestions for activities. Shy teenagers tend to benefit more from activities than just hanging out and trying to talk to a new friend.
- Make your home as welcoming as possible as a gathering place. Usually the provision of food and the presence, but not over-involvement, of a warm parent or relative can help make this happen.

- Sports, dance, art, religious education, and volunteer activities can expand teens' world and give them the opportunity to meet others with similar interests and values. Although friends from school and other children in the neighborhood are usually the most convenient way for children to develop friendships, sometimes that doesn't work out. Your teen may not have friends at school. This is where other activities can play a big role.
- A part-time job also increases access to other people who may be from different social networks and can increase social skills in a different environment.
- Support can come from not only families and peers but from community institutions. A part-time job, or religious, educational, and community agencies can still provide a teen with a sense of place. Involvement in a larger cause—a nonprofit or political organization—provides the opportunity to make a contribution and connect them to a sense of purpose.
- Limit screen time, watching television, and especially social media. Start when your children are young and continue to monitor screen time.
- Try to keep dinnertime smartphone-free. As described in Chapter 4, if family dinner is to be meaningful, smartphones should be elsewhere. You have to be willing to put your own phone down to show your teen that they can live without theirs for a while, too.
- Take periodic family media vacations. Every now and then, for just for a day or even a few hours, agree that all family members will be banned from looking at audiovisual media. This includes websites, magazines, television shows, Instagram, and more. You can turn it into a contest to see who can stay offline the longest. If your teens crave entertainment, they can read a good book, listen to music, spend time with friends, or engage in a hobby—and relax physically and emotionally.
- Help your teen develop media literacy, especially challenging the advertising of products that fuel body dissatisfaction.
- Do not undercut your teen's relationships with friends, unless there is a question of safety. You do not have to like them and you may not see what attracts your teen to them, but it's not your social life. You may feel judgmental, but share any concerns with your spouse or partner or a friend, not your teen.
- Do not tolerate comments that are body bashing, slut shaming, racist, or homophobic. Take this stance because it is the right thing to do and because a family needs to be a place to create acceptance. If you do this, your teens will feel safe if they feel "different" in some way.

- Do not tolerate bullying. Bullying tends to happen more in early adolescence, so if your teen tells you about it, listen carefully. Express support for them or any other targets. Empower them to understand that they do not need to accept the situation. If your teen is a target, use the motivational interviewing techniques described in Chapter 4 to help them determine how they want to handle the situation and ask how you can help.
- Follow the same strategy if your daughter tells you about online sexual shaming or body bashing.
- With your teen's permission, contact school authorities about bullying.
- Do not contact the parents of the bully. Research suggests that they are not receptive to such information.
- Do not accept a school or teacher's attitude that "boys will be boys" or "girls need to work on getting along"; don't settle for peer mediation, either. These programs don't work because bullying, by definition, involves a power differential, while mediation requires a level playing field and is therefore not appropriate for dealing with this problem.
- Remind your teens that they should try to intervene if they observe bullying.
- Advocate for the schools to have a bullying prevention program and a zero-tolerance policy for bullying.
- Get support for yourself as well. Raising an adolescent can be a difficult journey, so the more you can share with other parents, the better you will feel.
- If you are a single parent, social support is all the more important and, of course, challenging. Single parents, especially single mothers, often work all day, then want to be available for their teenage children and then must get ready for the next day, leaving very little time for their health and well-being or for socializing. This is where extended family can be helpful or you might find another single parent to share activities and exchange emotional as well as practical support.

During the first song in the popular Broadway musical, *Dear Evan Hansen,* I began to cry. This is not that unusual—I tend to cry during many musicals—but, as it turns out, I'm not alone in my experience of this play. The popular talk show host Stephen Colbert revealed that he cried throughout the play as well. The poignancy of the social anxiety experienced by Evan Hansen, his loneliness and inability to make friends, as well as his mother's struggle to help him are profoundly moving. Evan gets into enormous difficulty after he lies about having been a close friend of a young man who committed suicide. After ultimately confessing his lie, he is able to gain support from his mother, friends, and the larger community. The end of the show is quite a moving tribute to the power of social healing, with a song titled "You Will Be Found." If you want to understand more about our universal need for connection, I recommend seeing the play or watching the many excerpts on YouTube.

Remember that you can use the power of social support to assist you in your goal of helping your teen navigate the complicated world of relationships. We can't and shouldn't protect our teens from all social discomfort, but we can be available to help, to listen to them, support them, and model the many benefits of social connection.

CHAPTER 10

Time Out for Self-Reflection

We have covered a fair amount of material, so this is a good time to take a break from reviewing strategies and take a step back. Reflecting on the thoughts, feelings, and behavior that occur during your interactions with your teen can enhance and improve the relationship. You want to help your teen become emotionally healthy, and the material in this book can help you do just that. It's quite possible, however, that as you are attempting to utilize the techniques and communications skills we've covered so far, some come more easily to you than others. That is to be expected; we are covering a lot of psychological territory and it's not easy to change quickly.

At the same time, you are an individual with a specific psychological, family, and cultural history. If you spend some time reflecting on your own history, you will be able to identify patterns of behavior—those that facilitate or interfere with your parenting style and best judgment. You may not understand why some of the communications strategies and techniques in this book are difficult for you to implement. By looking at your own childhood and family interactions, you can come to a greater awareness of patterns that may not be clear to you at first. Understanding their impact will help you improve some of the skills of optimal parenting, including flexibility, conflict management, and navigating relationships. Reflecting on your family of origin is not about deeply probing the depths of past distress but making sense of it in order to recognize the impact it may have on you so you can behave with increased freedom and clarity of thought.

There are additional reasons to engage in this endeavor. Just as adolescent moods, with the rapid changes between highs and lows, is often compared to a roller coaster, raising an adolescent might be a bit like operating a roller coaster. As the operator, it's best for you to remain calm during the highs and lows, the stresses and joys along the way, to keep the roller coaster from going off the tracks; your reactions to the highs and lows can make the situation better or worse. For example, if you respond to a teen's anger or irritability with escalated anger or irritability, the interaction is not going to end well. If you remain calm and curious about all that emotion, you may learn what's going on.

FAMILY HISTORY: GRATITUDE

If you felt comfort, support, and warmth from your family of origin, you are more likely to be able to create those feelings with your teen. That model and experience of strong family functioning promotes growth for subsequent relationships. For the first part of self-reflection, take a moment to be mindful and appreciate the areas of life with your family and your teen that are going well. Think about any meaningful moments, enjoyable meals, holidays, activities, family travel, or the process of learning new information and ideas from your teens. You can be grateful for your spouse or partner, parents, relatives, teachers, and friends who have shown you the way or supported your growth in relationships.

By examining your psychological, familial, or cultural history, you may find some answers. Remember, though, we are entering another guilt-free zone. Productive self-reflection requires that you consider your feelings and behavior with a clear view, not one clouded by self-blame and recriminations.

CONSTRUCTIVE FEEDBACK

Perhaps your spouse or partner, a dear friend, relative, or teacher gives you constructive feedback on some aspect of your parenting. It may be difficult to hear at first, but constructive feedback can help you see your parenting from a different point of view. When Rita came into my office one day after a parent–teacher conference, she was annoyed. She had expressed her worry, as she often did, about a problem her daughter, who had a learning disability, was experiencing at school. During the conference, her daughter's fourth-grade teacher paused and said, "You know, you might want to enjoy this child more." The implication, of course, was that Rita was worrying too much and needed to make room for some joy in her parenting. In my opinion, the teacher made a good point, although her delivery was somewhat blunt. Rita and I explored this; her mother had a full-blown anxiety disorder and Rita was much calmer by comparison. She came to see that there was some truth to the teacher's comment, and they knew each other rather well, so the teacher wasn't speaking in a defensive way. She had given excellent short- and long-term counsel. By trying so hard to be an involved parent and advocate for her daughter, Rita was losing sight of some of her many positive qualities and strengths. If we are open to them, such conversations can be gifts we can use to develop our parenting.

PSYCHOLOGICAL SELF-REFLECTION

Negative Reactions

Start by thinking about your irrational negative reactions to some of your teen's behaviors. You may withdraw when you feel unappreciated. Perhaps you resent it when he doesn't seem to understand his privileges. Maybe you have difficulty tolerating sadness or you become enraged when he comes home late. And you can add more to this list. Many of these are understandable reactions to adolescent development. However, when you feel you are overreacting, under-reacting, or detaching, it is beneficial to think about why.

Psychological reflection allows you to think about your tendencies toward specific conditions or diagnoses. It is possible, for example, that you have struggled with depression or anxiety in the past or have some cognitive vulnerabilities in the way you think. Or you may be depressed now. Depression is a familial disease: Rates of depression in teenagers whose parents are depressed are three to four times higher than those for teens whose parents are not depressed. There are several possible explanations for this statistic, including genetics, which we cannot change. Your current behavior is one thing you can change, but this change is likely to depend on your understanding of your own past. There is also evidence that helping parents individually helps a teenager; some research shows that treating depression in a parent improves the mental health of their children. This has been shown to be true for mothers; we know less about fathers because they have not been the focus of research on parenting until relatively recently.

Anxiety may also get in the way. I have seen women who have tendencies toward anxiety still do quite well at work and in relationships. They seem to be able to control most of their worries and fears. Yet when they become mothers, there is often an explosion of new fears. This makes sense, because the birth or adoption of a baby brings an enormous amount of uncertainty along with an equally enormous amount of responsibility. Therefore, separation anxiety, concerns about potential medical problems, and fears about normal development, just to name a few, may take over. Alison Gopnik, author of *The Carpenter and the Gardener,* suggests that there is additional anxiety among today's parents because, unlike previous generations, many grew up in small families and did not observe the care of babies and young children. Thus, they missed out on the family knowledge and skills that previously were observed or passed down from older siblings and relatives during childhood.

Milder anxiety based on childhood experience can also get in the way, without necessarily being a traumatic or deep problem. A friend of mine grew up in a large city and was afraid of swimming in the ocean. This fear had not interfered with her life as she was never near the ocean. Then she moved to a seaside town in New England and had two daughters. She decided to join "Mommy and Me" swim classes when the girls were babies so they would learn to swim and not repeat her past. That growth also meant that she would be ensuring that she and daughters would be comfortable in her new environment by the ocean.

Your Family History—The Shadows

The term *family of origin* means the immediate family we grew up with, whether biological or adopted, and other significant caregivers. Our experiences with our families of origin directly and powerfully influence how we view others and ourselves in relationships. Early attachment and a sense of security can form the basis for warm and healthy relationships later on. In contrast, unresolved conflict and struggle can create shadows over your current family.

You may remember Kevin's father, Brendan, from Chapter 4. Brendan believed he was a good father because he had dinner with his children every night and he wanted to advise them well. In contrast, Kevin's view was that his father lectured him every night in a boring manner. Kevin hadn't minded it when he was younger, but grew resentful when he reached his teens. Brendan revealed that his own father was a serious alcoholic and that dinnertime in his youth meant feeling tense and worried about who would erupt next, his angry mother or his intoxicated father. Brendan justifiably believed that he had made great progress from his family of origin and, in fact, he had. But the legacy of his father's alcoholism was that

Brendan did not have very good communications skills and was very rigid in his responses. His extensive dinnertime lectures were an attempt to control his family in a positive way, just as he was unable to control his father's intoxication and parents' disputes as a child. When Kevin and Brendan were able to talk about these issues, each of them learned from one another and the reasons for the dinnertime problem were clarified. They still had a long way to go—old habits do indeed die hard—but they were no longer resentful of one another.

Like Brendan, we all react to parenthood in ways that are partially based on our families of origin. Parents' reactions occur throughout a child's life but change over time. Perhaps when your child was a newborn, you were overwhelmed by the responsibility, but you grew into the role. When your child moved out of the cocoon of the family into day care or preschool you might have been unsettled, but you grew into it. Family interaction during adolescence requires greater flexibility. Whereas earlier childhood stages require parents who are consistent and in charge, teenagers need a spirit of cooperation within general parental limits to provide a balance between supporting their autonomy while still maintaining some control. It's common for a parent whose family of origin was strict and rigid to struggle in dealing with a teenager's drive for autonomy. You may know what you don't want to do—replicate your parents' behavior—but it's hard to know how to behave differently.

If you have a spouse, partner, or co-parent, parenting becomes more complicated because you may have the shadows of two families of origin. However, by sharing your stories, you can learn more about one another. You can help one another with any "blind spots" and then create and agree on a general plan for the issues that tend to arise during adolescence. You don't have to agree on 100% of the issues; teenagers can tolerate viewing their parents as individuals rather than one parental unit. However, you do need a united front for important boundary and safety issues.

If you are a single parent, your current situation may be different from that of your family of origin. You may be divorced, widowed, or never married; you may be gay, lesbian, or trans. Your current family structure may be different than your family of origin and so you may feel that the model from your family of origin does not apply to your current situation. Not true. The qualities of warmth, support, acceptance, and flexibility matter, not the family structure. It is true, though, that if you are a single parent without a partner or co-parent, raising an adolescent can be even more challenging. This is a time when extended family and close friends or support groups can be enormously supportive and helpful. I have noticed that in single-parent families, there may be more power-sharing with teenagers at an earlier age, but those teens also take on more responsibility. Once again, mutual support, respect, and communication matter more than family structure alone.

Trude was a recently divorced mother of two teenagers who came to see me because she was very worried about Molly, age 16. Molly did well in school and had friends but "wasn't dating yet." When Trude came to see me, I saw that she was extremely attentive to her appearance—her hair and makeup were perfectly done—and she tapped her Ferragamo high heels and fidgeted with the hem of her twin set while we talked. Trude was tearful and furious that her former husband, who had begun dating, could be happy again so soon, after 6 months, whereas she was struggling. In contrast to her concerns about Molly, Trude described her 14-year-old Peter as doing well. He was an athletic boy who also enjoyed science.

As I got to know Trude in more depth, I learned that her own mother's role-modeling was negatively affecting Trude's view of Molly. Trude's father was a family physician in a rural area, a quietly supportive man who came home late, ate briefly, then retreated to his study. He was a local hero who "gave all to his patients." Her mother was chronically depressed and confided in and complained about her life to Trude, the oldest of six children. Her father wasn't around much and the family did not have a lot of financial resources because of the cost of raising six children and her father's small, rural practice. Trude tried to help out with her younger siblings to assist her mother, but she finally realized, probably accurately, that she could not make her mother happy. Her mother was too heavily burdened and resented her family life but didn't feel able to negotiate more shared responsibility from her husband. She emphasized that Trude needed to "make a better match."

Trude had dated a lot in college and married Roger, a charming man who was 2 years older, when she graduated. Although many of her friends wanted Trude to join them in graduate school or in starting high-powered careers, Trude did not want to follow that path because, she said, she never "felt that smart," did not want additional education, and was content to work part-time in a small gift shop after she married Roger until Molly was born. Trude had carried from her family a core belief that she was not important as an individual; instead, her "match" and her role as a helper were what mattered. Out of step with the times, Trude had very few individual goals, even before she met Roger.

When Roger joined a large law firm, Trude was happy to leave her parents in Iowa, move to the Northeast, and stay home with her two children. She acknowledged that Roger, who had become a busy trial lawyer, criticized her a fair amount during the marriage and did not really enjoy family life.

Trude had decided she was better off than her mother because there were more family resources, and two children "were a lot less work than six." Trude was devastated by the divorce but even more by Roger's beginning to date so quickly. She resisted going out, spent time on Facebook and Instagram, and believed that her alimony and child support were reasons not to look for a job. Roger began to spend even less time with the children. Trude became bitter, simultaneously different from and very similar to her mother.

Trude had lots of reasons to be angry with Roger, primarily his lack of commitment to family life, his criticism when they were married, and his neglect of the children after the divorce. Over time, it became clear to me how much Trude's neglect by both parents led to her negative core belief. Additionally, she overemphasized marriage alone as a source of meaning in her life because she was trying to follow her mother's advice. Trude's primary adult experience was being a mother. Trude's need for Molly to be more social was based on a pattern from her own family of origin, even though it had not worked out well for Trude. This shadow clouded her view of her daughter, who in fact enjoyed her friends, field hockey, and school. I suggested to Trude that hanging out in groups has replaced dating for many of today's teens and that her concerns about Molly's social life appeared to be unfounded at present.

Trude's distorted view of Molly clarifies the impact of psychological and family history on parenting. Trude could not see Molly accurately because of her current anger and shadows from her family of origin. These shadows, alongside untreated anxiety or depression, can interfere with this process. There is evidence that teenagers whose parents' view of their personalities matched their own self-assessment developed higher levels of self-esteem from age 17 to 29.[1] When Molly did come in to see me, I discovered a happy, active 16-year-old who had little interest in dating, but her mother didn't believe that Molly could really be content. Trude's dissatisfaction with her own life led her to be overly worried about Molly's social life. You can imagine that Molly might begin to question herself if Trude wasn't able to change, and this dynamic would create a third generation of dissatisfied women.

Just as our teens are going through development, so are we as parents. Trude was happy when Molly and her brother were younger, but adolescence

1. Zyan Luan, Poorthuis A., Hutteman, R., Asendorpf, J., Denissen, J., Van Aken, M., . . . Gerstorf, D. See me through my eyes: Adolescent–parent agreement in personality predicts later self-esteem development. *International Journal of Behavioral Development*, 42(1), 17–25, 2018.

triggered Trude's worries about Molly's future. In my practice, I have seen some parents view their children through a variety of lenses. For example, a mother who had very strict parents and became exasperated with her son's defiant behavior might say, "You are too impulsive, I could never have behaved that way at your age." A father might have an intense negative reaction to his daughter's blossoming sexuality because his parents divorced after an extramarital affair during his teen years. In both of these situations, it is likely that the parents were not seeing their teens' behavior clearly and the parents' clouded views interfered with their teens' development.

Trauma

If you have experienced trauma and have never had treatment, you may need some assistance with parenting. Most researchers define adverse childhood events as neglect, sexual and physical abuse, intimate partner violence, and extreme family conflict. The children of parents who experienced four or more adverse childhood events have over four times the rate of psychological problems of other children. Terms like *adverse childhood event* are used in research because they seem neutral or objective, but if you have experienced an adverse childhood event, you know that it was not neutral in any way. It was likely extremely disturbing and may have had long-lasting effects. Untreated trauma can interfere with your life in general and especially with your parenting, as you can be triggered by events even slightly similar to those in your past. Bessel van der Kolk, a pioneer in the treatment of trauma, has written that, with one out of eight children in the United States being subjected to maltreatment, "early exposure to family violence and emotional abuse is the largest and costliest public health issue in America."[2]

You may not have had a traumatic past nor experienced abuse or neglect, but had parents who were preoccupied, detached, or not particularly warm. That does not mean that your situation as a parent is hopeless. A large study of over 6,000 couples found that people who reported healthier families of origin or had come to terms with those families' difficulties reported higher satisfaction with their current relationships. Even if your family of origin was not ideal, if you come to accept and understand it, you can create a

2. Besel van der Kolk. The politics of mental health. *Psychotherapy Networker*. May-June, 33–54, 2019, p. 34.

better family environment for yourself and your children. In *Lab Girl*, Hope Jahren describes her experience as a parent: Even though she came from a distant, unaffectionate family, she notes, "Every kiss I give my child heals the one I had ached for but was not given. Indeed, it has turned out to be the only thing that ever could."[3]

One day, Kevin, who you'll remember from Chapter 4, came in to share a significant experience. His father, Brendan, had been in marital psychotherapy for a while and then sat Kevin and his sister down to tell them about a traumatic event from his past. When Brendan first got his driver's license, he was driving on a foggy late afternoon, and a women who suffered from dementia walked into the street. Brendan tried to brake but the woman was killed on impact. No charges were ever filed and the staff at the nursing home as well as the woman's family tried to console Brendan that the woman often wandered. (This was well before nursing homes became more vigilant about patients with dementia.) Still, Brendan spent one night in jail because he was afraid to call his explosive father. He had flashbacks of the "poor woman's startled face" for many years but never sought treatment. He was supported by a priest from his church, and those conversations had been helpful. He had told his wife Donna about the episode but had never wanted to talk about it. Brendan was beginning to understand that the trauma also fueled his lectures as a desire to "teach his children" about the world so that they would be safe.

I had mixed feelings about this information. It was fortunate that Brendan finally shared his secret with his children as it led to greater understanding and a feeling of connection. At the same time, I wished that trauma, secrecy, and shame had not increased the suffering of two generations in this family.

CULTURAL SELF-REFLECTION

As a parent, you are the connection between your teenager and your culture. Culture plays a role in parenting skills and practices. You can think about culture in terms of family roles, flexibility, nuclear versus extended families, multigenerational families, and holiday traditions, just to name a few. For example, in Euro-American cultures, the nuclear family is the primary unit of living and decision-making, whereas in many other cultures, including Asian, Hispanic, African, and Middle Eastern cultures,

3. Hope Jahren, *Lab Girl*. p. ??.

"the family" often refers to an extended network of grandparents, aunts and uncles, and cousins. Regional and racial differences are also important; in the United States, an African American family in Mississippi may have different norms than a family with a Scandinavian background from Wisconsin. There is no right and wrong here; the goal is to understand how your family's culture affects you and your children.

In my clinical practice, when students want me to meet their parents, they sometimes perceive me as a cross-cultural translator who can help parents understand why, seemingly all of a sudden, their student is changing. This is, in part, a natural progression of adolescent development, but the extent to which this is true varies. Many parents from all backgrounds are confused by the changes in their children. The confusion is a result of the adolescent growth, social changes, and multicultural values that many college students adopt.

If your spouse or partner is from a different culture than yours, discussing family expectations is an important part of developing intimacy. You can also discuss and decide how you want to raise your children. Exploring cultural issues and values is a great way to connect with your teens as well.

You may agree that understanding your history is important to your parenting and want to examine your past but not know how to get started. Here are some suggestions:

- Find a quiet moment to pause and think. Five minutes between picking up your kids and making dinner is not enough time for self-reflection. Remember that taking care of yourself is important and that allowing yourself some space to reflect is part of self-care.
- Notice your patterns of behavior and reactions in response to your teenager. Common issues are limit-setting, social issues, safety, and autonomy. Is it possible that when setting limits you overdo it and then undo all your previous efforts when you start to regret it?
- You could also start with your feelings. Do you have a particular trigger or feel a twinge (or even a surge) of panic when you feel that your child is involved in something that may or may not be safe? There are numerous possibilities. Start with your uncomfortable feeling or your behaviors that seem irrational and make a note to yourself, either in your mind or on paper.
- Talk to your siblings, close childhood friends, or cousins. What do they remember about your family?
- Write a family vignette. When I'm teaching medical residents, one of our seminars is a narrative experience. We do a home visit to a patient from the residents' practice. This usually takes about an hour; we've

been graciously welcomed into many homes all over the state. When we return from the home visit, we take some time to reflect on our reactions and write a narrative. We learn about the reasons for people's behavior and our various reactions to the visit. The residents often have transformative insights into why their patients behave the way they do. For example, they come to see a patient they previously viewed as "noncompliant" because she does not take her medications regularly as a resilient survivor after we've seen the poverty, physical chaos, and multiple responsibilities of her life. You can do the same thing when thinking about your family of origin. Just take some time to think back to any particular time or occasion and reflect on how you felt in your relationships with your parents, grandparents, siblings, and so on. What was the typical family dinner like? Write it down. Take a few minutes and read what has come to mind.

- Remember that the stories don't have to be negative. You may well have fond memories about family traditions. Most families are neither all bad nor all good. Think about the nuances as well.

- You may have difficulty writing an open-ended narrative; it would be understandable for it to feel like too massive an endeavor. In that case, you can try two other exercises. You could aim to write 50 words or less, which may feel more like a cognitively framed paragraph rather than a large assignment. Or you could try writing even less: Aiming for 10 words would be more like a haiku. Here is an example of the latter:

  Thanksgiving
  We heard the turkey
  slip off the platter
  to the floor.
  We gasped
  then laughed.

- Looking at a family photo is another productive exercise. See if you can find a candid one rather than one of those staged holiday card photos. Notice who is physically close to one another, the expression on their faces, and their body language. You may find that the images evoke more intense emotional reactions than written words.

  - What do you see with respect to your culture in the photos? Do family gatherings include the nuclear or extended family, close friends, or even a community? What was the food like? How did people dress? What were some of the traditions? What were the expectations for the children's behavior? Are you continuing these traditions?

- Depending on the material, you can discuss family patterns with your teen. I know one single mother who, after a heated argument about curfews, said, "I'm a mother of a teenager for the first time, just as you are a teenager for the first time. I didn't have older siblings and my parents were super strict. So maybe we can talk and learn together. And we have to work together."

- Whether or not you're having difficulties with your teenager, sharing your family of origin's stories with your partner or close friends can be a learning experience.

- If your family of origin had a substance abuse problem, many 12-step programs like Al-Anon and Narc-Anon can be extremely beneficial, comforting, and enlightening.

- If you have a history of depression or are currently depressed, during stressful times be sure to monitor your feelings and symptoms in addition to your overt reactions to your teen. Be sure to take care of your emotional needs, for your family and for yourself.

- To look at issues from the other direction, you may know that you have experienced family trauma but are not sure of its impact. Think through what happened and whether any similar events have occurred in your current family. Remember, the issue regarding parenting is not whether or not you suffered in your family of origin; it is whether you have come to terms with the suffering in some way. Cognitive behavior therapy (CBT) or family-oriented therapy can help you address unresolved issues and symptoms of trauma or depression.

- If you find that you have not been able to come to peace with your family of origin, there are many ways to get help. First, you can share your difficulties with your spouse or partner. A close friend or other parents could give you additional feedback and support.

- There are also programs for developing adolescent parenting skills in many adult education and community-based programs.

Trude ultimately decided to seek therapy in order to help her reduce her anxiety about Molly and adjust to the divorce. Over time, Trude became better able to distinguish her issues from Molly's.

The goal here is to increase your parental self-efficacy, the concept we explored in Chapter 5. Knowledge of parenting skills is not enough if you past interferes with using them. Based on this newfound self-assessment and increased self-understanding, you can return to communicating with your teen and implementing strategies for change with a greater sense of freedom.

PART III

Vulnerabilities and Strategies for Change

CHAPTER 11

How the Principles of Cognitive Behavior Therapy (CBT) and Other Evidence-Based Therapies Can Help Your Family

Make not your thoughts your prisons.

—William Shakespeare, *Antony and Cleopatra*

So far, we have covered positive values and lifestyle issues to promote growth and flexibility in children and teens. The next few chapters will present specific techniques that you can use to help your teenager reduce the likelihood of depression by defeating negative emotions. Some of these techniques were originally approaches to the treatment, rather than the prevention, of depression. All of these strategies, though, can be used to develop aspects of personality that support growth and resilience and buffer against depression. They can be useful for targeting one or two symptoms of depression, thereby preventing the onset of a full-blown depressive episode. I also find that many of these strategies can help in managing our busy, everyday lives. After you learn and try out some CBT techniques, you'll be able to identify those that can be helpful to you and your family.

One day, I walked into a seminar a bit early and the one student there said, "Man, I need some CBT for this mood!" I wasn't sure what Paul meant; he was having a bad day, and after we talked about it for a while, I realized that he really wanted a referral to a mental health professional. I also realized that he was not using the term *CBT* specifically, but instead to refer to all therapy. Although CBT is the most widely used evidence-based type of psychotherapy today, it is not the only one; there are, moreover, numerous types of CBT. Paul was not alone in his misunderstanding, though: Over the past 70 years, there has been a great deal of research to determine the most effective strategies for the treatment and prevention of depression, and the popular press often oversimplifies this research. In this chapter, I will clarify what we now know.

There's an alphabet soup in the world of therapy: CBT, BA, DBT, ACT, IPT—where to start? To make matters even more complicated, even though CBT is now the most commonly used evidence-based practice, most psychotherapists use strategies from a number of schools of psychotherapy. All of these types of treatment have some commonalities. The most important one is that they share an educational focus; that is, the strategies and ideas are not mysterious. You can learn them, and so can your teenager. They all have positive philosophies, tend to be active rather than reflective, and are effective and evidence-based.

The First Wave

Cognitive behavior therapy, or CBT, is a combination of cognitive therapy and behavior therapy. Before the advent of CBT, during the middle of the twentieth century, various forms of psychodynamic therapy dominated mental health treatment. These were originally based on the work of Sigmund Freud. Although some scholars attempted to make the ideas accessible, the basic concepts, especially unconscious motivation and the treatment approach of psychoanalysis, made psychodynamic theory difficult for laypeople to understand. It was also almost impossible to measure progress. After World War II, psychologists looked for treatments whose effects could be measured so that they could determine the impact of a particular intervention. The empirically validated or evidence-based treatments could then be standardized and taught to psychotherapists.

The first wave of behavior therapy (BT), then called *behavior modification*, was at first primarily in institutions—prisons, hospitals, and schools.

The premise here was that implementing basic rules of reinforcement could change behavior. Want more of an action? Reinforce it. Want less? Ignore it, punish the subject, or withdraw a reinforcement. While based on the pioneering work of John B. Watson and Edward Thorndyke, B.F. Skinner developed BT more fully. You may have seen drawings or photos of B.F. Skinner's rat being trained in the operant conditioning chamber, or "Skinner box." The rat, or other animal, could press a lever to obtain rewards of food or water. Different stimuli, like sounds or lights, could be added. The Skinner box was used to conduct research to ascertain and understand the most effective patterns of reinforcement. Skinner believed that conditioning could be used to improve education and serve as a way to improve society. If you gave your son or daughter a time-out when they misbehaved, or if you received stickers in elementary school for good behavior, you've already experienced behavior modification.

BT can also be used for self-management. *Functional analysis* is a term that means using observation to examine precisely what factors triggers a behavior and all of the positive and negative consequences. A change in environment can then modify a problematic behavior. Self-management strategies have been used for many years in helping people with weight problems, chronic pain, and numerous other conditions. For example, a person who overeats learns to minimize triggers for eating unhealthy foods and create new ones for healthy behaviors—like leaving sneakers by the bedside to encourage physical activity. This is called *stimulus control* or *environmental planning*. Smokers learn to avoid situations they associate with smoking in order to reduce the triggers to smoke.

I often use self-management techniques—I even used them while I was working on this book. I enjoy the process of writing. The administrative and referencing work? Not so much. If I've done administrative work for an hour or two, I use self- reinforcement by then scheduling a pleasant break—going outside for a bit, a short chat with family or friends, or listening to music. I also set the stage for writing the night before; this is stimulus control or environmental planning. The next time I want to write, I have everything I need to get started: my computer charged, legal pad and pens in place, and water bottle at the ready. My mini-rewards are also nearby—music (classic Motown) and my collection of brightly colored paper clips and floaty pens, given to me by dear friends. I also eliminate triggers that could distract me, primarily by limiting my access to email and the Internet.

In general, behavior modification for teens is most helpful in teaching basic learning skills and behavioral self-management. Parental praise also continues to be a powerful reward. It is clear that reinforcement is more effective than punishment and, of course, corporal punishment is never justified for controlling behavior.

Another example: What is a parent to do if a teen becomes verbally abusive? First, the rules of your home should be clear. For example, you can say, "We don't speak to one another or behave in that way." You'll need to be sure that you and your spouse or partner agree on the rules. Then, if your teen becomes abusive, you'll need to remind them of the rules. If they continue, the best course is to stop engaging so that you deny punishment or reinforcement. This is called *extinction*. You are also gaining control by ending the interaction. Finally, you can use a negative consequence, or punishment, like no car privileges or additional household chores. The important elements of the negative consequence are to implement it as soon as possible, be consistent and persistent, and be clear on the behavior. You are punishing a behavior, not invalidating a person. You want to avoid a shouting match, which would model the exact sort of behavior you want to eliminate. A similar process can be used for other behaviors like breaking a curfew or taking the car without permission. At another time, you'll need to emphasize empathy, listen, and explore what is going on with your teen to build better interactions.

The Second Wave

In the 1960s, Aaron Beck, MD, introduced cognitive therapy as a treatment for depression. Beck was influenced by Albert Ellis, who had introduced rational emotive therapy, which also has a cognitive focus. David Burns' best-selling book *Feeling Good: The New Mood Therapy* popularized cognitive therapy and its effectiveness in treating depression. The premise of cognitive therapy for depression is that people have distorted types of thinking that lead to maladaptive feelings and, over time, depressive symptoms or a depressive episode. Cognitive therapy helps a person identify these "cognitive distortions" and challenge them, replacing them with a more realistic and growth-promoting view. Beck's cognitive triad, also known as the *negative triad*, implicated three key elements in the belief system that leads to and maintains depression. The triad is a set of automatic thoughts that are seemingly uncontrollable and pessimistic about the *self, the future,* and *the world*. Following are some common distortions and corrections, called *cognitive restructuring*.

Overgeneralization involves taking a single event and assuming it's part of a global, constant, negative pattern. For example, this automatic thought reflects a negative *self*-schema: "Of course Joan rejected my invitation to go out for coffee. I am a loser." The negative view of the *future* involves selective abstraction as reflected in a thought like "No one else will want to have coffee with me either." Then comes the conclusion, which is based on a negative view of *the world* and overgeneralization: "Most people don't want new friends. I am hopeless and may as well give up on making friends." You can see how this string of automatic thoughts could lead to withdrawal and hopelessness. However, the only fact in that series of thoughts is that Joan turned down an offer to go out for coffee. The cognitive therapist would help examine the reality. What are all the other possible reasons that Joan said no? She may have been busy at that time, might not like the coffee shop, or may be shy. Contrary to some misunderstandings of cognitive therapy, a cognitive therapist would not reassure the teen that everything will be fine, but would instead comment on the teen's good attempt at socializing and help create a new plan, based on other evidence about Joan or other acquaintances and opportunities to socialize.

Dichotomous or *all-or-none thinking* is an oversimplified process in which people evaluate themselves and events in exclusively black or white categories. Teenagers tend to think this way, in part because they're not yet able to deal with nuance. But all-or-none thinking limits growth. For example, a high-schooler may declare, "My history teacher is a mean nag," or, on the other side of the coin, exclaim, "My history teacher is great! I got a 5 on the AP exam!" However, something like "My history teacher is detail-oriented and strict but helps us do well" might be a more accurate assessment. The principle in challenging all-or-none thinking is that few things are ever really that simple. The conductor Victor Yampolsky, from the Northwestern University School of Music, made a comment that I think is an apt metaphor for the restrictions of all-or none-thinking: He said that you can learn the basic melody of a symphony on only the black and white keys of a piano, but by doing so, you sacrifice the many colors of the orchestra.

Depressed and anxious people can also filter out the positive because they have the cognitive distortion of negativity, or a negativity bias. People who are vulnerable to depression and anxiety experience greater psychological impact from negative events than from positive experiences. An example is: "I gave a class presentation, but Jane was frowning. I must have been boring." In contrast, evaluating the evidence without the distortion might lead to a conclusion less likely to feed negativity, like "Most of the class looked engaged. One person did not."

Catastrophizing is a thought process that follows if you only see the negative and therefore predict the worst possible outcome. Often the catastrophe is the endpoint of a negative chain of thoughts: "I'm having trouble concentrating on my studies. → I will fail the exam. → Then I will feel worse. → Then I'll mess up on the next exam. → Then I'll fail the course. → I may flunk out. → I'll be a real failure." In this case, someone who is catastrophizing fast-forwards the negatives, moving directly from "I'm having trouble concentrating" to "I'll be a failure."

Even worse, a teen can then project similar negative outcomes for similar instances in the future. Socially anxious teens who may have suffered one rejection often project into the future, "I won't be able to make any friends" or make global generalizations, for example, " I am always so awkward." The challenge to catastrophizing, appropriately termed *decatastrophizing* is to stay in the present rather than fast-forwarding into the future. With the example of the exam, you would encourage your teen to stick with the one fact, avoid predicting the future, and try to focus on present concerns. In the moment, it might not be helpful to point this out, but it is additionally worth reminding her that even if she did fail one exam, that itself would only be one fact and not a chain of increasingly disastrous events.

Contrary to some criticism, cognitive therapy also takes the past into account in an assessment. The concept of core beliefs suggests that a depressed person has a deep belief that she is incompetent or a "loser." Beck would sometimes see a teenager's negative core belief as the result of early childhood experiences. If a child was treated poorly or scapegoated by parents, a negative core belief characterized by pessimism and a negative explanatory style would then follow. It might also interest you to know that Beck was originally trained as a psychoanalyst.

One of the most troubling outcomes of negative thoughts and attributional style is that hopelessness can develop in their wake. This is especially problematic with teens because of their impulsivity. Adolescents who struggle with hopelessness can fall victim to more self-criticism and suicidal ideation. One of the major advantages of CBT is that its problem-solving focus is ultimately optimistic, and this is the attitude you want to convey to your teen. CBT is an empowering experience because it creates an opportunity to see the world from a new perspective and develop new problem-solving skills.

As stated earlier, CBT combines the principles of cognitive and behavioral therapy. CBT is based on the present and is interactive, problem-focused, and action-oriented. It combines the cognitive restructuring techniques of cognitive therapy with behavioral analysis and developing new skills of behavior therapy. In sum, the CBT approach helps a person recognize negative patterns, challenge the cognitive distortions, and self-correct, while at the same time learning new responses by increasing reinforcement. Through CBT thoughts, emotions, behaviors, and the interactions among these three realms can be examined. For example, stress or early negative events may lead to a negative core belief and the negative automatic thoughts and distortions that result from one. These thoughts, in turn, lead to negative emotions and maladaptive behaviors. Once you learn to identify the patterns and distortions, it can be a transformative experience to change them, and it can be a bit of a fun challenge as well. In-depth examples of this process are provided in Chapters 8 and 12.

Other Forms of CBT: The Third Wave, also called Clinical Behavioral Analysis

Behavioral Activation (BA)

Advocates of BA therapy suggest that when treating depression, change can occur from the outside in. It uses the principles of the aforementioned behavior modification in a very specific way. Using functional analysis, BA encourages a person to take action, almost any action. The concept is that doing something will make you feel better. Peter Lewinsohn and colleagues have suggested that depression is caused by too little reinforcement and too much punishment from the environment. Therefore, the goal should be to increase reinforcement. To that end, people with depression collaborate with a BA therapist to develop a hierarchy of rewarding activities and then track their goals as they participate in each activity. For example, if you were stuck feeling depressed and sitting on the couch, you would create a list of potential activities, from easiest to hardest. The first step might be to text or email a friend. Then you would be encouraged to go to the next step, perhaps meeting a friend for coffee. With respect to anxiety, BA often involves exposure to a fear, as I describe in my work with Rebecca's fears about her Bat Mitzvah reading in Chapter Twelve.

A second BA approach is to identify negative loops, patterns in which a coping mechanism may provide immediate relief but is dysfunctional in the long run. For example, a teen may avoid a problem to reduce conflict but become isolated over time. BA would be used to develop alternative responses in order to break the loop. Similar to functional analysis, the acronym for this process is TRAP—Triggers, Responses, Avoidance Problem, and TRAC—Triggers, Responses, and Alternative Coping strategies. In the case of avoidance as conflict reduction, the TRAP could be that your teen had an argument with his best friend at school (trigger). His response is to try to avoid school the next day by pretending he is sick (avoidance problem). This might help reduce anxiety in the short term, but in the long run it makes it worse: Now he's missed classes and possibly called attention to himself, and he'll still have to see his friend when he does go back to school. The TRAC, meanwhile, would be to understand that the argument (trigger) is upsetting but then respond by developing an alternative coping strategy, perhaps texting his friend that night or trying to see him in the morning before classes. The result is that he has learned how to communicate better, he and his friend are in a good place, and he hasn't missed any school.

BA is an evidence-based treatment that is also recommended for depression. There have been studies in the UK and Europe that suggest that BA is as effective as more wide-ranging traditional CBT in treating depression in community mental health centers. BA has the advantage of being able to be practiced by junior (bachelor's level) mental health workers.

Dialectical Behavior Therapy (DBT)

In the late 1980s, Marsha Linehan of the University of Washington created DBT, originally for people who had been diagnosed with borderline personality disorder. In this case, the dialectic between change and acceptance leads to a synthesis of new responses. DBT has four key modules: meditation and mindfulness, distress tolerance, emotion regulation, and interpersonal effectiveness. DBT is described in more detail in Chapter 8, on distress tolerance.

Mindfulness-Based Cognitive Therapy (MBCT)

We discussed many of the advantages of mindfulness and meditation in Chapter 8. New research suggests that mindfulness-based cognitive therapy and MBCT can help prevent recurrences of depression. One study found it to be as effective as maintenance anti-depression in preventing recurrences. Zindel Segal, Mark Williams, and John Teasdale developed MBCT over a decade ago. The goal of the treatment is to help people disengage from negative self-criticism and rumination. The 8-week group program of 2 hours each also includes yoga and body awareness and homework. At the same time, there is promise that it has a moderate effect on treating depression. With respect to adolescents, a study in Belgium found that a school-based MBCT program reduced the symptoms of depression, anxiety, and stress. However, MBCT is not readily available because of the need to train more clinicians skilled in this modality.

ACT is less concerned with changing thoughts and actions than with using mindfulness and other strategies to be open to unpleasant feelings, but not dwell on them or avoid situations that may elicit them. Instead, it focuses on values and leading a meaningful life. Created in 1982 by Steven Hayes at the University of Nevada–Las Vegas, ACT encourages people to let cognitive distortions and symptoms go and focus on acceptance, self-compassion, and committed actions instead. ACT therapists suggest that although symptoms are not the targets of therapy, they decline over time as therapy progresses. One goal of ACT is to increase cognitive flexibility, as discussed in Chapter 12. Other core processes include being present in the moment, reducing the impact of negative thoughts, and focusing on values. Evidence of the effectiveness of ACT with depressed adolescents is limited to pilot studies but is still worth following. (By the way, ACT therapists use the whole word, pronouncing it like the verb *act*, rather than pronouncing the letters individually, like CBT or DBT).

Now that we've covered almost 100 years and three waves of behavior therapy, let's look at a final set of letters—interpersonal therapy, or IPT. Created by the partnership of Myrna Weissman and Gerald Klerman, IPT sees the *restoration of relationships* as the key to treatment of depression. It is a short-term, attachment-focused therapy and is an effective, evidence-based treatment for depression. The goals are to improve communication skills and develop a strong social support network. Chapters 1–3 and 9 describe some elements of IPT. I consider IPT to be extremely powerful because supportive relationships can help progress continue long after therapy has been completed. It has been adapted for use with adolescents, called IPT-A, and is particularly helpful with the psychosocial problems teen face. IPT has also been adapted for the treatment of social anxiety, with small studies showing some success.

Anxiety and depression respond similarly to similar treatments that we discuss elsewhere in this book: The same class of medications, selective serotonin reuptake inhibitors (SSRIs), are commonly prescribed for both, and some studies have found that in cases where a patient has both diagnoses, CBT applied to one can also affect the other. Given their overlap, it may not surprise you to learn that some clinicians have proposed that a single treatment approach, the Unified Protocol for the Treatment of Emotional Disorders in Adolescence (UP-A), be used to treat adolescents suffering from anxiety, depression, or both.

CBT, BA, and IPT have been shown to be effective in treating depression. MBCT has been shown to prevent recurrences, and ACT has some evidence that it reduces symptoms of depression and anxiety. Some studies suggest that CBT is at least as effective as antidepressant medication and lacks the side effects of medication. Some additional evidence suggests that CBT offers protection from relapse. CBT and IPT appear to offer similar outcomes when used to treat major depressive episodes.

Several programs to prevent depression have used principles of CBT, including the Penn Resiliency Project (PRP) and the Coping with Stress (CWS) program. The PRP is based in schools and aims to prevent depression by targeting the features of students' cognition and behavior identified as risk factors for depression. Employees of the schools offering the program hold 12 group sessions that last between 90 and 120 minutes. Studies of the PRP have found that in the 6 months to 2 years following participation in the PRP, students reported a reduction of depressive symptoms. One study of 11- and 12-year-olds showed that girls' depressive symptoms were reduced, and another found that low-income Latino children reported "significantly fewer depressive symptoms" than the study's control group.

The aim of CWS is to help at-risk teens develop mood management and conflict resolution skills. According to one study of the efficacy of CWS, teens who participated in the program had fewer occurrences of depressive symptoms than the control group. In a follow-up 1 year after their treatment, only 9.3% of the CWS participants reported symptoms corresponding to the diagnostic criteria for major depression, while 28.8% of the teen control group did. Beardslee and colleagues have developed interventions for families in which the parents are depressed. Gladstone has detailed these interventions and other programs.

We have reviewed the types of therapy presented in this chapter so that you can establish a shared vocabulary. Should you need to select a therapist for your teen, you will now have a better understanding of the "therapy alphabet," which can help you and your teen make a more informed decision about the approaches of the therapists you are considering. Going forward, you'll learn more about how to use the techniques yourself and share them with your teenagers and your family. You'll be able to create a family environment for positive change and embrace a growth-promoting outlook.

CBT Tips: How to Get Started

The next chapter offers many suggestions about how to use ideas from CBT with teens who are perfectionistic. Meanwhile, here are some tips on how to get started using CBT.

- In general, the best attitude is that most problems can be solved if analyzed and a plan for change is made. This makes all CBT approaches optimistic in outlook.
- One of the best strategies to use with your teen (and yourself) is to avoid projecting into the future, creating that chain of automatic thoughts. One problem is not a disaster.
- If you and your teen brainstorm a plan to deal with a problem and the plan doesn't work, that, too, is not a failure or a disaster, but rather additional data from which you can create a new plan.
- The third-wave therapies also allow that some distress may occur and if it does, it's best to accept the distress but not become entangled with it.

These principle can be extremely helpful for families but often a teen may need additional assistance. If you think your teen could benefit from CBT or another evidence-based treatment, Chapter 14 gives suggestions for how to find a psychotherapist.

CHAPTER 12

Transforming Malignant Perfectionism and Encouraging Flexibility

Let your imperfections be an invitation to care. Remember that imperfections are deliberately woven into Navajo rugs and treasured in the best Japanese pottery. They are part of the art. What a relief to honor your life as it is in all its beauty and imperfection.

—Jack Kornfield, *The Tyranny of Perfection*

Providence, Rhode Island, where I have lived for many years, was once home to textile and the jewelry industries, but both long ago relocated to the South and then overseas. Consequently, we have many repurposed mill buildings, and I recently attended a sale at a glass blowing studio in one of them. I ran into 18-year-old Rebecca, a former patient. When I see adult patients outside of the office, they will make eye contact and perhaps smile and nod, but then continue on their way to protect their privacy or, perhaps, mine. Teenage girls are a whole other story. Rebecca quickly glided across the wooden floor in her ballet flats, her curly blonde hair flying, to hug me enthusiastically and gushed, "Oh Dr. Landau, I'm so glad to see you! I am loving college!" I was delighted to hear this good news. We might not have predicted this 6 years ago when Rebecca's parents came to see me. My work with Rebecca and her family is a gratifying example of how early intervention and use of the cognitive behavior therapy (CBT) techniques we reviewed in Chapter 11 can help prevent a teen from developing depression or anxiety in college. Rebecca refers to me as a member of her "Bat Mitzvah Girl Team." The Bat Mitzvah Girl Team was composed of her rabbi, her Hebrew tutor, and me.

Rebecca's story illustrates how CBT techniques can be used to modify perfectionism. When Rebecca was 12 years old, she was terrified of reading from the Torah during her coming-of-age ceremony. Both her tutor and her rabbi reported that she was progressing quite well in her studies. Her parents, on the other hand, revealed that Rebecca was "a nervous wreck" and "was doubting herself because she was sure that she would make an error and freeze during her reading." Rebecca's initial therapy was a relatively straightforward combination of anxiety reduction techniques and positive visualization. My initial assessment revealed that she was indeed well prepared, at least in academic terms. Although her Hebrew was excellent, she was extremely anxious. Research on phobias indicates that public speaking is the most common of all fears. Therefore, it is not surprising that the idea of a performance, especially at the vulnerable, self-conscious age of 13, was nerve-wracking for Rebecca. Reading in Hebrew, especially in front of a large group of family, friends, rabbis, and teachers, would be somewhat stressful for almost everyone. In fact, if I were to help a patient construct a hierarchy of fears about public speaking, from the least to the most intense, the elements of the Bat Mitzvah might provoke the most anxiety.

Our first step was to help Rebecca separate her anxiety from reality. With her permission, I consulted with her tutor and her rabbi. They reiterated that they believed she could perform well; she knew her reading and had good language skills. I emphasized this to her; Rebecca had been magnifying the potential for failure, when the evidence was quite to the contrary. This reality testing, or examining the evidence for her fears, helped give Rebecca an initial boost of confidence.

Next, we moved onto anxiety management with deep breathing exercises. When she would feel the first bit of fear, Rebecca learned to stop herself, breathe slowly and deeply, and focus only on her breathing. This technique helped her control the physiological elements of fear—rapid, shallow breathing, increased heart rate, and sweating. We rehearsed her Torah portion, with the instruction to try the breathing exercise first. We then collaborated on creating a positive visualization, a scene in which she would perform well and in a more relaxed state. The breathing exercises, reading rehearsal, and positive visualization became her daily homework assignments.

We next collected more evidence to counter Rebecca's fears. People who are anxious tend to be so self-conscious and catastrophize so they overestimate the impact any failure will have on others. I asked Rebecca if she had ever seen anyone else briefly stammer during a Torah reading. When she had to think a while and then replied, "I guess so, yeah," I then asked her if it had been a disaster for them. Rebecca shrugged and acknowledged that it was not.

At this point, Rebecca's perfectionism became evident. Although she had not been completely aware of it, her expectations about the reading were negative and at times, dramatically so. We explored the statements she was making to herself and realized that her high standards led her to engage in catastrophic fears and all-or-none thinking. We used a cognitive technique of corrective self-talk to counter thoughts like "If I make a mistake I'll panic and it will be a disaster" with "That's unfortunate, but I'll keep going." It took time, but with a collaborative approach of identifying her harsh standards and fears and using homework to apply self-correction, Rebecca progressed from all-or-none catastrophic thinking to more nuanced thinking: "I'll probably do OK but if I make a mistake, I know I can recover and keep going." She came to accept that, with practice, she could overcome any small barrier if she didn't panic and become overly self-critical.

As we had hoped, Rebecca's Torah reading went well. She was anxious and read slowly at first, but as time went on, she was able to read more fluently and enjoy her Bat Mitzvah. Two years later, though, she returned with another specific request: Could I meet with her and her parents to talk about her college applications? Rebecca was now beginning to feel an extreme amount of anxiety about disappointing her parents. She had several colleges in mind but felt that they would not be "good enough" for her high-achieving, professional parents. This was especially stressful because her older brother had gone to an Ivy League university to study engineering and was now successful at work.

TYPES OF PERFECTIONISM

Rebecca was struggling with perfectionism. The Bat Mitzvah anxiety was one part of this personality trait. She held herself to a set of extremely high standards, was self-critical, and tended to ruminate about any mistakes. She also experienced external pressure to be extremely high achieving owing to her parents' expectations and the culture of her competitive high school. These are all elements of maladaptive perfectionism. Maladaptive perfectionism creates a negative cycle that leads to problematic behaviors and psychological issues. Teens with maladaptive perfectionism are especially concerned with how they will be evaluated and, because they hold extremely high standards at the outset, their perfectionism leads to harsh self-criticism. This in turn lowers self-esteem, creates shame and humiliation, and then produces pessimism about the future. Teens like Rebecca believe they will be failures because they have set standards that are unrealistic. Research on maladaptive perfectionism reveals that it is associated with a number of psychological problems, including depression and anxiety. We can understand this as a result of the negative chain of thoughts and feelings. Perfectionism is similarly a major stumbling block when I work with young women who struggle with eating disorders and with people who have obsessive-compulsive disorder.

And there's more negative fallout from maladaptive perfectionism. Perfectionism negatively affects social relationships. Like Rebecca, many of the depressed and anxious young people I have seen have negative cognitive filters; they screen out positive data in favor of the negative. It may take a lot of encouragement, for example, to say "Hi" to someone they don't know well in the halls of their high school. Then, if the other person only nods or doesn't say much, the perfectionist's creative mind can go wild: "I said something stupid" or "She'll never like me anyway." These reactions can lead to overgeneralization and pessimism: "I'm a social failure and will always be an outcast at school." To correct these distorted thoughts, the patient and I look for hard evidence and alternative theories for the other student's muted response. It's possible, for example, that the other person was just coming from a class that was difficult, had been chastised by a teacher, and was preoccupied or in a hurry. One of my patients, who has been in therapy for a while now, jokes with me and says, "I know, I know, what is my evidence?" before I get a chance to ask him, "What is your evidence? or "What are alternative theories?" Our interaction reveals that since elements of CBT are educational, over time, people can learn to implement them on their own and that, of course, is the ultimate goal.

With all cognitive techniques, especially those that involve humor, it is important to me as a psychologist and you as a parent to make sure your teen first feels validated and understood. Otherwise, we too can be perceived as being critical or making fun at their expense. In fact, one of the most destructive consequences of perfectionism is that it interferes with the effectiveness of treatment. If perfectionism isn't targeted as part of therapy and doesn't change, the results are worse. You can imagine that very perfectionistic people would harshly grade themselves, the therapist, and the therapy. These individuals may also have difficulty accepting some of the nuanced elements of therapy because of all-or-none thinking or might want to do any homework assignment in therapy "perfectly" and, consequently, may avoid it. By wanting to be the "best patient" they may fail to reveal parts of themselves that are extremely important for the therapist to understand. These are all reasons to be sensitive but persistent in addressing perfectionistic standards, and the earlier the better.

There is additional troubling news: maladaptive perfectionism is increasing. A large study (40,000) of American, Canadian, and British young people found that they are more demanding of themselves and others than previous generations, from 1980 on. The authors of the paper, Thomas Curran and Andrew Hill, concluded that this is a result of the cultural emphasis on individual competitiveness and achievement and on tying self-worth to achievement. And it's true: This is a winner-take-all society, with little regard for anything other than "success," defined as monetary or career achievement alone.

THE GOOD NEWS: ADAPTIVE PERFECTIONISM

The news about perfectionism is not all bad, though. There is another type of perfectionism, adaptive perfectionism. Adaptive perfectionism involves working for achievement but based on internal rather than external standards. Adaptive perfectionists are aspirational; they accept that hard work is valuable in its own right but may not necessarily lead to attaining some rigid, unrealistically high standards. For those reasons, adaptive perfectionism is a positive trait and is associated with conscientiousness and higher academic expectations. During adolescence, teenagers are struggling to find their own standards, independent of their parents' and teachers' expectations. Parents and teachers can seize this opportunity to help students reduce malignant perfectionism or transform it into adaptive perfectionism, especially if they start as soon as possible.

At age 12, Rebecca was at the "in-between" stage, just beginning to separate her goals from those of her parents and teachers. When I met Rebecca and her parents again, the first goal was to help Rebecca express that she felt tremendous pressure to go to a college of her parents' choice rather than of her own. Rebecca's parents were prominent in their fields (marketing and law). Her older brother was still shy, but comfortable in the lab where he worked. They were a close-knit family and Rebecca was especially emotionally connected to her father. Rebecca was not afraid of her parents' possible criticism but was more concerned about disappointing her father. This fear of letting parents down can be just as strong an element of perfectionism as the fear of outright judgment. When, at her request, I met with Rebecca's parents alone, it became clear that there was a disagreement between them. Her father strongly believed that if Rebecca followed in her brother's footsteps, she would have a more successful life, and he wanted to make sure Rebecca had the same opportunities. Her mother, on the other hand, felt that Rebecca differed from her brother in a number of ways; she was not a scientist, she loved art and especially dance. More important, Rebecca was extremely sensitive, and had diverse interests—movies, novels, and environmental activism. Her mother thought that Rebecca might be happier at a smaller, less intense college where she would feel freer to explore all her interests. Rebecca's parents were relatively comfortable discussing their differences. I believed that, although their input could help, it should be Rebecca's choice and that as a family, they could openly discuss the pros and cons of each college or university.

Ultimately, Rebecca applied to a large number and variety of colleges. She was accepted at several of them and chose a small liberal arts school. When she saw me at the glass blowing studio, she wanted to share that she enjoyed it, had friends, and was comfortable in college. I appreciated her follow-up and was happy that she was able to explore friendships, new artistic activities, and hike in the rural area surrounding her college, not just confine herself to a narrow view of education as another rung on the ladder to achievement. Rebecca was fortunate that we were able to discuss her concerns openly and that her parents could directly share how they disagreed. By applying to many colleges and discussing them with Rebecca, they came to a decision that they all could accept. Not everyone is so fortunate. Rebecca's story also helps us understand that parents can self-correct when they realize that they may have instilled maladaptive perfectionism in their teens. And the standards are not always (or only) academic. Teens can feel pressure to be perfectionists in sports, extracurricular activities, jobs, hobbies, appearance, and weight.

GIVING UP MALADAPTIVE PERFECTIONISM

Challenging malignant perfectionism is a complicated issue for many parents. We'll be spending some time on this subject because maladaptive perfectionism is one of the most powerful risks for depression, and family dynamics play a major role in its development. As we saw in Rebecca's family, it is important to listen to our teens and then challenge some of the beliefs that can drive maladaptive perfectionism, to create a healthier family foundation. Now, despite what you've read so far, you might still be asking yourself, "Why should I lower my standards with my children? Shouldn't they be the best they can be? How else will they be successful?" I believe that we need to reject the idea that personal worth is based on successful career or financial achievement alone. Whether it's getting into college, getting promoted at work, making more money, or being the best dressed, if we limit ourselves to rigid standards and then evaluate ourselves accordingly, we miss other valuable aspects of the human experience—flexibility, compassion, a sense of emotional balance, commitment, recreation, creativity, intimacy, and community, just to name a few. In this way, rigid standards can get in the way of the kind of success we want for our children.

It is not difficult to find examples of people who have achieved a lot in their professional life to the detriment of their personal lives. In addition, setbacks can occur through no fault of their own, but for maladaptive perfectionists setbacks can lead to profound self-doubts. For example, some high school students feel enormous disappointment and failure when a very small number of elite colleges do not accept them, despite some of the admissions criteria being arbitrary and out of their control (geography, legacy status, etc.). So, the question is: How do we support teens and help them make choices, knowing that they still have our respect and love even if they may be disappointed?

Even well-meaning parents continue to hold unfortunate beliefs, feeling the need to push their children extremely hard for them to succeed. A corollary of this is the attitude "Anything worth doing is worth doing well." I like to add, "but maybe not perfectly." I remember going to a seminar on women's health where I learned, and grew to love, an expression to the contrary: "Everything worth doing is not worth doing well." For example, spending time with your children in a relaxed atmosphere is more important than having a spotless kitchen. Of course, some children need encouragement to work on their goals, but others need to be a little more relaxed because of their anxiety and self-criticism.

Another belief is that praise will make a child arrogant. I've noticed that there's a lot of criticism of helicopter parents, parents who may be overinvolved with and overprotective of their children. Taken to an extreme, this trait can be detrimental, but in my experience, it is not as detrimental as parents who deliberately withhold praise. It's true that global praise about being "special" or better than other people does not encourage empathy or growth and can lead to entitlement. On the other hand, praising children for their good behavior, especially for taking on new challenges or working hard, is extremely important for their optimal development.

MALADAPTIVE PERFECTIONISM IN YOUR TEENAGER

If you observe maladaptive perfectionism in your teen, as always, the most important first step is to listen to them and to validate their concerns.

Teens in particular are vulnerable to the idea that "everybody" will notice their failures. Anxiety and perfectionism can be part of adolescence, which, as a developmental stage, features intense self-involvement, so self-consciousness and embarrassment naturally follow. Teens can be tough on one another at times, so family support can be an important counterpoint.

As it was for Rebecca, it can be a relief for teens to understand that they will not be judged, especially not by their parents. Many psychologists believe that the key element of perfectionism is profound insecurity about family attachment, the belief that parents will not accept anything less than perfection. When teens challenge us about perfectionism, it can be painful, and as parents, we can be defensive. But this, too, can be a result of needing to be a "perfect" parent, so it's complicated. Maintaining open communication, especially active listening, as discussed in Part II, is the foundation for change and healthy development.

So as parents, we need to self-reflect on our own level of perfectionism. The following statements are some of the items from a perfectionism subscale: "If a person asks for help, it is a sign of weakness"; "If you cannot do something well, there is little point in doing it at all"; "If I fail partly, it is just as bad as being a complete failure"; and "If I ask a question, it makes me look inferior." If many of these statements sound familiar, you may well have maladaptive perfectionism. It might be difficult to gain some objectivity in self-monitoring perfectionism, so this is where your spouse, partner, best friend, or children can come in handy by providing feedback. If you realize that you have elements of maladaptive perfectionism, it is important to examine your behavior toward your children and determine how to stop a vicious cycle.

Countering maladaptive perfectionism is not just learning a set of techniques, although strategies can help repair relationships. It requires changing the family culture to one of acceptance, to make clear that you will continue to love your children independent of their achievements, no perfection required. Teenagers need to know that we all make mistakes but can learn from them and not resort to blame or self-blame.

Much of the help for perfectionist teens is educational. We need to give them the information to help them understand the destructive force of maladaptive perfectionism. It may be difficult for them to give it up. Here is when you can join them by saying something like, "I just realized that I am a perfectionist and that it can be destructive. Maybe we can look at the issue together." Many teens do not understand that they are successful, in spite of their perfectionism and not because of it. Harsh pressure, extreme anxiety, and unrealistic standards are confining and do not promote achievement. The distinction between maladaptive and adaptive perfectionism is usually clarifying. As mentioned earlier, your teen may let you know that she is under too much pressure from you. But it's also possible that other factors are at play: school culture, the larger social pressure to achieve, and competition with friends.

Even though you may at first feel defensive, it is critically important to listen and validate, rather than follow the instinct to make counterarguments. Here is an example of addressing maladaptive perfectionism in parents and their teen:

> "So, you're saying that your mom and I are too hard on you?"
>
> "Yes, you always ask about my grades and only act pleased if they are A's."
>
> "Ok, I wasn't aware of that. I'll try to be more flexible. I hope you know that I admire all the work you do."
>
> "Ok, but at school it's even worse. It's all about elite colleges, SATs, extracurriculars for applications."
>
> "Well, would you like to work on rejecting those pressures and figuring out what you want for yourself, not for us or the school?"

Try to avoid the generic "How was school today?" It is an open-ended question, which is good, but few teenagers will respond with anything other than "fine." Of course, as a parent, you do want to know how your teens are doing in school, but a better approach would be a comment based on what you know, like "I know you were worried about your exam today" or a non-academic question like "Did you and Jane talk about going to the swim meet?" These questions can open up the conversation to feelings, expectations, and other non-evaluative reactions.

Although most teachers are supportive, some can inadvertently foster competition. I've seen numerous younger siblings who've been compared to older ones in a competitive fashion. I've also seen schools that heavily promote that their students are admitted to elite colleges, when I know that many of those same students are super-stressed, abusing alcohol, or not particularly good citizens. Everyone feels the achievement pressure. Over time, though, your values will be more powerful than any one teacher. Your teen needs reminding that you love and like them as a person, because of their values and their unique combination of a variety of gifts, independent of their achievements.

With this validation, you can help them self-correct their assessment of events, especially by moving away from harsh self-judgment. For example:

> "I worked really hard on my figure skating. But when it was my turn, I made a mistake. I'm so stupid."
> "It looks to me like you showed a lot of determination."
> "But I felt like I really screwed up."
> "Do you think one error is 'screwing up?'"
> "Yes, I'll never be any good."

These dialogues let your teen know that you don't see them as a failure. When you get to "I'll never be any good," you can use the examining evidence approach:

> "You know, when we started with figure skating, we knew it would be an exacting sport with a lot of pressure."
> "I do love it most of the time."
> "Ok, great. Now what does your coach say?"
> "She said it wasn't so bad, I just need to practice my short program more."
> "Sounds to me like that's not stupid or a failure but a work in progress. Do you think so?"

EMBRACING A GROWTH MINDSET

A related concept that can defeat perfectionism is psychologist Carol Dweck's growth mindset. She and her colleagues found that when parents praised intelligence or abilities, rather than effort, children developed a fixed mindset, and the children felt that every challenge was a test of whether they were smart or not. That is a maladaptive perfectionist approach. Consequently, these children were less persistent and showed less enjoyment when presented with new problems to solve than those with a growth mindset. In contrast, a growth mindset leads to an openness to change, develop, and learn. Even more important, Dweck found that college students with a fixed mindset were more likely to be self-critical and to ruminate and become depressed than were students with a growth mindset. The children with growth mindsets had learned to take constructive action rather than to worry. For example, students with a fixed mindset may avoid courses that could be challenging but exciting because they focus only on good grades.

I've noticed that successful athletes and athletic teams allow themselves some time to feel bad, but then they turn to what they have learned from the loss. Dweck's work reinforces the belief that praising hard work and problem-solving is more beneficial to children than creating all-or-none, unchanging standards. A family with a growth mindset is more likely to develop an accepting and encouraging environment than one that is harsh and pressured.

TACKLING PROCRASTINATION

I never put off till tomorrow what I can possibly do the day after.
—Oscar Wilde

Oscar Wilde's comment reveals that procrastination is common. But it's not really all that funny for teens. Perfectionism may also be revealed by procrastination. Some teens avoid activities associated with evaluation because of anxiety. People who procrastinate delay the anxiety about evaluation, but delaying it only makes it worse, of course, because then they run into a time crunch. Then the fear of evaluation can be countered by the thought, "I would have done better if I'd had more time." They avoid anxiety temporarily, but in this way, procrastinators rob themselves of the joy of real achievement. Everything becomes burdensome and stressful.

You can help your procrastinating teen in several ways. If you and your teen see the procrastination as part of perfectionism, you can utilize the strategies we've reviewed so far, especially collecting any evidence that they can perform the task at hand.

People who procrastinate often believe the myth that they must feel motivated in order to begin work on a frightening task, but the anxiety will definitely overtake that motivation. In reality, just starting the task in any way will become motivating. One good approach, then, is to get your teen talking about the assignment to help them see that they do have ideas.

In addition, they may ask for your practical help. If so, you can first see if there is any new way they'd like to approach the task, such as dictating text rather than writing it. You can also help them break down a task into smaller tasks. For example, if they are avoiding writing a term paper you can suggest this list:

- Brainstorm: jot down *any* ideas about the subject.
- Outline.
- Write topic sentences.
- Write the introduction only.
- Now go back and fill in material after the topic sentences.

You could also ask your teen how they would break down the task. We all need rewards, so you can collaborate on developing a schedule of rewards for each task. The rewards should be short term—read a funny book, watch a YouTube video (for a limited time), take a walk, and so on. You can also check out the Pleasant Events Schedule, described in Chapter 8. By encouraging flexibility, instilling confidence, and alternating a small task with a rewarding activity, your teen can chip away at procrastination.

DISRUPTING RUMINATION

One of the most destructive elements of perfectionism is self-critical rumination. Rumination, or worrying to an extreme degree, about causes and consequences of a negative emotional experience is introverted and isolating. It is also associated with several psychological conditions, including depression and anxiety. Maladaptive perfectionists have difficulty accepting that they may have made a mistake. This can lead to a cascade of thoughts, as in "I made a mistake. Why did I make that mistake? I must be a failure," and so on. It's like the internalization of a harsh, critical voice and is associated with depression. I had a patient once who, as a teenager, overheard a teacher say, "Diane is not that smart" when they were discussing scholarships. This triggered a negative expectation that Diane was lacking in ability. Diane is now a successful CEO, but when she makes a small mistake, she begins to ruminate and hears that voice. To help her understand the damage and negative power of that old voice, we named it "Cruella." This scenario raises another negative result of rumination: It leads to disconnection and avoidance of people, the opposite of what we want in order to prevent depression. Diane was so preoccupied with the old voice of Cruella that she couldn't see that her hard work had made her successful and that she was surrounded by supportive colleagues and friends.

Another way to counter the process of rumination is to invoke what I call the reverse golden rule, or "Do Unto Yourself What You'd Do for Others." For example, you can ask, "What would you say to a friend in the same situation?" Most people will admit that they would reassure a friend and show compassion. This is one way to help a teen learn self-compassion and avoid harsh self-judgment and rumination. In fact, a recent study showed that techniques aimed at increasing self-compassion are more successful than trying to change some of the perfectionist thoughts alone. So rather than challenge the thought, "I didn't do well in that track meet, now I'm a failure" by saying, "No, that doesn't mean you'll be a failure," a more effective approach would be to say, "I understand. That's how you feel now but it's just a thought. Everyone has ups and downs. It's better to be kind to yourself." This can help your teen avoid taking the thought literally and to downplay it rather than attack it.

And, because the perfectionist cycle is generational, as parents, we must have self-compassion as well. This is important for parents who want to be less perfectionistic with their teens. I've seen many parents who have themselves been scarred by extremely critical parents and have internalized maladaptive perfectionism—they are harsh and critical and lack self-compassion. I have admired these parents as they tried to overcome their own upbringing by raising their children in a more relaxed and comfortable family atmosphere. Yet even these parents, struggling so valiantly, forget one thing: We continue to be role models. So, if we teach our children to be less perfectionistic and more accepting but they observe us being harshly self-critical, the message is at least partially undercut.

Increasing self-compassion and rejecting harsh perfectionism are not easy goals, given the current culture, where we all are exposed to such statements as "Losing is not an option" and where materialism and individual achievement are glorified. Individualism to the neglect of community is now the norm. However, we can still teach our teens a contrasting set of values of connection, community, and compassion, knowing full well that we are rejecting an increasingly harsh larger culture.

We must remember that the goal here is to help our teens develop into robust and resilient children, and that is probably why you are reading this book. We need to create family environments where parents and teens alike can aspire to attain goals while also being more forgiving. We can escape our past by focusing on growth and self-compassion in the present and enjoying our teens for who they are now and in the future. Promoting these qualities goes against the current social and political climate and can be challenging. But remember that we value the growth process, not just one perfectionistic outcome.

CHAPTER 13

Growing Up Different

LGTBQ Issues and Teens Who Are Overweight

What happens when a teenager is "different" in some way? Because adolescents have a strong need to be accepted, standing out in a negative way is stressful, especially if they are subjected to bullying. This chapter looks at the stressors that result from growing up different and how parents can help reduce their impact. There are many types of difference, including (but certainly not limited to) racial or ethnic minority status, immigration status, being physically limited, or having a learning difference. We will look at the concerns of many groups when we discuss campus life in Chapter 16. This chapter focuses on two of the groups that are most vulnerable to depression, LGBTQ and overweight teenagers.

At first glance, it may seem that LGBTQ teens and overweight teens have little in common. To better understand the commonalities, we need to look at what's known as the Meyer minority stress model, which suggests that stigma, discrimination, harassment, and prejudice, alongside low levels of social support, all lead to poor health outcomes and, specifically, increased psychological distress. Classmate and parental support can buffer the effects of stress on teens, but it can be lacking for some teens who are LGBTQ or overweight. Bullying is an additional factor, as these are two of the groups that are most commonly targeted. LGBTQ or overweight teens often suffer in a social situation worse than mere isolation; living in a hostile culture takes a toll on a teen and their emerging sense of self. Depression can develop as a result of the combination of increasing social isolation and fear that often occur from persistent exposure to this hostile culture.

Supporting your teen during adolescence, then, is especially important when she feels rejected by her peers. The processes for helping LGBTQ and overweight teens serve as examples of the general principles for working with your own teen, no matter what her perceived difference. First, of course, is warmth and communication. It is crucial to demonstrate that you accept her and to let her know that you love her and will support her, no matter what. Don't accept your teen's periodic fear that her difference defines her entire identity and limits her. You understand her in a deeper way. You need to let her know that you are aware of her values, strengths, and gifts.

To engage in an open conversation, you may need to learn the vocabulary your teen uses to talk about her difference. This process is more than learning new words; it also includes avoiding hurtful words that are a result of negative stereotypes. Words are powerful; words can hurt or heal; words can isolate or include.

LGBTQ TEENS

Lucas, a first-year college student, came to see me because of some developing sleep problems. Lucas had seen a therapist during high school and knew the advantages of seeing someone before more serious symptoms developed. He was a slight young man, dressed in black jeans and tight-fitting T-shirt. Lucas' large green eyes illuminated his pale face and his hair was dyed very black. Despite his insomnia, Lucas assured me that he felt a lot of freedom in college. His eyes filled with tears of relief when he shared that he no longer had to be afraid of pushes, shoves, comments written on his locker, and taunts from some members of the football and hockey teams in his large, consolidated rural high school. Like many teens, given the heightened awareness of LGBTQ issues, he had come out to his family when he was 14. The average age for coming out varies by country, but the historical trend is clear: The age is dropping. For people in their 30s, the average coming out age was 21. Some American reports have found that the average age to come out in the United States has also declined, moving from 18 to 14. Lucas' mother and his sister were accepting and supportive. However, being out at a younger age can also expose teens to a longer period of harassment. Lucas said that he felt a knot in his stomach every single day for 4 years. Like 80% of gay and lesbian teens, Lucas felt profoundly isolated and at that time was sad and withdrawn and had fleeting thoughts of suicide. At home, his mother was concerned, but because he was also subjected to cyberbullying, he still felt somewhat unsafe. Lucas' response to sexual minority stress and harassment is representative, as LGTBQ teens have twice the rates of depression and suicidal ideation as those of straight teens. Being in an accepting college environment, he said, was the first time he felt "it was safe to be me."

LGBTQ students are at significant risk for depression because of their minority status and subjection to bullying. The research is unequivocal: Being LGBTQ by itself is not a mental health hazard. Instead, the major risks to health and well-being are the results of homophobia and harassment. The alarming statistics about the lives of LGBTQ teens reveal that the vast majority of sexual minority teens are targeted by bullies; over 90% report having property destroyed, being physically threatened, and being taunted by hateful terms like *dyke* or *faggot*.

Here is what the school experience can be: like Lucas, over 55% of LGBTQ teens have overheard adults at school make sexist or homophobic comments, and only 16% report receiving help for homophobic harassment. School becomes the exact opposite of a safe place. Imagine that you dreaded school every day and feared for your safety.

The situation is even worse for bisexual teens. One study found that bisexual men have a 6.3 times higher suicidal rate than that for heterosexual men, and for bisexual women the rate is 5.9 times that of heterosexual women. This may be a result of feeling "in between" and not fully accepted by gay or lesbian or straight people. Lack of social support may be a factor as well, with only 28% of bisexual respondents in one study reporting that the important people in their lives knew about their sexual orientation, compared to 71% of lesbians and 77% of gay men.

Transgender Teens

Gender identity is a deep feeling of being female or male. A *transgender* person is someone whose gender identity, expression, or behavior is different from those typically associated with their assigned sex at birth. A *cisgender* person is one whose gender identity is aligned with the sex they were assigned at birth. There are transgender people from every social, class, religion, race, and educational and ethnic group. Unfortunately, transgender teens are subject to violence and physical abuse as well as harassment. They are challenging the social norm of binary sexuality and thus must develop their gender identity within a primarily unaccepting community. Transgender teens who do not feel safe at school have lower grade point averages and less desire to go to college. Over half of female-to-male transgender teens attempt suicide.

The abuse suffered by many transgender children and teens is exemplified by Suneel (a) Mubayi, a male-to-female transgender teen who contributed to the latest edition of the classic book, *Our Bodies, Ourselves*. Named Suneel by his Hindi parents, he was taunted as a young child and called "Suneela" by bullies with accusations of being weak and effeminate. Suneela reclaimed that name and now writes, "I claim the right to choose my ultimate gender beyond my traits, looks, qualities and features even if it is different from the sexual organs I possess."[1]

Parents of LGBTQ Teens

The parents of LGBTQ teens suffer as well. Lucas asked me to meet with him and his mother, Hannah, when she came to visit because he wanted me to reassure her that he was faring better psychologically in college. When I met with Hannah and Lucas, I could see that she was much more than "concerned," as Lucas had described, She was dominated by her worries and anxiety about Lucas, his sister, and many other issues. Hannah fidgeted a lot as we spoke and was wringing her hands. Her anxiety level was so high that I could feel her tension when we shook hands in the waiting room.

Hannah was a devoted mother who had been divorced from Lucas' father when Lucas was about 4. She was dedicated to her two children. Hannah reminded me of many of the people I grew up with in the Midwest—straightforward and hard-working, in her case, as a reference librarian. However, Hannah spent her life dominated by worry. When I asked her to describe her thoughts, she said that she had been a shy and slightly worried child but coped well in the small town where she grew up and with a lot of supportive family and friends. Later, when she was first married, she felt secure and that she did not have so much to worry about. However when she had children, and certainly after Lucas's father left the family, her worries "took off."

She said that she woke up most mornings worrying. It's "like there's a conveyor belt running in my brain, and the topic of the day or the hour hops right on it." Her challenges with the harassment that Lucas faced only made the situation worse and she found that she couldn't stop worrying.

1. S. Mubayi. I claim the right to choose my ultimate gender, in Boston Women's Health Collective, *Our Bodies, Ourselves*. New York: Simon and Schuster, 2011.

While he was in middle school, Hannah worried about what might be happening to him almost all the time. I also noticed that Hannah was a "shallow, rapid breather" and that she had a strong startle response. She jumped when she heard the sounds of someone gunning a motorcycle on the street outside my office.

Lucas and I were able to reassure Hannah as to his current happiness and acceptance in college. Both Hannah and Lucas' eyes filled with tears when he was able to help his mom worry about one less issue.

I described to her the diagnosis of generalized anxiety disorder. Hannah shared most of the characteristics: She was chronically worried, and sometimes well out of proportion to the issues at hand. The harassment Lucas suffered would be a worry to most parents, but Hannah also worried about less important issues—being on time, her daughter's friends (Lucas said that his sister, Jenny, was happy and had great friends), and innumerable "what ifs." She felt on edge most of the time and suffered with insomnia as well. It's always gratifying when you describe a syndrome to someone and they react with a response like "Yes, that's me exactly!" This realization and *naming* a phenomenon can propel a person to get help. In Hannah's case, I recommended that when she returned home, she could consider CBT for anxiety and perhaps medication with an SSRI.

I felt a kinship with Hannah because, as a mother, I too would hate to see my child harassed. Hannah did not have a partner to share her parenting problems with, which made her even more worried. And given the way Lucas was treated when he was younger, her fears was not catastrophic; they were grounded in reality. Yet Hannah's high levels of anxiety caused Lucas to worry about her, as well as about himself. And so the cycle continued. Hannah described that she came from a long line of anxious women. She had a close-knit family but remembered a few early events that had upset her. Once her mother was late to pick her up from school in first grade. Another time, when she was younger, she lost sight of her father, only for a minute or two, when they were in a large department store. As a parent, Hannah had done the best she could. For example, despite her anxiety, she had gone to many meetings to advocate for Lucas and other LGBTQ teens when he was in middle school. Lucas was relatively resilient, and now, in a more nurturing environment, he was able to come into his own.

Lucas returned to see me the following week, stating that he felt much better because not only was his mother reassured but he now understood her better. This is not to blame Hannah in any way. Then several weeks later, Lucas reported that his mother had started CBT. I was hopeful and relieved for both of them.

Vocabulary

Because the vocabulary associated with LGBTQ issues has gone through such dramatic changes in the past few years, I have provided major definitions in Appendix 3. It is adapted from the guidelines of the American Psychological Association and the Gay, Lesbian & Straight Education Network (GLSEN pronounced "glisten"). If you look at the appendix you'll see that it is an extensive list, but don't be overwhelmed—we all have a lot to learn. One major result of the growing acceptance of LGBTQ people is the elimination of outdated and harmful words. There are also changes in words you may have seen as neutral. The word *homosexual*, for example, is rarely used in the LGBTQ community; people are specifically lesbian, gay, bisexual, asexual, transgender, or pansexual, whereas heterosexuals are referred to as "straight." In any case, as always, the most critical issue is to listen nonjudgmentally. You will learn much more than new words from your teen.

Family Communication and Support

The statistics about the stresses on LGBTQ teens and the resulting psychological problems are troubling, but parental acceptance and support can make an enormous difference. Here are some important facts. A review of 42 peer-reviewed articles by scholars at Cornell University concluded:

> We found 25 studies showing that accepting behavior by parents toward their children's sexual orientation or gender identity is linked to the health and well-being of LGBT youth. Another 17 studies found that family support in general (i.e., not necessarily in response to children's sexual orientation or gender identity) is linked to the health and well-being of LGBT youth. The upshot is that families that engage in rejecting behavior raise the risk of significant harms for their LGBT children.[2]

Moreover, in one report, 92% of LGBTQ teems with extremely high family support believed they would become happy adults, and almost 70% of them wanted to become parents themselves. By contrast, only 35% of

2. Cornell University. What does the scholarly research say about the link between family acceptance and LGBT youth well-being? What We Know: The Public Policy Research Portal. Retrieved from https://whatweknow.inequality.cornell.edu/topics/lgbt-equality/what-does-the-scholarly-research-say-about-the-acceptancerejection-of-lgbt-youth-2/

LGBTQ youth without parental support believed that they would become happy adults, and only 10% of them wanted to become parents. With respect to transgender teens, those who have greater amounts of family support have higher levels of self-esteem and a more positive view of the future.

If we take a deeper dive into the statistics, we can see how much families matter. The Family Acceptance Project at San Francisco State University reports that "LGBTQ young adults who reported higher levels of family rejection during adolescence were over 8 times more likely to report having attempted suicide, 6 times more likely to report high levels of depression, over 3 times more likely to use illegal drugs, and over 3 times more likely to report having engaged in unprotected sexual intercourse" when compared to peers from families that reported no or low levels of family rejection.[3] Not surprisingly, these peers also have greater life satisfaction and well-being and are at lower risk for developing medical problems as young adults. These enormous differences demonstrate the impact families have on the lives of their children.

Let's say your child wants to come out to you. Remember that coming out is not a one-time event but a process, so you will have many opportunities to talk if you are open to the dialogue. Of course, you want to create an environment of acceptance in general. You may at first be uncomfortable talking about any dimension of sexuality with your teen. You can motivate yourself by knowing that close support from family and friends is a major barrier to depression. Your teen needs to know that you love them and that any additional information about them will not change your unconditional acceptance.

Just as you want to understand vocabulary, it's also an excellent idea to be aware of your attitudes. It would be difficult to have grown up in this society and not have absorbed some anti-LGBTQ attitudes. Think back to when your teen was younger: When discussing sexuality, were you inclusive? Did you acknowledge that some people were attracted to the same sex? Have you ever made remarks that reinforce regressive gender norms, like "He throws like a girl," "Man up," or "She just needs to meet the right man?" If so, you should be aware that if your child is gay or lesbian or trans, it will be more difficult for them to come out to you. Even if you have some internalized homophobia, you can reassure your teen by saying, "I know that I have a lot to learn and I hope you can share with me." You can

---

3. Caitlin Ryan. *Supportive Families, Healthy Children: Helping Families with Lesbian, Gay, Bisexual & Transgender Children*. San Francisco: San Francisco State University, 2009.

reinforce this attitude by being sure to welcome your teen's LGBTQ friends into your home.

If a teen believes that she is transgender, you can accept her feelings as legitimate, explore them over time, help her find her way, and get specialized, gender-affirming psychological and medical care. An example of the enormous discrimination faced by transgender people is concert pianist Sara Davis Buechner, who started her career as David Buechner. In her 30s, despite her obvious talent and many accomplishments, after she had transitioned to Sara, Buechner found that she could not get work. She writes,

> Conductors who once routinely engaged me stopped returning calls, prestigious teaching offers were withdrawn, and concert opportunities vanished. Changing managers did not help. I recall one particularly low point as the time I received a check from a Florida recital presenter several weeks before my appearance—having booked David Buechner, they paid Sara not to come.[4]

Finally, after being invited to teach in Canada, Sara reemerged and concert audiences are once again able to hear her brilliant performances.

If you are having difficulty accepting your teen, PFLAG (Parents, Families and Friends of Lesbians & Gays) can be enormously helpful. PFLAG is a national organization with local chapters that can provide you with education and support and referrals to LGBTQ community resources. You will be able to learn from the experience of other parents, which can be a powerful, positive experience. After Hannah had engaged in CBT for a while, she attended her first PFLAG meeting and found it to be enormously helpful. In other cases, I have been impressed by how some parents grow into supportive advocates, when previously they were not at all accepting of their teen's sexual orientation or gender identity.

Friends and Role Models

If your teen is unhappy at school, suggest activities outside of school that are welcoming. There are chapters of Youth Pride in many areas. Your teen probably has a variety of interests that can help them meet others with similar interests. Remember the power of the example. If there are other LGBTQ members of your family or extended family, remind your teen that

---

4. Buechner, S. D. (2018). Transgender issues. Retrieved from http://saradavisbuechner.com/transgender-issues/

he can talk with them. In many communities, there at least some adults who are out and successful who can serve as mentors. Many schools have teachers who are LGBTQ or allies.

Television has played a role in changing attitudes toward LQBTQ people, from *Will and Grace, Buffy the Vampire Slayer, Glee*, and, more recently, *I am Jazz, Transparent, RuPaul's Drag Race, Modern Family*, and, of course, *Ellen*. The show *13 Reasons Why*, which I find troubling in many ways, nonetheless features several grounded and supportive gay characters. These media examples also reflect good news about our wider society: Millennials and younger generations are much more accepting of LGBTQ people than previous generations. However, it is still not easy for LGBGTQ teens. So if you live in a community without local resources, many resources are available online, like the Trevor Project and the It Gets Better project. Others are listed in the Resources section.

Advocacy

Advocacy begins at home. If your home is one of acceptance, your nuclear family may not make homophobic remarks. It will be important to stand up to others in your extended family or at social events if you do hear any homophobic comments. On the societal level, bullying and cyberbullying remain major problems for many LGBTQ teens. If your school system has an anti-bullying program, you can consider getting involved or starting one if the school is lacking one.

If your family is religious, you may need to speak to clergy to make sure that your teen has an accepting spiritual community. If the clergy in your family's local religious place of worship are not accepting of your teen's sexuality or gender identity, you may want to advocate for acceptance and point out the rejecting message that is being given. You may decide to reach out to other clergy to find more support for your teen. The Resources section at the end of the book includes a list of welcoming religious communities.

OVERWEIGHT TEENS

Rates of being overweight in the United States have risen dramatically, and worldwide, they have tripled since 1975. Technically, being overweight may not be a demographic minority for long, with estimates that 39.8% of Americans could be categorized as obese. However, weight bias and discrimination have increased by 66% in the past decade; it is socially acceptable in the United States and UK and is rarely challenged. Teens who are overweight are exposed to many forms of weight bias and discrimination, including teasing, ridicule by peers, social exclusion, and bias or different expectations from adults. In addition, the more recent health focus on childhood obesity is complicated and may have increased bias and discrimination, as the medical concerns are seen as justification for blaming and shaming individuals who suffer with excess weight. This occurs in part because most people are unaware of the genetic, environmental, and sociological factors that contribute to being overweight.

Vocabulary

Lance Armstrong, the now-disgraced cyclist and former winner of many Tour de France races, was interviewed on the Oprah Winfrey show in 2013. When confronted with his mistreatment of a teammate's wife, he admitted to her, "I called you crazy. I called you a bitch. But I never called you fat." Let that sink in for a bit. It was, apparently, worse to call someone "fat" than "crazy" or "bitch." Sadly, Armstrong is not alone. In our appearance-focused, Instagram-driven culture, even looking fat in one photo can lead to being shamed. Another word with negative connotations is *obese*. Technically, in medical terms, *obese* means having a body mass index (BMI) of 30 or being more than 20% over ideal weight, but the word is not used that way socially and is usually spoken with a tone of disgust. This is one reason I prefer the neutral word *overweight*.

The words *weight stigma* or *bias* refer negative attitudes expressed toward individuals who are overweight. *Discrimination* refers to unequal, unfair treatment. For example, an applicant for a job who is equally or more qualified may be rejected because of weight discrimination. A study of over 2,200 adults conducted by the Rudd Center for Food Policy at the University of Connecticut revealed that weight discrimination was more prevalent than discrimination based on physical disability, ethnicity, or sexual orientation. Notably, women experienced discrimination at lower weights.

Because you can't hide being overweight, overweight teens are easy targets for bullies and others making negative comments. Prejudice can be contagious. In one study, if individuals overheard a person express discriminatory attitudes, they accepted it and remembered it even a month later. "Fat shaming" is common everywhere—in school, on playgrounds, on television, in the movies, and in public. There are few overweight people, especially women, on TV or in the movies, and they are usually seen as humorous sidekicks who take more than their share of "kidding." Samantha Bee revealed that in broadcast news, the B roll (supplemental footage used with the main story) about overweight people is called "B-roll for fat people: Headless guts and butts." It was impossible for her producers to find footage of overweight people in everyday life.

Although girls are treated more harshly, it is not easy for overweight boys, either, especially if they are not athletic. Then they have two strikes against them, according to the demands of traditional masculinity. Almost all teenage boys must endure a culture based on nicknames and taunting, with the more socially powerful boys choosing the nicknames. So, an overweight boy could be "Big Guy" if he is lucky, but if not, he may constantly hear himself addressed as "Lardo," "Fat Ass," or worse. I have never understood why many teachers do not address this type of humiliation. Yes, teasing is a bit of male teen culture, but if it is often cruel and stigmatizing, it is unacceptable.

In a monologue that quickly went viral, James Corden, the multitalented late-night television host, responded to comedian Bill Maher's vitriolic attack on overweight people that included the idea that we needed more, not less fat shaming. Corden's video was alternately humorous, evidence based, and poignant. He stated, "Let's be honest. Fat shaming is just bullying. . . . The issue is not a lack of shame. If making fun of fat people made them lose weight, there'd be no fat kids in school and I'd have a six pack by now." NBC's Al Roker quickly followed suit on the *Today* show, pointing out that fat shaming scars people and that Bill Maher "doesn't know what he's talking about." I was delighted to see these men, who have important platforms, speak up. It's extremely unusual for men to comment on this issue and a very positive step forward.

In a study that appeared in the *British Medical Journal*, the views of over 1,700 overweight young people ages 12–18 were listed. This partial list of their thoughts reveals how weight bias becomes internalized. "It's on my conscience all the time." "It's down to me." "It's like a girl thing?" "If you're fat, then they don't like you." "If I had the choice, I wouldn't be this size." "I don't want to stick out." "Day after day, you're terrified." Also, so true: "Easier said than done."

You might believe, as I do, that a good coping strategy for overweight teens is to increase physical activity and decrease screen time, but here's the problem: Another body of research has revealed that when teens experience weight bias, they experience not an increase but a decrease in their motivation to exercise, an increase in calorie consumption and patterns of disordered eating, a drop in their perception of their overall health, and higher levels of cortisol. Thus, the results of weight stigma make a teen less likely to take the single best course of action. We can look to programs like the non-stigmatizing approach at Spellman College, a historically black women's college, which launched a blame-free wellness program that focuses on overall health and increasing physical activity, not weight loss, and uses the motto "Eat better, move more, sleep well."

Communication and Support

It is true that being overweight, in the long term, can create additional health risks in some people and leads to discrimination. Fortunately, there is an approach called Health at Every Size (HAES), a weight-inclusive philosophy that respects people of every size and focuses on healthy eating and physical activity. The goal is fitness, not weight loss. HAES points out that weight alone is not a good measure of health; fitness is.

It is clear that, in general, blame and criticism don't change behavior; support and acceptance do. Therefore, it is much more important to understand the effect of fat bias and stigma on teens than to try to push for weight loss.

What if Your Teen Is Both LGBTQ and Overweight?

Only recently has a study examined weight-based victimization in LGBTQ teens, but one from the Rudd Center found that in a group of almost 10,000 LGBTQ teens, 44 to 70% of them reported weight-based teasing from family members, 42 to 57% reported weight-based teasing from peers, and about one-third of adolescents reported these experiences from both family and peers. This suggests that having two minority conditions could lead to additional stress.

When Helping Can Hurt

Communication about weight, especially between mother and daughter, can be a minefield. Let's start with what not to do. Some well-meaning comments you want to avoid are as follows: "Why do you wear such baggy clothes?" "Do you really want to eat that?" "You have such a pretty face . . ." Most overweight teenage girls will take offense because they have heard similar comments so often. Also, teens are just plain tired of hearing talk about weight loss.

A study in the journal *Pediatrics* revealed how well-meaning parents can make matters worse for their overweight teens. Teens who were overweight and whose parents suggested dieting fared worse as adults than those whose parents did not. A long-term research project followed teens into adulthood and indicated that those whose parents encouraged dieting were not only more likely to be overweight and engage in unhealthy weight control behaviors like food restriction and binge eating, they were also less satisfied with their bodies 15 years later. Results also showed that parents' emphasis on dieting was being passed down to the next generation.

It is clear, then, that a lot of good can come from changing family communication patterns. Research has repeatedly revealed that how family and friends talk about appearance and body size during childhood and adolescence can have long-term negative effects in adulthood. Research has also found that girls whose fathers teased them about their weight and shape are more likely to develop discomfort with and shame about their bodies; the same is true if fathers objectify their daughters' bodies and critique them. What's more, dads who are preoccupied with their own weight and who are critical of their own bodies often pass the negative torch to their daughters. Whether mother or father, hearing a parent disparage their own body can create a negative legacy, causing a teen to cast a similarly fault-finding eye on her own physique and internalize those negative comments and apply them to her body.

The first step, then, in improving communication about weight is to eliminate any fat-shaming vocabulary and teasing from the family. This also includes "helpful" comments and suggestions from grandparents and aunts and uncles; you will need to advocate for your teen and perhaps explain that such comments are counterproductive. When your child brings up her weight, and most girls will, express concern for her feelings. You can tell your daughter that you are pleased she shared her concern with you and ask facilitating questions. Listen. You can ask about harassment at school or elsewhere. I once saw a young woman who was the brunt of nasty remarks about her weight from teenage boys yelling at her as they drove by while she was running. This is an outrageous example of being harassed while trying to become healthier. In this instance, as a parent, you can add that you are sorry for what happened. You might comment that this is harassment based on body size and an issue of diversity. This won't stop the pain, but it names the behavior as a social injustice. This will let her know that, even theoretically, your teen is not alone.

The same dialogue can occur with boys, but they tend to be less forthcoming. The male culture we discussed earlier doesn't leave a lot of room for sharing sadness and even less for humiliation. With younger boys, you may have more opportunities. As mentioned previously, pay attention in the car if you drive him and friends somewhere. You may overhear telling remarks. At one time, this was a tried and true method; it is less so now due to constant texting, but it is still worth trying. You can follow up later. If you hear someone referred to by a hostile nickname, you can ask if he has one or if he uses mean-spirited nicknames for others. It never hurts to ask, if you are supportive in your tone.

Always ask if you can be helpful before making any suggestions. Your teen may want help paying for or arranging transportation to a gym or physical activity program. Or she may want you to listen uncritically. If you jump right to suggestions, you may cut off dialogue. In my experience, increased physical activity and less screen time is the best plan for the whole family. "Going on a diet" is a bad idea for many reasons, the main one being that it suggests a one-time, temporary change.

Friends and Role Models

Classes and activities outside of school may give your teen access to general social support. Similarly, look for accepting teachers, coaches, clergy, and so on. Friends and role models may be more difficult to discuss with your teen; here's the problem: Given the pressure on overweight teens to lose weight, they may not want to identify with other overweight people, hoping instead that they will change. That's fine. But if you hear them make self-hating remarks, like "Overweight people are lazy" or "It's impossible for a fat person to be successful," you can point out that those are unfair stereotypes and counter with some examples. The best examples are people they know. Some public role models who are overweight are the actor Rebel Wilson, *Saturday Night Live* great Aidy Bryant, and Queen Latifah. Few voices can match Adele's or Aretha's. John Goodman and Charles Barkley are funny. James Corden created the brilliant "carpool karaoke" series and has starred on Broadway. Michael Moore is an activist to be reckoned with. Note that many of these people do try to lose weight, and that's part of the point. Life can be hard; we can struggle but still manage to have a good life. Nonetheless, these role models are talented, with productive and accomplished lives.

Supportive friends, overweight or not, can make all the difference. In the movie *Booksmart*, best friends Molly and Amy are talking about a conversation Molly overheard in the bathroom, when several teens shamed the way she looked. When she's about to repeat the slurs, Amy loudly interrupts her that she won't even hear them. Similarly, Molly encourages Amy to pursue a sexual relationship with another girl in their class. *Booksmart* made me more optimistic because, although an idealized "buddy movie," it reflects the power of friendship and, to a certain extent, the more accepting attitudes of younger generations.

Advocacy

Advocacy begins at home. In addition to the ideas in the previous section, you can start with the anti-bullying issues we described with respect to LGBTQ teens, at school and any community organizations you are involved with. Many school anti-bullying programs fail to include body diversity as a concern, so you can educate the educators about this. You can speak up when you hear prejudicial remarks; this can challenge not only the speaker but also any bystanders. I have found that people are not always embarrassed about fat-shaming comments, but that doesn't make them right. You don't need to proclaim, "That's fat shaming!" in a loud tone of voice but instead note that science is clarifying how complicated it is to lose weight. Or you can note that there is no evidence that overweight people are lazy.

You can teach your child media and advertising literacy; they may benefit from knowing that the goal is to persuade the audience to buy a product, not to communicate facts. One media literacy example is when a friend of mine and I were looking at ads for mascara. My friend commented, "You realize that they are all wearing false eyelashes, don't you?" Of course I did, but only after it was pointed out to me. Similarly, photos in advertising are now universally digitally manipulated, and many advertisements from the billion-dollar weight loss industry are just plain false. You can choose not to buy products from companies that promote only the thin ideal and support companies like Dove for their campaign for Real Beauty. You can get involved in programs that deal with health, not weight alone, like Michelle Obama's Let's Move. The Rudd Center has an excellent comprehensive website with a section called "Action Through Advocacy" and resources on decreasing weight bias (see Resources section).

Here are some examples of the power of family support:

- Adam Shankman, film director, producer, and choreographer, has said his parents were so supportive of his being gay that they outed him to himself.
- Itzhak Perlman recalls that, as a child growing up in Israel, despite his talent, no one believed he could have a career as a professional violinist

because of his polio, but his parents continued to do everything they could to support him.

- Author Frances Kuffel is grateful that her parents were supportive of her when she was an overweight teen. Her advice to parents: "When the topic does come up, I beg of you, take the attitude that my own parents did: 'When the time is right, you'll take care of this. I know you will. You are a strong person. And I will help if you ask'."[5]

The same principles of support outlined in this chapter can be used to buffer the effects of discrimination on other groups. For example, there are ethnic differences in social anxiety disorder. Some studies suggest that Asian American and Latinx students have a higher rates of social anxiety disorder than European American students. This may be the result of discrimination from peers. The social stress of giving presentations, speaking up in class, group assignments, and even going to a teacher for help can interfere with school performance.

Asian Americans also are least likely to receive mental health services, compared to all ethnic groups in the United States, whether in an educational, psychological, or general medical setting. The increased stigma of having a psychological problem and the relative lack of Asian American psychotherapists may account for this underutilization. Aleta Bok Johnson, a former psychotherapist at Brown University and in independent practice for 25 years, argues that it is important that college mental health professionals validate students' experiences of racism, acknowledge the strength of racial/ethnic identity, view activism as valuable, and avoid devaluing or stereotyping cultural differences with Asian American students.

The same principles hold true for psychotherapists working with Latinx and African American and other minority students. In a review of articles on racial differences, of the 461 associations examined, depression and anxiety were significantly associated with racial discrimination in 76% of outcomes examined. Less often studied are Arab Americans and Muslims, who now face enormous discrimination and harassment in the United States. As with any mental health problem, a clinician needs to take the cultural context into account, with every person, without stereotyping whole groups.

5. Frances Kuffel. Don't talk to your overweight teen—act! The shame and pain of being an overweight teen. *Psychology Today*, June 30, 2013.

These steps should provide support for your child who is perceived as different and help you let her know that you will be there for her and advocate for fairness. Getting back to the issue of depression, remember, it's important to be proactive. This means monitoring symptoms as discussed in Chapter 3. You can also be direct and ask about the symptoms and your teen's overall mood whenever discussing with her the issue of being different. Be sure to notice if your teen becomes sad and withdrawn or irritable. Notice if she is pulling back from friends or is socially isolated and fearful about going to school or other activities, as severe social anxiety can be devastating. Try to engage her and listen carefully to any talk about her emotions or loneliness. Pay attention to appetite and sleep changes. Sleep is especially important for overweight teens, as there is an association, not completely understood, between being overweight and not getting enough sleep. You can make the difference, with unconditional support for your teen and prompt attention to symptoms of depression and anxiety.

The NPR commentator and host of the podcast *Pop Culture Happy Hour*, Linda Holmes, was informed by physicians that she had no psychiatric disorder all throughout her teens and early 20s. She was targeted for ridicule as an overweight middle-schooler. Once she went to a psychiatrist for psychological help, but was told to go on a diet. However, as it turns out, Holmes was suffering from undiagnosed persistent depressive disorder. Fortunately, she had a supportive family and early on, learned and valued that she loved writing, which ultimately became her career. Holmes' diagnosis wasn't made until she was in her 30s. We don't want that to happen again, to any teen, especially when the treatment of depression is so effective.

It is possible that you, the parent, are also LGBTQ or overweight. This can affect communication in many ways. Your child may hesitate to bring up the issue for fear of hurting you and protecting you from the transfer of hate she has received. A younger teen may be harassed about her gay or lesbian parents even if she is straight. You can be direct about this, though, and ask if that has happened. Another approach is to ask, "Would it help if I told you how I handled the situation?" In this specific situation you need to be on solid ground as a role model, rather than only sharing sadness.

When in doubt, listen. Your teen needs to know that she can share any concerns with you. If she has come out to you, you can ask, "I know that sometimes lesbians (or gay men or overweight teens) are harassed or bullied at school. Has that happened to you?" Many teens are hesitant or embarrassed, so if she says no, you can follow up with "Ok, but I do want to know if that happens. I will not do anything about it without your permission, but please tell me so we can talk about it."

CHAPTER 14

No Shame, No Stigma

When and How to Get Psychological Help

We all need help from time to time. You may notice that your teen has symptoms of depression and anxiety and that the strategies in this book have not helped enough or the situation may be getting worse. When you notice that, it's time to have a supportive and direct conversation about psychological treatment. Teens, especially girls, will often agree—this generation is much more open to therapy than previous ones. In fact, some teens are the first ones to ask their parents for help. Others are more reluctant. Your first task is to be supportive and make sure that your son does not feel like a failure just because he could benefit from therapy. You might need to reassure him that they he is not inadequate, "crazy," or "a loser."

If he requests help at college, there are many options. Here is a process for obtaining help when your teen is still living at home or when he is at college but needs or wants to go off campus for treatment.

Once your child has requested help, the next step is to consult with your pediatrician or adolescent primary care professional (PCP). I have taught residents in primary care medicine for over 30 years and know that most of them are becoming increasingly more sensitive and knowledgeable about psychological conditions like depression or anxiety than in the past. In fact, PCPs provide more psychological care than mental health professionals (MHPs). Your PCP will usually be able to refer you and your teen to an MHP. Another important reason to consult with a PCP first is that certain medical illnesses or medications can cause symptoms of depression and should be ruled out before a psychiatric condition in diagnosed. Such medications include some birth control pills and isotretinoin (sold as Accutane, a medication to treat acne); the medical illnesses include thyroid disorders and type 1 diabetes. Any medication or beverage that contains caffeine can cause increased anxiety, as can some medications used to treat attention deficit–hyperactivity disorder (ADHD); the bronchodilators, including inhalers, used to manage asthma; thyroid medication; and some medications used to control seizures. You can see why your PCP is the best person to sort this out and perhaps adjust the dosages. For more complicated medication issues, I recommend a referral to a psychiatrist.

If, for some reason, your teen doesn't have access to a PCP, teachers, guidance counselors, school psychologists, friends, and members of the clergy can be excellent resources for referrals.

Here are some guidelines for selecting an MHP:

- The individual should be licensed by your state's health department. This information is usually available on the health department website. There are licensing laws for physicians, psychologists, nurses and nurse practitioners, social workers, and, in some states, mental health counselors. Each discipline has requirements for education, supervised practice, continuing education, and ethics, and the licensed individual has to have met these requirements.
- Make sure that the MHP has ample experience and expertise with adolescents. Many MHPs have had specific fellowship training or extra credentialing. If not, your PCP should be able to advise you about the person's expertise in a specific area, and it's perfectly acceptable to ask the MHP questions about their experience.
- As we've discussed, the most validated, evidence-based treatments for depression are cognitive behavior therapy (CBT) and interpersonal therapy (IPT). They are effective, active forms of therapy and are often short term.
- Some qualities of a good therapist are warmth, being nonjudgmental, and being interactive. A therapist needs to be qualified, but you also want your teen to experience a connection with them and feel understood.
- If your teen has gone to one therapist and it was not a good match, try again. You can ask your teen to be specific as to what was lacking from the appointment in order to get suggestions for a different person.
- You also want someone who understands that depression and anxiety are family issues. Typically, with your teen's permission, an MHP will want to see you and your spouse or partner in order to get a full developmental and family history. They should, with your teen's permission, check in with you and then get your perspective.

- At the same time, your teen needs to have confidentially with the MHP and know that the MHP will not share information with you or anyone else without your teen's permission. Trust is the foundation of the therapeutic relationship, and if your teen does not trust the therapist, it is unlikely he will talk honestly about his feelings and behavior. However, it is also true that there are limits to confidentiality. If a teen is a danger to himself or others, the MHP must let you know. So, you do not need to worry that you would not know about a dangerous situation.
- It is also possible that, after an initial assessment, the MHP will recommend group therapy or family therapy for additional treatment. These types of therapy are not evidence-based treatment for depression but can be very helpful. Group therapy can be extremely powerful because it can feel validating to have the acceptance of peers, and teens are also more likely to accept problem-solving ideas from them. Family therapy has several advantages. The effects of teenagers' psychological problems create a two-way street. Your teen's depression has an effect on the family, and family stress or relationship problems can precipitate or worsen depression and anxiety. The entire family can benefit from having a safe forum for self-expression. Finally, family therapy can communicate the foundation of parental and sibling support.
- Most insurance plans cover psychological and psychiatric treatment; this is mandated by law. Some insurance companies have care coordinators who can help you with the referral process. Find out the complete details about coverage, co-pays, and reimbursement so you can make an informed decision.

ANTIDEPRESSANT MEDICATION

Your teen's MHP or PCP may suggest a trial of antidepressant medication. Many parents have a negative reaction to this suggestion, in part due to news stories about the dangers of antidepressants. For that reason, we can examine the guidelines from the American Academy of Child and Adolescent Psychiatry (AACAP). First, antidepressants are appropriate if your teen is diagnosed with a major depressive episode or a very persistent chronic depression. (They are also recommended for the treatment of obsessive-compulsive disorder, but that is not the focus of this book.) The AACAP recommends that more severe depressive episodes will generally require treatment with antidepressants.

Several of the SSRI (serotonin selective uptake inhibitor) medications are approved by the FDA for the treatment of adolescent depression. The most common side effects are gastrointestinal issues. Other side effects are sleep changes including insomnia and vivid dreams, restlessness, headaches, changes in appetite, and sexual dysfunction. With teens, antidepressants may also cause impulsivity, irritability, and agitation. I know, quite a list! However, not every person will have troublesome side effects and most of them tend to wane over time, usually within a few weeks. One problem with antidepressants is that these side effects, including increased feelings of anxiety, occur almost right away, but the actual antidepressant effect can take up to 8 weeks to manifest itself, so it definitely requires being patient and understanding this process.

For all of these reasons, especially with teens, antidepressants need to be started slowly and monitored carefully by the teen, the parents, and the physician. This should be part of an ongoing conversation, and the physician should answer all your questions and let you know what the plans are for coverage and for phone calls regarding your concerns and the types of situations that would necessitate immediate contact.

Another reason to monitor the situation closely is the slightly increased risk of suicidal thoughts with SSRIs. In 2004, the FDA required a "black box warning" on all SSRIs indicating that they can cause suicidal thinking and behavior in people younger than 25. This notice decreased the number of antidepressant prescriptions, especially by PCPs, and some have suggested that the warning had the unintended consequence of increasing suicides in teens, because some teens who could benefit from the treatment with an SSRI were not receiving it. The American Academy of Pediatrics recommends that if your child is prescribed an antidepressant, be on the alert for the following:

New or more frequent thoughts of wanting to die, self-destructive behavior, signs of increased anxiety/panic, agitation, aggressiveness, impulsivity, insomnia, or irritability, new or more involuntary restlessness (akathisia), such as pacing or fidgeting.
There is an association with treatment with the SSRIs and venlafaxine with a new onset of mania, although it's not clear whether the medications cause an excited state or if they trigger an underlying bipolar disorder. So if you notice an extreme degree of elation or energy, fast, driven speech, and new onset of unrealistic plans or goals, be sure to contact the prescribing clinician.[1]

1. Benjamin Shain. Suicide and suicide attempts in adolescents. *Pediatrics, 138*(1), p. E8 2016.

In some communities, psychotherapy is not readily available, and in some situations, your teen may refuse psychotherapy but be open to taking medication. If so, you need to weigh your concerns about any side effects with the need for your child to receive help. I believe that it is generally wise to consider medication for severely depressed teens who have not responded to CBT or IPT-A, provided that someone is closely monitoring the medication's effects. For a teen who is not severely depressed and has never had treatment before, I recommend starting with a trial of CBT or IPT-A. These take 8–12 weeks to show benefit and have essentially no negative side effects. They also provide long-lasting changes. One study of teens who refused medication found that CBT significantly reduced symptoms in teens ages 12–18.

I've mentioned that many teens will accept help, but what if your child refuses? In one study by the Jed Foundation, even though 49% of students said they would suggest psychotherapy to a friend, only 22% said they would go themselves. Twice as many female students as males responded that they would be willing to accept psychological help, so it is often a young man who refuses. If he's not in imminent danger, then first listen to why he doesn't want to engage in therapy. You can then try using problem-solving and motivational interviewing techniques to elicit more information. Here's an example:

YOU: Martin, I've been thinking that it would be good for us to find a psychologist for you to talk to.

MARTIN: I don't want to do that; everyone will think I'm a loser! Besides I can handle this myself.

YOU: Ok if I tell you a little bit more about therapy?

MARTIN: Eh.

YOU: Did you know that one out of every five teenagers has some psychological problem? Also, therapy is private. Nobody needs to know about it unless you want them to.

MARTIN: I didn't know that, but still it makes me uncomfortable.

YOU: I wonder if any of your friends have been in therapy?

MARTIN. I'm not sure. Oh yeah, Maybe Sarah, when her parents went through the divorce.

YOU: Do you think you could think about it?

MARTIN: Maybe.

YOU: Can we talk about it again?

MARTIN, Well, OK.

YOU: Or you can think about going to see someone just once.

MARTIN. Hmm.

YOU: Ok, think about it and let me know if there's anything I or anybody else can do to help.

If you or if anyone else in the family has had therapy and you have their permission, you can share those experiences as well. This can be the start of an ongoing conversation. Just like anything else, attitude change may take time. Of course, if the situation becomes a crisis, the next section gives you additional suggestions.

Kai's family contacted me so that she could see me in outpatient therapy for sadness and worry. Kai, age 16, felt pessimistic and was beginning to withdraw from her friends. But Kai wasn't suffering from other symptoms of a major depression, such as changes in sleep, appetite, or concentration. I told Kai's parents I'd be happy to see her but that it would be better if Kai contacted me.

Kai's father said, "OK, but you'll need to hit a homerun." I would go on to learn that this was an athletic family. Kai had agreed to an initial first session only. Her parents thought that that she might be depressed because she was lesbian, even though she had been out for 2 years and her parents were supportive. We agreed to meet and Kai started by saying that therapy was kind of a weird situation. "You walk in, you meet a stranger, and you're supposed to spill all of your secrets." I agreed with Kai that we were in a what could feel like a strange situation and encouraged her by asking questions and letting her know that she didn't need to answer everything that day.

We began with her parents' concerns so that she could feel free to complain about the fact that they had pushed her to come see me. I acknowledged that fact and suggested that we just see how it went, without any long-term commitment. With the pressure taken off, Kai was be able to relax a little and slowly started telling me about her worries and growing isolation, her feeling distracted during classes, and her concern that she might get cut from her much beloved high school basketball team. She often came to her appointments after practice, wearing her basketball uniform covered by a Nike jacket and pants. I grew up in Michigan and attended a high school where sports were king and so gained some credibility by being an educated audience for some of Kai's basketball stories.

That was enough for Kai to begin to talk more and to continue a deeper conversation after several sessions. Being a lesbian wasn't worrying her. Kai was worried because her parents had been arguing quite a bit about her younger brother Bruce, who was autistic. She was afraid they might get a divorce, and then what? She was also concerned about Bruce's long-term prognosis and her ability to take care of him some day. We were able to clarify her concerns and then invited her parents to join us for a few sessions. Her parents explained that their arguments were not serious, but the situation *was* stressful as they were trying to come to an agreement about Bruce's education. The family had never discussed what would happen in the long run and Kai was relieved to know that her parents were saving money and had engaged a lawyer to help in case Bruce needed long-term care. Her parents were touched that Kai had such deep concerns about Bruce.

Kai's story raises a few issues. First, as parents we may well be wrong when we try to guess what's troubling our teenager. In addition, this was a basically healthy family under the stress of providing for a child with special needs, and Kai was the one to express the need for help. Parental conflict tends to be frightening, even to teens. With some help in sharing all of their concerns directly, the family established better communication and agreed to talk more in the future.

SUICIDE

Suicide is perhaps the most frightening issue for parents. It is heartbreaking and terrifying to learn of the suicide of a young person. It is true that suicide is the second leading cause of death in the age group 15–19. It is also true that most suicidal people are depressed. But that does not mean that most depressed or anxious people will attempt or commit suicide. Depression and anxiety are common; suicide is rare.

Here are some facts:

- Girls make more attempts than boys.
- Boys succeed more often, because they use more immediately lethal methods, like guns or hanging.
- Factors that increase the likelihood of suicidal behavior include previous attempts, exposure to violence, substance abuse, victimization by bullying, and a history of physical or sexual abuse.
- LGBQ teens are at greater risk, especially trans teens, for suicide, most likely due to victimization, substance abuse, lack of social support, and family conflict.
- Suicide rates are highest for American Indian and Alaskan Native women ages 15–24, a much neglected group.
- The rate of suicide attempts by African American teens rose by 73% since 1991.

A wrongful death lawsuit against Harvard University by the family of undergraduate student Luke Z. Tang has cast light on the complicated issue of suicide among Asian American young people. There is some evidence that Asian American students have higher rates of suicidal thinking compared to white students. Asian American young people do not have a higher suicide rate than the other groups, but the number gradually went up between 2011 and 2015, according to the Centers for Disease Control and Prevention, and in 2015, suicide was the leading cause of death among Asian American young people ages 20–24. One-third of Asian American deaths were a result of suicide, with the corresponding rate for whites being 19%; Latino males, 15.3%; Latina females, 16.2%; and blacks, 8.1%. However, it is also important to remember that the term *Asian American* is used to describe a group of many diverse nationalities, so more research is needed.

We've discussed the need to get care for depressed teens; concerns about suicide should be shared with a PCP or an MHP right away. The following may precipitate an attempt: hopelessness, despair, agitation, or unusually impaired problem-solving. These should all get your immediate attention. It's always good to ask your teen to contact the therapist or prescribing physician, but if she refuses, you should do it to ensure her safety.

How to Talk about It

Sometimes parents are afraid to bring up the topic of suicide because it will "put this idea in his head." This is a myth. If a teen has not been thinking about suicide, your bringing it up will not change that, and if he has, he will probably be relieved that you asked. You can find a way to bring it up. As we have discussed before, you always want to listen, first by asking an open-ended question about mood. You can try, "You've seemed really down lately. How are things going?" Then, if suicidal thoughts have not come up in the responses, you can add, "Sometimes when people are depressed, they feel like life isn't worth it. Do you ever feel that way?" Or ask directly: "Are you having thoughts of hurting yourself?" "Do you have a plan?" You should always ask how you can help and ask if he would like anyone else to help. Explore whether anything specific happened to make him feel so bereft. Many suicidal teens are victims of bullying or abuse but suffer alone. Often, it's a relief for your teen that you bring up this topic for discussion so he doesn't feel so alone with his thoughts. If your teen expresses significant suicidal thoughts, even if you make an appointment with a therapist or physician, monitor the situation to keep him safe until the appointment.

There is a difference between self-harm and suicidal behavior. Self-harm is sometimes a suicidal act, but non-suicidal self-injury, often cutting and burning with cigarettes, can be viewed as a coping strategy, although a dangerous one. Teens injure themselves because they want to avoid painful emotions, and self-injury can create a sense of control over these unwanted feelings. A study of teenage girls who self-injured found a correlation between emotion dysregulation and family and peer conflict. It follows that one intervention is teaching young women better coping skills, as outlined in dialectical behavior therapy (DBT). An additional serious issue is that some self-injurious behavior can inadvertently be lethal. Like depression, self-harm behaviors in teens have also increased.

Many depressed people have some thoughts of suicide––up to 20% of college seniors have had such thoughts at some point during the year––but when you hear that plans are developed, a place has been identified, and the means are available, it is time to instill hope and reassurance and get help immediately. If you must have firearms in the home, they need to be locked at all times.

There are several options to help you and your teen with a psychiatric emergency. With an acute threat you should take your teen to the emergency department at a local hospital. The physicians there are very experienced in handling psychiatric emergencies. If the situation is not imminently dangerous you can text START to 2741741 or call 800-273-TALK (8255). The Trevor Project also helps the LGBTI community. You can call 866-488-7306 or text TREVOR to 212-304-1200. They will listen in an empathic and nonjudgmental way and help you access the best resources. If you are concerned about your college student who is not nearby, please refer Chapter 17, on getting help at college.

WHAT NOT TO DO

- Do not allow shame or hesitation get in the way. Conditions like depression and substance abuse, though common in teens, often bring up a fair amount of guilt and shame in parents. This is in part due to feelings of failure, despite a desire to be the best parents possible and the need to protect our children. But it's not about our failings, it's about your child's safety.
- Don't feed into your teen's ambivalence. Starting therapy can be frightening for many teens, especially boys, but they may not be able to articulate their concerns. It's best to take a positive approach throughout as to how therapy can be a life-changing experience (or, to a teen, at least not a complete drag).

- Do not be lured by a fancy website. A person being camera-ready or employing a good Web designer does not make them a good therapist. A website should present the therapist's credentials and experience. Sometimes viewing a short video can show you and your teen a bit about the therapist's style.
- Many therapists are happy to a schedule a short phone call for you or your teen so you can ask general questions and get a sense of what the person is like.
- Don't wait. If your family has made the decision to get help, act promptly, despite the distractions of a busy life. Early intervention is the key to preventing more serious depression.

PART IV

Changing Times

Campus Life, Depression, and Anxiety

CHAPTER 15

College as a Land of Opportunity

Family, Friends, and Faculty

"It takes one parent, one teacher, and one friend" for a child to thrive. I can't remember where I first read this statement about children and psychological health, but it rings true to me with respect to happiness and success in college and in life. Of course, gaining the knowledge and skills to start building foundations for a career and to help navigate the transition to adulthood are some of the major goals for college students. If we can support our students and listen to them, if they can find one inspirational teacher or mentor, and if they experience the joy of friendship, then, in my opinion, college is a success. The college experience provides numerous opportunities for students to find their way, but there can be barriers as well. In this chapter we will explore what we want for our children, college as a land of opportunity. In the next chapter, we will examine the barriers, challenges, and mood triggers that can get in the way.

There are so many good reasons to be excited about your child starting college. College provides students with an opportunity to learn, to develop critical thinking and problem-solving skills, to begin preparation for a career, to be exposed to peers from a wide variety of backgrounds, to meet and get to know faculty, and to explore a range of interests. If the college is not near home, students can also get to know another community. As the author Louise Penny observed, "University was a time of education, and not all of it in a classroom. It was a time to experiment. To grab life. To consume at random, like the first time at a buffet."[1]

IT TAKES ONE PARENT

Although your student is moving away from her dependence on you, she will always be your child. Your involvement can reflect a respect for her growing autonomy as well as your ongoing availability. One decision you will need to make is frequency of contact and what form of communication you will use. In addition to the phone, you can be available by text, email, Facetime and social media. There is no right or wrong answer to the question of how often you should keep in touch. The answer is dependent on your child's needs and your best judgement. I see many students and young people on the street, constantly talking on the phone. Many of them use this travel time as a convenient way to check in with a parent. The contact should be based primarily on your student's needs, although we all like to hear our children's voices now and then. It is reasonable to get a general idea of her schedule. You may be accustomed to quick responses to texts, for example, yet your daughter may have labs that last 3–4 hours or a job that takes most of a day. You will miss her, but she needs to develop independence from you and greater connection to her peers and to campus life.

If you are tempted to stay in touch in order to solve her problems for her, she will not acquire the wisdom and problem-solving skills to do so on her own. There is a danger in having too much information. Before the digital revolution, a student might have called home once or twice a week, so a parent would get an overview of the week. Now, you can hear the news in real time, whether it is a roommate problem, an academic struggle, or even just a cranky mood. You may become preoccupied by any of these, only to find that your daughter quickly moved on. I had one patient whose daughter appreciated talking with her frequently. As I came to know Helen over time, I knew that even though she might come in to a session weighing the pros and cons of the potential solutions for her daughter's dilemma, it was likely that her daughter had already solved her own problem. It was the "info dump" and the listening that Helen's daughter needed, not the problem-solving.

If you are very interested in your student's activities, you might be tempted to follow her on social media, but I don't think that is a good idea.

1. Louis Penny. *Glass Houses*. New York: Minotaur, 2017, p. 166.

Again, she needs space and you are not her primary (or even secondary!) audience. If you want general information, you can subscribe to the student newspaper or check the college website, where there is usually a "News" section.

This is a change in your role as a parent, and like all change, it can take some time to get used to. Of course, during times of stress, like exams, an academic failure, or a breakup, you may be needed more often. Most of the time, though, availability rather than proximity and periodic nonjudgmental listening and support will be your main responsibilities now.

IT TAKES ONE TEACHER OR MENTOR

Students successful in knowing even one faculty member closely are likely to feel more satisfied with their college life and aspire to go further in their careers.[2] A close relationship with a faculty member is one of the joys of college. To me, there's really nothing more important. Research backs this up. If your student can find a faculty or other mentor in college, her educational experience will be enhanced, with better academic self-concept, enhanced motivation, and achievement. Students who experience informal interactions with faculty also tend to feel more a part of the college culture and are more motivated, engaged, and actively involved in their education. Some would say that it is the type of student who seeks a mentor that leads to active learning and success. However, a study that assigned students to mentors found that those with mentors achieved higher GPAs, completed more courses, and had a lower dropout rate compared to those without mentors. These results were independent of gender or ethnicity.

Given all these benefits, the question becomes how a student develops a mentoring relationship. One option is to identify some of her areas of interest. These do not need to be in her ultimate major. These commonalities may provide your student with enough initial confidence to approach a professor. At the same time, sometimes a student is so inspired by an outstanding teacher that she discovers a totally new interest. As an undergraduate, it took me some time to figure out how to choose good courses. This was long before student evaluations were available online. After I had taken

2. Gary Rosenthal, Domangue, T. J., Folse, E. J., Cortez, N. G., Soper, W. B., & Von Bergen, C. W. The One-to-One Survey: Students with Disabilities Versus Students without Disabilities Satisfaction with Professors During One-on-One Contacts. *Journal of Instructional Psychology*, 27(2), 2000, p. 90.

my required courses, I realized that the best thing to do was to seek out faculty who had the best reputation as teachers and go from there.

Encourage her to push through anxiety or shyness. Remember that during the first few months, your teen is still *learning how to become a college student*. I have seen more than a few students who misunderstood the functions of faculty office hours. Some see going to office hours as a sign of weakness or an admission that they couldn't keep up. It is true that office hours can be used as a time for questions, but they can be much more. Office hours can be used to discuss potential research papers, to inquire about other courses, and to get to know the professor and their field in general. Some students fear that they would be burdening the professor. This is also false. Almost all faculty are happy to hear from an interested student. Of course, some students are just plain shy, so they might need some extra help. Some other possible approach strategies include visiting after class, attending other lectures the professor gives, and enrolling in a smaller seminar. Email is a way to break the ice or ask a quick question that can be followed up by a meeting.

Another excellent opportunity on many campuses is to serve as a research assistant or do a summer internship with a professor. In addition to the primary teaching relationship, a faculty member can become a mentor, who can help guide a student in her academic interests, suggest projects, introduce the student to professional associations, and serve as a recommendation for graduate school or a job. In the best of circumstances, a mentor can also be a good role model, as long as they are someone who values education and research and also has a balanced life. This is one reason why students appreciate spending time with faculty, informally or with their families.

Another type of mentor on campus may not be a faculty member but rather a staff member associated with a student activity, a dean, a coach, or a college chaplain. People in all of these roles can be involved and provide supportive relationships that facilitate positive growth and development. Common interests, encouragement, and showing a student new possibilities can come from many people.

Unfortunately, on some college campuses, the demand that faculty produce research has reduced faculty members' ability to concentrate on their teaching. I find this to be especially true at some of the most elite colleges, ironically enough. On some large campuses, teaching assistants (TAs) are primarily responsible for teaching many courses. According to the US Department of Education, over 50% of academic appointments are for adjunct positions, meaning that the faculty hired in such a role may not spend a lot of time on campus and may not hold the position for more than a semester. Another 25% of appointments are not in tenure-track positions. Despite these institutional conditions, TAs and adjunct faculty can become mentors as well and may particularly appreciate serving in that role.

Perfectionism can, in some cases, be a barrier to finding a mentor. When students are too perfectionistic, they may judge people harshly, so it's possible that when extremely high standards are applied to faculty, none of them will live up to expectations. That's when it's time to encourage your student to look a little more deeply and less critically. Another aspect of perfectionism is when a student believes that she needs to know everything about a faculty member's area before approaching her. That is simply not true—in general, faculty expect to be imparting new material to students. After all, teaching is all about sharing new information with people who didn't know it previously.

A close relationship with a faculty member may last a few years or a lifetime and makes an enormous difference at all levels of education. Carl Jung, the Swiss psychiatrist and psychoanalyst, summarized it well when he wrote, "one looks back with appreciation to the brilliant teachers, but with gratitude to those who touched our human feelings. The curriculum is so much necessary raw material, but warmth is the vital element for the growing plant and for the soul of the child."[3]

IT TAKES ONE FRIEND

As we reviewed in Chapter 9, having enough social support will make any transition easier. New students are usually excited and anxious to meet their roommates. Even though there are now social media groups for incoming classes and the ability to text, message, or talk on the phone, meeting in person and living with a roommate is a new experience. Most students hope that their roommate will become a close friend. We will discuss this more in the next chapter, but it is best to be flexible about the roommate relationship. You can suggest to your student that she doesn't need to limit her hopes for close friendship to one person. There will be other people—in the cafeteria, in the dorm, in the library, in sports or activities, in the gym, and in classes. These can all serve as good opportunities for meeting and forging new relationships. These non-roommate relationships may require a little more outreach, but remind her that everyone is in the same boat,

---

3. Edward Hoffman (Ed.), *The Wisdom of Carl Jung*. London: Kensington Publishing Corporation; New York: Citadel Press, 2003, p. 94.

all looking for new relationships and trying to appear to be more confident than they actually feel.

Social media, as we have examined, has advantages and disadvantages for college adjustment. It can provide ongoing connections with friends from home and high school and in that way can reduce homesickness. However, as the semester goes on, there needs to be a balance between old friends and new, leaning toward the new.

Another disadvantage of social media is the ending of the high school romantic relationship, a common occurrence in the first or second semester of the first year. Many students find this to be a heartbreak as well as a reminder that their lives are changing in major ways. This can lead to anxiety, in addition to the sadness of loss. If Instagram is the way a student discovers that her high school boyfriend is seeing someone new (as is increasingly common), it could intensify her sense of betrayal and compound it with the embarrassment of learning this news in such a public way.

There is a certain developmental process over the 4 years of college. The first year is often an expansive time for friends. In fact, after some months, first-year students may be overwhelmed by the number of new relationships. Sophomore year can be a continuation or require social adjustment or, in some cases, starting over if there was a breach or falling out in the first-year relationships. This was true for Nick, from Chapter 6, who quit the wrestling team. Belinda Johnson, former Director of Psychological Services at Brown University clarifies:

> For those first-year students whose main friendships were forged in their dormitories, the sophomore year requires a significant adjustment if those friends scattered across campus. Now having company for dinner or just hanging out requires a degree of planning that wasn't necessary when she could just knock on a neighbor's door at the last minute. Students can be taken by surprise by how isolated they feel at the beginning of the sophomore year, and you may need to provide encouragement to your student to be the one to reach out to old friends as well as new.[4]

Students with social anxiety or depression are less likely to take a realistic look at their new situation and more likely to blame themselves when they don't have a ready-made peer group available.

During junior year, there tends to be a bit of pruning of the social network as students value deeper friendships rather than a large number of

4. Belinda Johnson, Personal communication, May 23, 2019.

them. Senior year brings thoughts of who will remain friends after college or, as Jill Ker Conway, an Australian American scholar and the first woman President of Smith College, wrote, "Some friendships in life sustain themselves only to the particular life stage, products of some mutual developmental problems to be resolved together, or of some external circumstance being housed in the same dormitory. . . . Others grow out of a deeper spiritual and philosophical affinity which continues throughout life."[5]

Alexandros, whom we met in Chapter 5, had some difficulty finding good friends on campus. He had joined a fraternity in order to feel close to a smaller group of students, but it didn't turn out to be a comfortable environment. Alexandros later became involved in Model UN and, through that network made friends across the United States and, later, internationally.

Every student has a distinct set of needs for college, based on her family and cultural background, previous education and interests. If your daughter is a first-generation student, mentors can be more important because the family is new to the college and professional world. She may benefit from extra encouragement from you, relatives, or family friends. Becoming active on campus in an organization is another way to meet people and feel more connected to campus life. If your student has a religious affiliation, on-campus religious organizations are a quick way for her to meet people with shared values. In addition, some colleges now have groups for first-generation students, and these groups often have faculty advisors who can serve as an entree and guide to the college culture. This model may be true for LGBTQ students, Latinx students, students with disabilities, and many others.

What if your teen discovers that her career goals may not fit neatly into any of typical post-undergraduate careers? I know some students who decided that they wanted to be nurses, emergency medical technicians, fine carpenters or chefs. In these situations, they got involved in healthcare or technical or restaurant settings off campus and then ultimately attended training programs after graduation. They didn't regret having gone to a 4-year college because of the many opportunities and general educational experiences, but ultimately, they had different careers in mind.

Volunteering in the larger community can also be enormously beneficial. It may help your student find another mentor or colleague, but it can also remind him that there is a much the larger world beyond the college gates and that he need not focus individual achievement alone. The volunteer experience, along with religious life on campus, can encourage a form of moral development, another key change that takes place during college.

5. Jill Ker Conway. *True North: A Memoir*. New York: Alfred A. Knopf, 1994, p. 145.

For these reasons, many colleges have service-learning courses or centers that combine off-campus projects with an academic perspective

WHAT DOES YOUR STUDENT WANT?

I have based all of this material on research and what I've learned from students and their families. In my experience, the really important consideration is what the student wants. We need to sit down with our students early on to understand their goals. Some of this happens when students select colleges for their application list. If they are fortunate, a college guidance counselor can help. A student committed to STEM probably doesn't want to attend a small college where the focus is visual arts. But more than content, listen to what your teen wants the experience to be—friendship, sports, small seminars, research skills? Before she leaves for college you can ask her what her initial goals are, so she can remember them later, even though they may change over time.

Another meaningful experience is to let her know what you think, not about college but about her as a person. The melancholy goodbye at the dorm may not be the time for the conversation, but going off to college is a major and meaningful life change for you and for your student. You can embrace this and use it as an opportunity for communication. Tell her what you admire and value about her, how proud you are, how you see her strengths, academic and otherwise, and what you hope for her. Marshall P. Duke, at Emory University, suggests that you can do this in a letter, especially if you are overwhelmed by emotion or have difficulty communicating your thoughts.

IT MAY NOT BE A STRAIGHT LINE BUT A CIRCUITOUS PATH

Most involved parents are solution focused and want success for their college students. And many students today hope to start a career or go to graduate school after college. Sometimes though, finding a career they love is not a straight line but rather a meandering path.

Illustration: My Path

I wanted to be a clinical psychologist starting in eighth grade, when we were allowed to go to the gigantic University of Michigan library to research different career paths. For a bookish girl like me, this was very exciting. I chose psychology as a career immediately, ironically because I thought that psychological assessment tools like the Minnesota Multiphasic Psychological Inventory were so cool. Of course, using formal assessment tools has been the one area of psychology that I have not pursued, but the choice has still been an excellent one for me. Every day I learn more about human behavior and resilience, I am engrossed by my patients' stories, and I enjoy helping people identify strategies for change.

However, my path was not direct, because the psychology department in my college was not encouraging about clinical (as opposed to experimental) psychology, and it offered very few courses in my areas of interest. In addition, when I was a first-year student, we were required to take a language and that led to unexpected consequences. I had taken French in high school and so signed up for an intermediate course, yet I quickly discovered that many of the young women in my French class had studied abroad or had had long-term French tutors, whereas I had been taught by a high school teacher who might have visited France a few times at most. I was justifiably concerned about my accent and fluidity of the spoken word. In addition, Monsieur H. was a cynical and, to me, frightening, Parisian.

The class would engage in open-ended conversations and I found it to be so difficult and anxiety provoking that I sometimes had stomach pains before class. Then, one day we were discussing the book *Les Misérables*, and this led to a discussion of injustice. Somehow my language took flight, I expressed my values and feelings about economic opportunity and racial justice. After I finished speaking, Monsieur H. looked at me with just a hint of a smile and said, "La passion, Mademoiselle Landau, la passion." I had briefly overcome my anxiety about speaking, owing to the intensity of my feelings. That might be one lesson from the experience, but for me it was more. My experience in that French class ultimately revealed that my passion would be activism and a concern for social justice, both of which still motivate my clinical work and teaching to this day. By taking courses in sociology, religious studies, education, and American civilization and by participating in community activism, I discovered what was important to me. After college, I worked in a psychology outreach program, then went on to graduate school, and so was ultimately able to integrate my interests.

Others' Paths

Then there is Chef Carla Hall. In the podcast *The Sporkful*, Dan Pashman, an insightful, funny, and curious journalist, interviewed Carla Hall about her career and education. Hall originally wanted to be an actor, so she applied to a conservatory. She was rejected, so she decided to follow her sister to Howard University, where she studied accounting. She later realized that her original college rejection made her settle for a career she ended up hating for a few years. She was under pressure from her mother to have a solid profession, but in her heart, she wanted something else.

Hall later became a model in Europe, fell in love with food, and then went to culinary school, where she focused on French cuisine. She enjoyed being a chef, but said that during that time she rejected her African American roots and the regional traditions of comfort and soul food from her home town of Nashville. Hall revealed that it wasn't until one episode of her TV show *The Chew* that she realized that she needed to assert herself and allow her authentic passions to come out. In their conversation, Pashman and Hall created a metaphor of shopping in a large grocery store. You've gone through the store and realized that you're in the frozen food section, but you forgot something back in the produce department. You're too tired so you remain in the frozen food section when really you should go back. Similarly, in college and afterward, we can become trapped in careers we don't want, just like becoming trapped in that frozen food section. Hall gave up her African American heritage for a while, but came back to it as a chef, television host, competitor on *Top Chef*, and cookbook author.

Can we blame Carla Hall's mother? Of course not. These days especially, we want our children to be able to support themselves in a challenging global economy. If a student is fortunate, she can be educated and then find a career she loves, but I also believe that working for a few years in most jobs can be a meaningful experience. It teaches responsibility, persistence, problem-solving, and self-sufficiency and can help pay off student loans.

Some students know very early on what motivates them. The concept of "True North," based on the direction from the earth's surface to the North Pole, is used to mean your internal compass toward what really matters, your values, and what motivates you. True North can guide a student to a career or a life plan. When I met with Adam Pallant, the Medical Director at Brown University's Health Services, we had a wide-ranging discussion about students' medical and psychological needs. At the end of our conversation, I asked Adam what advice he could give parents about their children and college. I don't know what I was expecting (maybe advice about health), but Adam replied, for students, "Don't let go of your True North." Many students identify their True North before or during college, and as parents we should help them follow it.

CHAPTER 16

College as a Land of Challenges

L et's suppose you have raised your son to communicate well, to tolerate distress, to have self-confidence, and to understand the need for self-regulation. Perhaps you've also addressed vulnerabilities to depression and anxiety. You've talked a bit about his expectations for college life and mental health, and you hope that his time in college will be successful and happy. Finally, the day comes: You drop him off at college and have a tearful, wistful return home. What challenges will he face? What could disrupt his mood? In this chapter, we will look at some common adjustment issues and focus specifically on those that can trigger sad feelings and symptoms of depression and anxiety. Sad feelings are natural, short-term reactions to loss or other stresses, but symptoms of depression are not. We examined many of these issues in Chapter 7; now we will look at how they are manifested in the college experience.

CLOSE QUARTERS

The first challenge will be sharing space with strangers—the roommate issue. The roommate relationship can vary; some roommates become best friends, and some see one another as the most annoying people on campus. You can help your student by emphasizing that he try to be as flexible as possible and as assertive as possible when the situation calls for it. Flexibility matters, because living with anyone requires the ability to compromise and adjust to the other person's schedule and habits. Your son may be used to having his own room, so the lack of private space may be a concern. Or he may have shared a room with a sibling or siblings, and be used to the way they did things. From either background, change and adaptability will be necessary.

It is tempting to hope that the roommate relationship will be easy, and that is often the case, but it is better not to make assumptions. In general, most roommates will be perfectly fine. If the roommate does not become a close friend but is reasonable about sharing the space, there will be many other choices for friends in the dorm, in classes, and student activities. Issues like sleep schedules, what kind of food to store in the room, neatness, noise level, and sex will require discussion and accommodation. On some campuses there are mediators to help with these issues if the roommates can't work out their differences.

During my many years in practice, I have heard about many roommates. Most were solid citizens. There have been a few quirky situations, like the young man whose father was terrified of fire and so kept questioning safety issues and suggesting fire escape plans ("You could throw that heavy table through the window!"), or the rigid roommate who was so preoccupied with neatness that she divided the room in two by using masking tape on the floor. I've collected a few roommate horror stories as well. These include a man who expected his boyfriend to live in the dorm room with him from day one, a woman who played the violin most of the day and night, a man who was addicted to heroin, and one whose mother came to stay in the suite every weekend. None of these situations is acceptable roommate behavior; they required self-assertion to establish a boundary. However, it's not easy to be assertive with someone you don't know well. If a direct discussion doesn't work, meeting with the resident advisor, housing office, or dean of residential life may be necessary.

You might be tempted to get involved if you hear about such struggles, but it's better to help your student navigate things himself. There also may be another side to the story. For example, the student who told me the masking tape story admitted that she was "one of the messiest people on earth." The exception here is safety. If the roommate who was addicted to heroin had not quickly dropped out of school or if the university had not been helpful to the student, I would have recommended that parents get involved, especially if the roommate was selling as well as using.

For young women with body dissatisfaction, living in such close quarters can lead to a preoccupation with comparisons of weight, body shape, and clothing. As Courtney E. Martin wrote in *Perfect Girls, Starving Daughters*, "College is a lab for body dissatisfaction."[1] It is very difficult

1. Courtney Martin. *Perfect Girls, Starving Daughters: The Frightening New Normalcy of Hating Your Body.* New York: Free Press, 2007, p. 279.

for young women in Western culture to avoid comparing themselves with other women when trying on clothes and getting dressed, and many times they end up feeling worse, no matter what the reality. Even women who can usually keep their body-image demons at bay will turn a harsh gaze on their bodies during times of extreme stress or when they face a major life transition like starting college.

We covered self-regulation skills in Part 2, particularly Chapter 6, and now, during college, your student will have the opportunity to test these skills on his own. Self-regulation skills, critically important for depression prevention, may be more difficult to establish and maintain in the new college environment, where parties, too little sleep, and too much exposure to alcohol and marijuana can be the norm. In addition, all of a sudden, there is no adult supervision. Many students learn over time what they can and cannot tolerate and still maintain an academic and social life, but those who are vulnerable to depression need to be more vigilant.

DYSREGULATING BEHAVIORS

One of the more troubling new patterns over the past 20 years is "drunkorexia," in which a student, typically but not exclusively female, diets or fasts in order to drink more alcohol. It is estimated that that 30% of women between the ages of 18 and 23 diet so they can drink more, and for 16% this is a regular practice. For some women, this is an exacerbation of an ongoing eating disorder like anorexia or bulimia, while others develop this new habit in the face of unlimited food and alcohol. It seems logical to them: A student interviewed by ABC News reported, "I've done [drunkorexia] for years and I'm still healthy. And I'm skinny," she said. "That's the best of both worlds to me, so it's not likely that I'll stop doing it any time soon." Many of the young women involved give each other tips on diets, purges, and workout plans.

Missing from their assessment is that drunkorexia is dangerous. It may seem like fun to get drunk quickly, but drinking on an empty stomach and the resulting unpredictable level of intoxication impairs judgment and increases the risks for binge eating, accidents, and unwanted sexual contact. A nutritional deficiency can develop because the process of metabolizing alcohol increases the need for some nutrients, which are being restricted. Drunkorexia can also trigger eating disorders, alcohol abuse, and depression. Drunkorexia is primarily a problem for women; conventional binge drinking, which has many of the same risks, is more common in men.

If your student has a history of depression or anxiety or a vulnerability to either one, drinking alcohol and using marijuana are dangerous. The material in Chapter 7 demonstrates that alcohol is a depressant and disrupts sleep, and given that the teenage brain is still maturing, binge drinking can have a major negative effect on cognitive development. We cannot predict which college students can drink safely and who will develop a substance use disorder, but we do know that alcohol and depression create a perilous combination. Some parents look back with nostalgia at their own drinking days in college and think, "I turned out all right," but those memories often overlook the experiences of a few friends who went on to develop serious alcohol problems. I have seen many students who start partying on Thursday night, when a lot of bars have happy hours, and are still recovering on Monday morning.

WHEN SELF-REGULATION FALTERS

I can see, via Skype, thatMatthew and Robin, parents of Nia, are worried. Robin's dark eyes are filled with tears as she looks down. Matthew is bent over, running his hands through his longish curly brown hair. It's May, and Nia has returned home from what her parents describe as a "tough year." Her grades were "mediocre" and she had revealed that she wasn't very happy. The close quarters with two suitemates exacerbated Nia's eating disorder: She "felt fat compared to them," so Nia had begun to periodically binge and purge. Nia was adopted and was very close to her parents and extended family. Her parents were successful in business, but neither of them had finished college. They had been concerned when Nia chose to go to college far away from home and the finances were stretched. Nia was biracial and never felt "quite right" in her mostly white community, so she was happy to escape to a more diverse setting.

Matthew and Robin asked to Skype with me because they lived in a suburb of a large city in Oregon and wanted to consult with Nia's therapist. Nia agreed happily, as she was hoping that I could reassure them. Nia was striking and enjoyed "dressing up." The first few times I met with her revealed her dramatic side: She first wore a free-spirited retro hippy look; then tight jeans and a revealing T-shirt, and once she came in with sophisticated makeup, her hair braided and wearing a long gray dress and tights. After we got to know one another, Nia settled on the jeans. Just beneath the dramatic surface, though, Nia revealed her struggles with depression and anxiety. Although she had been a very good student before college, Nia did not feel comfortable socially, especially with other young women in high school. She had loved elementary school but was very awkward meeting other girls as she grew older. Nia described a certain innocence that I saw later was very similar to the main character in the poignant movie *Eighth Grade*, with her social stumbles and experimentation with different personas. Nia had been ostracized by some of the "mean girls" (bullies) because she was too academic and "weird." Nia had always been concerned about her appearance as she was just a little overweight. She had periodically purged after meals during high school.

She had dated quite a bit by the time she was 16, as Nia was comfortable with boys. She had a sexual relationship with her boyfriend for the last 2 years of high school. During that time, she ate a healthy diet and did not purge. She joined a Pilates class with her mother and became an instructor. Before college, she broke up with her boyfriend, who stayed in Oregon for college. Coming East to college had been a bit of a culture shock, even though she wanted the experience with the diverse student body and more sophisticated students. Nia experienced some of typical struggles with her first roommate, but they worked it out.

The combination of multiple changes––college life, a new part of the country, and exposure to other young women's bodies––increased Nia's social anxiety and she started the binging-and-purging cycle again. At the same time, although she had been an A and B student in high school, she was getting mostly B's and even one C in her college courses. As a result, Nia was beginning to question her academic capabilities as well as her body and started ruminating about what she saw as her faults.

Then, one night, Nia was encouraged by a friend to go to a party. She had not planned on going out and had not eaten all day, but agreed at the last minute. However, when she arrived, she became socially anxious and quickly consumed a craft beer, which had helped her with anxiety in the past. She was offered punch and drank three glasses. Nia was not an experienced drinker and soon became inebriated. She remembered dancing, and the next thing she knew, she was awakened by noise and found herself in the room of Adam, whom she'd met earlier. Nia was terrified that she had been raped, so she went to the college health services. As it turned out, there were no signs of intercourse and Nia mustered her courage to confront Adam, who said they had "made out for a while but then we both passed out." Nia was now filled with self-doubt and told her mother about the episode. This was the final straw for Matthew and Robin—slipping grades and a dangerous drunken party. They wondered if Nia should be forced to come home.

Fortunately, Nia had been in psychotherapy during high school and had the ability to assess that she needed help. Nia and I talked about the fact that, like many former high school students with good grades, she might have to adjust to the increased demands of college and spend more time studying than she had originally allotted. One of Nia's academic problems was that her college required a "core curriculum" for first-year students. The fact that she had gotten mostly B's in subjects that were not her strengths was not a terrible outcome. Now that she was heading into her second year, she would have more choices, and I reassured her that if she spent more studying her grades would improve.

We then talked about the drinking episode. It was a singular event and Nia was unaware of the gender differences in alcohol metabolism that put her at greater risk than, say, Adam. The experience terrified Nia, so she decided to try to limit her drinking. We discussed strategies to decrease anxiety while drinking less, like identifying people at the party she knew, mentally rehearsing topics of conversation, deep breathing, and switching to soda after one or two drinks. Social anxiety is one of the many reasons that students drink alcohol. Students can also drink to excess because they see it as fun or experience social pressure. For others, though, it's an addiction. Like Nia, 33.6% of female college students (and 33.8% of males) regretted a decision they made as a result of drinking alcohol in the previous year. Matthew and Robin had done their best to listen to Nia over the school year--they tried not to be too judgmental--but when the drunk and dangerous sexual episode occurred, they had, understandably, reached their limit, and appropriately, looked for a way to become more involved.

Here are some college alcohol use facts:

- Alcohol-fueled sex more typically occurs during the first 6 weeks of the first year, when students are new to the college social scene and are less experienced in monitoring their intake and setting appropriate limits.
- Some older male students target first-year women for sexual advances when the women have drunk too much.
- There are apps that can let a student know where their friends are.

What you can do:

- Tell your student that you are primarily concerned about his safety.
- If your student is open to a conversation, review the facts about binge drinking from Chapter 7.
- If your student acknowledges drinking or using marijuana, nonjudgmentally suggest that, if so, he needs to know where whatever substance he is consuming has come from. Where was the punch made? What is in it? Who bought the marijuana?

- Let your daughter know about older male sexual predators showing up at parties, as described earlier, and that a good practice for students is to arrange to arrive together at a party or event and leave together.
- Create an agreement similar to the house rule of getting a safe ride by letting your student know that you will help pay for a cab or ride share.
- It is good to know the on-campus resources for problem drinking and for sexual assault so that you can encourage your student to contact them if necessary.

Initially terrified about sexual assault, Nia shared the incident with Adam with her parents, and they weren't sure what they should do. In the end, they did not need to deal with the issue. If they had needed to get involved, here are some suggestions. In addition to helping her access sexual assault services, you can be enormously helpful to your daughter by listening and providing care and empathy. A student being assaulted is an emergency; I believe parents should get involved, at least as major advocates and contacts, unless the student refuses. And let's not forget that sexual assault is assault, an attack. You should assess whether your daughter is in any continued danger of being assaulted, stalked, or harassed again. If penetration occurred, you can discuss with her whether she wants to go to a nearby hospital to be examined with a rape kit by sensitive professionals who have been trained to do this. Even if she doesn't want to have a rape kit done, she will also need to be tested for pregnancy and sexually transmitted diseases. This will be a highly emotional time for you and your student. You may feel that your daughter was foolish if she was put herself in a dangerous situation, but this is not the time for that kind of discussion. The most important thing is your support.

We had several Skype family sessions so that Nia could share what she was learning in therapy about substances, sex, and studying and so that her parents could feel involved. It was my opinion that, with the support of therapy, the fear she had experienced after the party with Adam and a session with the dean who did counseling about substances, Nia should continue in school for at least another semester and then re-evaluate. Matthew and Robin accepted this assessment. Nia also wanted to explore her feelings about being biracial and adopted. Her social isolation, periodic sadness, and anxiety were in part a function of feeling like an outsider. After the initial adjustment, Nia stated she was now meeting people "who looked more like me." Her body image issues were also somewhat related to being biracial because, as she said, "I always wished that I could be blonde and skinny like the other girls in school." I pointed out that this desire was common among American women and a result of social media, advertising, and cultural expectations. Nia understood that, but replied that it was difficult to completely reject these images. I agreed. We also agreed that she could turn some of her energy away from food intake and toward physical activity, as she had played field hockey for fun in high school.

Nia's story is a good example of early intervention to avoid depressive episodes. She has two symptoms of depression, depressed mood and some hopelessness, as well as social anxiety, but the fact that she could self-reflect and conclude that she needed help, limit her alcohol intake, begin to be have healthier perspectives about her body, and get more physical activity helped her to avoid a major depression.

GOT SLEEP?

If your student shares with you that he is feeling "off," but not necessarily depressed or sad, I'd first ask about sleep, exercise, and nutrition, as these habits can easily be disrupted, and many students forget their importance in the thrill of new college experiences. I have seen that exercise and nutrition (except for periodic pizza, nachos, etc.) are often part of the student culture now, but getting enough sleep is not.

As we have seen in Chapter 6, sleep is foundational for health and well-being. Some students can make up for their lost sleep on the weekend by sleeping late, but for others, sleep disruption can lead to daytime fatigue, irritability, and, in some cases, depressive symptoms. Sleep deprivation also increases anxiety, even in people who do not have a pre-existing psychological condition. I have been heartened by the fact that some students entering college with a history of depression have been educated about the role of sleep and so have learned to take care of themselves in this way. The Jed Foundation has found that students like these, who have learned to create a healthy lifestyle, have a better transition to college.

LONELINESS, LOVE, AND LOSS

It stands to reason that students who are vulnerable to or have a history of depression would have an especially difficult time with a breakup or loneliness. In the previous chapter, we reviewed ways for you to encourage your student to reach out for social connection. It's quite possible that your student will fall in love during college. College relationships can be more meaningful than high school ones, owing to more time together, ongoing development, and the overall depth of emotional experience during college years. It is also likely, however, that he will experience a breakup, since not many people marry their college sweethearts. Sadness, shock, and loneliness may well follow. In addition, many students perceived themselves as a couple and enjoyed that role, now lost to them. If the breakup occurs during senior year, not only is there heartbreak, but the image of the next phase of life as a couple together is shattered, as well as the imminent details like graduation events and celebrations.

You may get the call from a devastated son or daughter when a breakup occurs, especially when it was unexpected. As we have learned in other chapters, the most important thing to do is listen and validate the pain. It might be tempting to offer false reassurance or to engage in some ex bashing, but neither of those strategies tend to work. My client Jacqueline was a junior when her boyfriend of a year broke up with her in the second semester and this was a complete shock to her. She spent days crying alone in her room. Then her friends stepped in to remobilize her, force her to go to class, go to lunch, and so on, gradually increasing her activity level.

In reality, it took several months for Jacqueline to regroup. Her parents were furious with her boyfriend, whom they had met several times. And although criticizing the ex is understandable—that person hurt your child!—over time it's possible that your student will begin to see the benefits of the relationship and integrate it as an overall positive experience. Jacqueline refocused her energies and became involved in new activities on campus and later looked back at her boyfriend with some sadness, but with fond feelings as well.

If your son or daughter is gay or lesbian, the situation is similar—love and loss hurt—but it may be more complicated if it was their first same-sex relationship. Lucas, the gay student we met in Chapter 13, was so happy to be in an accepting college and then he fell in love with Daniel, but they broke up after 4 months. Daniel had come out early in high school and was Lucas' first important relationship. Lucas felt that his "stupid virgin self" had doomed the relationship, but Daniel was primarily interested in exploring additional relationships. The end of a relationship can be a time for self-reflection, although it's important not to drift into irrational thoughts or overgeneralizations, as Lucas was beginning to do. Lucas became more involved in a jazz trio and later he and Daniel became friends. LGBTQ students may feel less able to access social support because society gives less respect to same-sex relationships and, consequently, a breakup is not always validated by others as a significant loss. Here again, being a member of an accepting family can make a positive difference.

Here are some ideas for parental responses, based in part on skills described in previous chapters and what was helpful to Jacqueline:

- Help her understand that it will take time, but the intense pain will ultimately pass. Remind her that she can tolerate the loss.
- When she is better able to engage in a conversation, point out that she has an individual identity, not only as a part of a couple.
- She may have learned some important lessons from the breakup, but if she becomes overly self-critical about the relationship, encourage self-compassion.
- Suggest that if she finds herself ruminating about the boyfriend or girlfriend, try mindfulness or distraction.
- Encourage distraction—from daily, upbeat music to getting more involved in coursework or new student activities.
- Monitor substance use. In general, young men are better at distraction, but for them and some young women, substance misuse may be a tempting solution.
- Remind her of the social power of spending time with friends.

Sometimes the loss occurs in the family; the loss could be the death of a parent, grandparent, family member, or dear pet. You may be more involved in family matters than after a breakup because you are sharing a sad but meaningful experience. It is difficult to be away from family after a death, so if there is a way, help your student come home for the funeral. Even more important is to keep him in the loop after the funeral. You can let him know if people send cards or stop by to see the family, for example. Be aware that the first time a student returns home, the loss will become more real, so his grief may take longer to process or take a different form than that of other family members. If he needs support, campus chaplains are sensitive to the grief process and can be extremely caring and compassionate.

Death on Campus

Death is always a loss, but when a young person dies, it feels tragic and unfair. Yet deaths do occur on campus, sometimes from illness or an accident and sometimes from suicide. The students who remain feel vulnerable and frightened. I have found that on most campuses, many resources come into play at that time. Deans, faculty, chaplains, and staff from counseling and psychological services usually offer individual and group support sessions. Students come together to support one another. A student who is depressed or has suffered a recent loss might need additional attention at that time. As their parent, you can reach out to them to see if they are accessing services and support.

PARENTAL DIVORCE

Divorce is never easy for children, as we reviewed in Chapter 4. Although most children and adolescents cope well, about 25–35% experience clinically significant problems, including depression and relationship issues. A divorce that takes place when a student is in college elicits complicated reactions. If the family experienced a lot of intense conflict, a student may have looked forward to college as a way to escape, only to have to face a new set of problems, and worries. Where will he stay when he goes home? Will he offend the other parent? Are his parents okay? How are his siblings managing? He may also be concerned about financial changes.

Another reaction is that if divorcing parents did not argue in front of the children, the divorce may come as a surprise. A student may feel guilty that his parents repressed their feelings and stayed together for his sake until he left home. He may also go through some revisionist history, asking questions like "Did they ever love each other?" There is also the common worry of whether he caused the divorce in some way. In this situation, you should reassure your student that the divorce was not his fault and that you will be there to listen. You will also want him to know relevant details of the divorce and agreements so that he does not feel isolated from the rest of the family.

SEX ON CAMPUS

It took me a while to realize that I was confused listening to my patients talking about the "hooking up." It wasn't because I couldn't remember the definition of a hookup but rather that the term is used in a variety of ways, from kissing to having intercourse. A *hookup* is essentially an uncommitted sexual encounter, and the most recent data suggest that between 60 and 80% of North American college students have had some sort of hookup experience. This trend aligns with Jeffrey Arnett's view of emerging adulthood as an "in-between" stage, in this case the stage in between exploring sexuality and that of marriage. With the age of puberty lowering and the age of marriage increasing, there is a longer period of time for teenagers and college students to experiment sexually.

With respect to heterosexual hookups, there are some gender differences. In most studies, women have more negative reactions than men do. In addition, more women than men hope that a casual sexual encounter will develop into a romantic one. Women also have more thoughts of worry and vulnerability than men. As for hookup regret, one study found that large proportions of both men and woman expressed some regret. Not surprisingly, better-quality sex reduced the degree of regret reported.

It's clear that hookups are now a part of the college experience for most students, and in some ways this is a continuation of a trend started in high school, only with more alcohol and marijuana and greater freedom. Hookups are typically associated with marijuana or alcohol use. Over 60% of students said they had hooked up while drinking alcohol, with an average consumption of 3.3 drinks. This leads to some of the potential problems with hookups. First, there is the question of safety, with one study revealing that in a sample of over 1,400 college students, 429 (over 30%) of the students had engaged in oral sex, anal sex, or vaginal intercourse in their most recent hookup and less than half had used a condom. More troubling is that in some of the casual encounters, between 7 and 8% in one study, a consensual hookup turned into *non*consensual sexual activity.

There are psychological ramifications to hookups. In a study of 3,900 students on 30 campuses, researchers inquired about number of hookups and several measure of well-being. The authors concluded that "casual sex was negatively associated with well-being and positively associated with psychological distress."[2] In this study there were no differences between women and men. More research needs to address the behavior and needs of the LGBTQ community. Earlier studies about gay men were primarily conducted with respect to transmission of HIV and AIDS, and very few studies have examined the needs and behavior of lesbians.

There is an expression health professionals use: "If you go to Midas, you'll get a muffler." This was derived from a 1971 Midas ad, "If you've got a toothache, you go to the dentist. If you need a new muffler, you go to Midas." As a therapist, I don't want you to think that every student needs therapy, although you need to have sensitivity to symptoms of depression and anxiety and the appropriate treatment. I hope that the information in this chapter illustrates an attitude of optimism that you can share with your student who may be struggling in the first 2 years of college. Some

---

2. Melina Bersamin, Zamboanga, B., Schwartz, S., Donnellan, M., Hudson, M., Weisskirch, R., . . . Caraway, S. Risky business: Is there an association between casual sex and mental health among emerging adults? *Journal of Sex Research*, *51*(1), 43–51, 2014, p. 43.

of these mood triggers are quite predictable—the comparison with other students with respect to academics, appearance, and social skills; challenges in finding a group of friends and an academic pursuit; and, finally, a need for independent self-regulation. Sometimes a student like Nia will benefit from therapy. This is especially important to understand if your student experienced psychological problems before college. Other times, a focus on optimism, self-efficacy, and encouragement to be brave and reach out to people will be enough.

CHAPTER 17

Getting Help on Campus

Your daughter Lynne calls you at the beginning of second-semester junior year, having returned from a semester abroad in Scotland. Lynne had a bit of difficulty adjusting to college. She had come out as a lesbian the summer before sophomore year and hoped to develop a comfortable community at college. By the end of sophomore year, she did have a few friends and did well academically. Still, she couldn't quite find her place. Scotland provided a welcome relief and adventure. She enjoyed her classes as well as the charm of Old Town and the cultural opportunities in Edinburgh. She made friends and took weekend trips to the Highlands and St. Andrews. Now that she is back, she's been texting you more than usual and she seems a bit at sea, not sure of her courses, concerned about her future. Her new roommate hasn't worked out well, so she's been a little lonely, although she has a couple friends left from the previous year and keeps in touch with friends from Scotland online. Lynne finds herself crying from time to time and wonders how she'll manage. What should you do?

First, don't panic. This scenario is quite common. Students returning from a semester abroad often have problems readjusting to courses and campus life. The good news is you will be ready for this possible phone call, because this chapter will orient you to the types of services available on most campuses.

Let's say you've used your communications skills to listen and clarify how Lynne feels. She says she not really depressed, just feeling out of sorts and lonely. If she wants suggestions, you might encourage her to spend a little less time online with friends from Scotland and more reaching out to old friends who are on campus now. Lynne is reluctant and feels left out. You can point out that her old friends probably just maintained their social network while she was abroad and will likely include her again, but that she may need to take the initiative. Another option is to suggest that she try to connect with other students returning from abroad or with transfer students, who are also looking for new friends. Loneliness and roommate problems are among the most common concerns that resident assistants deal with.

If there is a specific interest Lynne has from high school that she let drop (music, art, sports, games, community or political activism, etc.), she can look for options where she can get involved. Some of these activities may take her off campus, giving her access to additional people from the larger off-campus community. These activities may help give Lynne a sense of purpose outside academics. If Lynne feels strongly about an issue (women's rights, the environment, economic opportunity, or a religious or spiritual commitment), she can tap into those values to gain strength and connection.

As for campus academic support, Lynne would benefit from talking to a dean or a concentration advisor about her courses. If she is interested in a specific area, she might seek out a faculty member with the same interest or ask a dean for suggestions. In my opinion, the relationship with faculty during college can provide an excellent education and, sometimes, inspiration for a lifetime. Some students fear imposing on faculty members, but many faculty members welcome contact with students who have genuine interest in their area of study. Moreover, the student does not need to be an expert in the area—one or two genuine questions are all that is needed.

Campus chaplains can also be very helpful. In addition to religion and spirituality, many chaplains are comfortable discussing a range of issues, from finding meaningful work to not knowing how to fit in. They can also provide support and counseling and are aware of other resources on and off campus. Students often find that there are so many opportunities that they have trouble deciding what courses to take or what future study, profession, or occupation they might pursue. Speaking informally with a chaplain allows them to be more expansive in their discussion before meeting with a dean.

Chaplains are also called on for pastoral support to lead community responses in times of crisis. When a student dies, for instance, a memorial service may be held on campus and a tree planted in the student's honor. Ceremonies like this can aid students, faculty, and staff in coping with the loss of a community member. Chaplains also help by giving support to a student when a close relative is seriously ill or has died. Helping with the grief process is important, especially in our culture, which allows very little time for grieving the loss of a friend or relative. Even friends who want to be supportive often don't understand that grief tends to last months rather than weeks, but chaplains do understand this. Most university chaplains do not limit their services to students from the same religious denomination.

Three weeks pass and now Lynne tells you that the situation is getting worse: She is having trouble concentrating and feels down a lot. She spoke to a dean and made some headway on figuring out her courses for the semester and, while Lynne appreciates your other suggestions, she hasn't been able to mobilize herself to take additional steps. She gets out of bed every day, but it is a struggle. Lynne says, "I just don't feel like myself."

Now is the time for Lynne to contact the counseling center; her symptoms of depression are getting worse. The sentence "I don't feel like myself" is often a summary statement indicating that a student knows something is wrong. CBT is probably the best option for Lynne. Almost all universities have counseling centers, also called psychological services or wellness centers. On some campuses, mental health services are housed within the health services. The central importance of on-campus mental health resources is reflected in the fact that you will usually hear about services during the orientation to campus. If you have concerns about your student's mental health, you'll want to pay close attention during orientation, because your teen will not be able to! They're typically so overwhelmed by all the information and new social dynamics that they can't keep track of everything.

Colleges and university counseling centers vary as to how much psychotherapy and medication they provide. Most provide emergency services and triage, short-term treatment, and a referral to a therapist in the community if longer-term care is necessary.

If Lynne hesitates to call, you can ask her to look at the counseling center's website. On many campuses, appointments can be made online. Lynne might also discover groups that interest her or other services she did not know about. However, you cannot make the call for her. Most therapists want to hear from the student directly. And you don't want to undercut Lynne's developing self-efficacy. If you feel the need to encourage Lynne or if she needs more structure, you can call or text her and ask her to call the counseling center and then text you back. If she is uncomfortable with a parent serving in this role, she can ask a friend or sibling to help her move forward with therapy.

Here are some of the concerns Lynne might have about obtaining mental health services on campus:

- One common concern is that psychological treatment will go on "the permanent record." This language is a bit of a throwback to high school fears. The permanent transcript of the university is academic only. Yes, the counseling center will maintain its own file. But that is separate from the college performance or evaluation record.

- Many students are concerned that they will not have confidentiality. The reality is that counseling centers care very much about keeping students' information confidential. They are aware that if they do not do this, students will be reluctant to use their services. Policies in this regard may differ somewhat from institution to institution, depending on state laws and the ethics standards of the mental health professionals. Many counseling centers have information about confidentiality on their Web pages and students can call to speak to a clinician about this. It's not as if the mental health professional will escort Lynne out of her office and then immediately called the dean's office. Similarly, if Lynne is having difficulty in a class and a dean feels she would benefit from mental health services, she will make a recommendation, but will not contact the counseling center without Lynne's permission.

- If Lynne is feeling marginalized due to her sexual orientation or any racial, economic, disability or other minority status, she may be less likely to go to the counseling center. There are usually many support groups on campus. Most campuses have centers for LGBTQ students, women, first-generation students, international students, Latinx students, and students of color. Student groups can be a gateway to meeting other students and offer connection for people with similar issues, help with problem-solving, and provide access to other campus resources. They may be able to identify particularly sensitive and culturally competent staff members at the counseling center. First-generation students may find it especially helpful to seek out a group because of concerns about stigma and letting down their parents.

- The exceptions to confidentiality are danger to self and others. If a mental health professional believes that a student is likely to hurt herself or someone else, confidentiality will need to be broken as much as is necessary to keep everyone safe. In most states there is a law allowing involuntary commitment, which gives physicians and licensed mental health professionals the right to commit a person to a mental health facility for up to 10 days if that a person is in danger of hurting herself or someone else. Mental health professionals also have a duty to inform other campus members who may be affected and may additionally need to inform the police, depending on the institution and state laws. But these situations are as infrequent on a college campus as they are in your community.

- Lynne may be afraid that she will be asked to leave school because of mental health issues. This is a rare event and only occurs when a student's behavior means she is unsafe on campus or a has a psychiatric disorder so severe that it disrupts the community, which is seldom, if ever, the case with depression. Although each college deals with these situations differently, the Americans with Disabilities Act prohibits a university from asking a student to leave due to a psychological condition alone.

• This leads to another concern many parents share. If your student is over the age of 18, the same rules of confidentiality apply to you. That is to say, a mental health professional cannot contact you without your student's permission, and if you phone, the center cannot tell you whether or not she has an appointment unless she has given permission to tell you. Some students fear that their parents will be disappointed or disapprove of their obtaining mental health services. Many counseling centers, deans, and administrators are trying to balance the issues of privacy and safety. I recommend that if you know your student is receiving psychological services on campus, you may ask that she sign a release so that you can talk to the mental health professional on a limited basis. Then you can find a way for your involvement that will not be overly intrusive but will allow you to know if your child requires additional help. Additionally, you may have information about family history that is relevant to the treatment.

In my experience, students who are depressed or anxious usually want their parents to be involved in some way. In this situation, your involvement is critically important. The first thing you can do is remember to be nonjudgmental and reach out to see if there is a way for you to help. Your daughter may not want you to text her constantly, but checking in on a daily basis and letting her know that you or other relatives and family friends are available could be extremely beneficial. If your child has some suicidal thoughts, you can collaborate with her and the mental health professional to develop a plan about what you'll do if her suicidal thoughts become plans and if other symptoms become more severe.

If your daughter does not want to sign a release or if she is reluctant to make an appointment at the counseling center, you can still call the center and request to speak with the director. In this situation, you could share the reasons for your con. You would be asking the director for advice on how you can help your student—without regard to anything they may or may not know from personal contact with her.

Lynne reaches out via email to Meghan, her roommate from Scotland, and Meghan reveals that she has been in therapy. Meghan, who is also lesbian, says she tried one therapist but it wasn't a good fit and the therapist didn't understand LGBTQ issues. Then Meghan tried again and, with a good connection with her new therapist, CBT helped enormously. Meghan adds that Lynne's concerns could be discussed openly with a therapist or physician at the counseling center or health services. Reassured, Lynne contacts the counseling center and begins CBT. When she calls you and you express concern, she replies, "Don't worry mom, Meghan is a big believer in therapy and she will make sure I follow through."

This would be a good time for you to pull back a bit. You can be relieved that now Lynne is in CBT and has a friend watching out for her. You can let her know that you are available when she needs you.

NEW APPROACHES TO MENTAL HEALTH SERVICES

Some universities are developing new approaches to reduce stress and psychological problems. Counseling centers are trying to respond to students needs by developing teletherapy and 24-hour hotlines. Meditation and mindfulness programs exist in many universities as part of the counseling center or in another department. Brown University has a mindfulness center that integrates research, training, and education. Here are a few other examples: Johns Hopkins has "Mellow Out Mondays," where students receive free massages. Carleton College offers art therapy experiences. Morgan State University's counseling center offers consultations to parents. Arizona State's counseling center offers DREAMzone, a resource for the Arizona State University community supporting undocumented students, DACA students, and students with families of mixed immigration status. They offer individual help, "support circles," and training to heighten awareness. George Mason University offers a residence hall devoted to stress management, health, and social support. The Massachusetts Institute of Technology (MIT) offers grants of up to $10,000 for cutting-edge ideas about wellness, mentoring, and grassroots solutions that are developed by faculty, students, and staff.

Many universities are using mobile technologies to reach out so that students can do anonymous self-assessments. The US federal government sponsors TRIO programs on campuses "targeted to serve and assist low-income individuals, first-generation college students, and individuals with disabilities to progress through the academic pipeline from middle school to post baccalaureate programs." The name "TRIO" refers to these three groups of students.

Because we know that stress and psychological conditions interfere with all learning, many universities are also including courses on stress management. The University of California at Santa Cruz has a three-session seminar entitled, "Embrace Your Life," helping students identify what they would like to change. The Engelhard Project for Connecting Life and Learning at Georgetown University incorporates psychological health issues into traditional courses. For example, in one course on mathematical modeling, the professor incorporates datasets involving nutrition, gambling, and alcohol.

Much of my career has been devoted to integrating the fields of primary care medical practice and psychological health, so I am pleased that this approach is beginning to be used in universities as well. The Jed Foundation is encouraging primary care professionals at college health services to screen students for some of the more common conditions, like anxiety and depression. Many universities, including Brown, are doing so. Penn State offers online monitoring directly to students so they can self-assess the existence of a psychiatric disorder.

So Lynne has many options for help on campus. If Lynne had needed off-campus treatment for continued treatment, you could follow the suggestions about therapy from Chapter 14. In addition, most counseling centers will be able to give her some suggestions of people whom they know well and have experience with college students.

WHY WAIT FOR THE PHONE CALL WHEN A LITTLE BIT OF PREPARATION CAN HELP?

If you are concerned about your daughter's vulnerability to depression or anxiety or especially if she has been in treatment or experienced a depressive episode, check out the student services before orientation. That way she can arrive with a plan prepared in case she needs it. If your daughter is a worrier and you can afford it, a quick visit to campus over the summer can allay some basic concerns of how to get around, where services are located, where the dorm is, and so on. This plan is also advisable if your teen has any physical limitations. A visit can alleviate anxiety and reduce some of the barriers to getting help on campus.

Lynne stays in CBT for 12 weeks, then feels much better. She discovers that her college has a chapter of Active Minds (www.activeminds.org), a student-run organization that provides education about mental health, aims to reduce stigma, and promotes stress-reducing activities on campuses nationally. Lynne joins and shares what she is learning with Meghan, who is thinking about started a similar group in Edinburgh.

In Lynne's case, she was able to access a timely course of CBT on campus, which is possible on many campuses. However, campuses differ widely in the quality and extent of services that are available to students. As much as the staff may want to provide all that your student needs, situations may arise in which the demand of the center far exceeds the ability to provide reasonable services to all who seek it. Universities are sometimes reluctant to acknowledge this.

If your student is dealing with mild depression, anxiety, or adjustment issues, it may be reasonable to have an appointment every 3 or 4 weeks. But if she is suffering from a more serious depression or has stopped attending classes, she really needs more frequent sessions. You could talk to her about asking her therapist to recommended off-campus resources. Students usually much prefer to have their treatment on campus because of the convenience of the location, as well as the clinicians' familiarity with campus culture.

Overall, then, you can help your daughter identify a variety of resources on campus. There are also times that going off campus for treatment is the best option, and you can help her sort this out as well. There are many avenues for treatment, education, and support.

CHAPTER 18

Is Taking Time Off from College a Good Idea?

Parents often ask me whether taking time off from college is a good idea. In general, my answer is a qualified "yes." I use the word "qualified" because students need to explore all their options first, and when a student is depressed, his negative outlook may prevent him from seeing them clearly. Many times, though, time away is a good idea.

I saw Derrick before his time away from school after the first semester of his sophomore year. By the time we met, Derrick was already in the process of withdrawing from school. One of his professors referred him to me. Derrick is African American and had been raised by Janyce, his mom, who was divorced and worked as a clerk in Buffalo, New York, his hometown. Janyce had sacrificed greatly for his education, first sending him to a local Catholic high school and later helping him apply for admission and financial aid at private colleges. Derrick had decided to go home to work for a semester and was "lining things up" for when he returned. I was to be part of his lineup.

Derrick was emotionally and academically exhausted when I first saw him. He had wanted to excel, for his own sake and to prove to his mother that all her sacrifices were worthwhile. He plunged into a double major in neuroscience and engineering with the hopes of joining a biotech firm after graduation. In many ways, Derrick did well in his first year of college. He made a few friends and played piano in a trio, but the price of Derrick's success was severe stress and it affected his mental health. To accomplish all that he wanted and keep up his grades, Derrick only slept for 5 or 6 hours per night. He was extremely bright, and his high school had not been very demanding for him. To his credit, he learned that he needed to become "super organized" in order to get everything done in college. But he was a bit perfectionistic as well: He wanted to get "mostly A's" and was self-critical when he did not. He also needed to work part-time in a lab for his financial aid package.

Let's review: too little sleep, a stressful schedule, concerns about disappointing his mother, and perfectionistic expectations—a growing formula for a depressive episode and increased anxiety. Yet when I met with Derrick, he was already cultivating the appearance of a young professional. He was more formally dressed than most students, wearing pressed chinos and a designer sweater over a button-down collared shirt. At the same time, Derrick seemed a little socially immature. I could tell that his laser focus on academics had taken a toll on his social development.

It took Derrick a few weeks to trust me enough to share a secret. His father had been incarcerated on drug charges for 5 years starting when Derrick was in kindergarten and had never been able to readjust, taking part-time, often temporary, jobs. He had not seen Derrick more than a handful of times. Derrick's mother also did not want him to spend much time with his father. They had gone through an acrimonious divorce and she thought he would be a bad role model. Derrick didn't share this part of his background with anyone on campus.

This privacy about his father made sense, because Derrick already felt "different." He was a racial minority, a first-generation student with fewer financial resources than most other students, the son of an incarcerated father, and, in the back of his mind, possibly a sexual minority. Being African American on a primarily white campus can be daunting. Michelle Obama describes what it was like for her at Princeton, after going through an orientation of mostly African American first-year students: "If during the orientation program, we'd begun to feel some ownership of the space, we were now a glaring anomaly—poppy seeds in a bowl of rice. . . . I 'd never stood out in a crowd or a classroom because of the color of my skin. It was jarring and uncomfortable, at least at first, like being dropped into a strange new terrarium, a habitat that hadn't been built for me."[1]

Derrick wanted to prevent what he called a "breakdown." He had experienced a mild depression after his first girlfriend broke up with him in high school. I wanted to know more about his family history, but Derrick didn't know much about his father's history. His mother had experienced what he described as some "spells of mild depression." Although Derrick

---

1. Michele Obama, *Becoming*. New York: Crown, 2018, p. 72.

was not suffering from a major depressive episode, he described fatigue and an increasing sense of anxiety and he had started to use marijuana to unwind. He said he was feeling less hopeful than usual and expressed fear that he was "losing the can-do attitude."

When Derrick said he just wanted to "go home for a while and sleep and eat," I didn't like the sound of the words "go home and sleep," so I did a suicide and safety assessment. I know that it is often difficult for men, especially men of color, to reveal the depth of their psychological pain to a stranger, in this case an older white woman. I considered that Derrick might have a tendency to cope with high stress by expending huge amounts of effort, at significant psychological cost. I admired Derrick's dedication and hard work but knew it was taking a toll on his mood and his development.

I told Derrick that I wanted to support his plans but that I would be uncomfortable if he returned to Buffalo without arranging therapy there and without my knowing that he was safe. Suicide is the second leading cause of death in people ages 15 to 34, so it is always worth doing a suicide and safety assessment with young people, especially those with symptoms of depression.

I also clarified that many college students of all backgrounds, especially those struggling with depression, had thoughts of suicide. Unfortunately, a survey of college-age students found that only one out of three of those with suicidal ideation was getting mental health treatment. And the rate of getting treatment is lower for students from minority groups and students from poorer economic backgrounds. That had not been a problem for Derrick because of his relationship with the professor who referred him to me.

Suicidal feelings related to depression can occur during a first depressive episode because a person hasn't learned that the feelings of hopelessness and sadness will eventually pass. That's one of the reasons adolescents have a higher rate of suicide; their age and relative lack of experience may lead them to act impulsively based on fleeting emotions because they are less capable of realizing that those emotions are fleeting.

I considered risk factors. Derrick had never had thoughts of death nor suicide attempts. His mother's family did not have a history of depression or substance abuse. We did not have a family history for Derrick's paternal side; we only knew that his father had used cocaine. High stress is also a risk for suicide. Derrick had not suffered a loss, but leaving school might be seen that way. As for supports, Derrick had his close relationship with his mother, his new friends at college, and the professor.

I was also concerned because, as described in Chapter 6, sleep problems are associated with suicidal risk, even independent of depression. However,

Derrick denied having suicidal thoughts or impulses when we talked about suicide. He revealed that he had had fleeting thoughts of suicide before he talked with his professor but then realized that he had options for changing his situation. He clarified that he was sad but that what he meant was that he literally wanted to sleep more. Derrick also explained that his sleep restriction was voluntary and not the result of insomnia, so we talked about sleep deprivation and the relationship of sleep to overall health and mental health.

Now that I was reassured, I could reassure Janyce. Derrick asked me to talk with her because she was very worried about the recent turn of events. I spoke with Janyce and explained that many students took time off, that it did not mean he was dropping out, and that the combination of therapy and work could help Derrick re-gather his impressive psychological resources. After I talked to her and she talked to Derrick, Janyce accepted the situation and asked what she could do to help. I responded that from what Derrick had told me, she had been a resolute and engaged mother and that listening and encouraging his plans would be the best course of action. Derrick also wanted a job that wouldn't require any "book work." Fortunately, he had worked one summer as a carpenter and so his mother suggested he call that company to get a part-time job.

The plan was coming together. I recommend that students who take time off have a job, a supportive living environment, and a therapist. Derrick had the promise of work, his mother, and therapy, which he could arrange because he could go back on his mother's health insurance since he was under 26. Derrick also had an additional source of support, as he and his mother had gone to the same church, he said, "as long as I can remember," which meant that there was a larger community of people rooting for him. Church had also given him access to additional adults who he could talk with when he needed advice or had a concern he didn't want to share with his mother.

Now he needed to make sure his options at school were protected. I suggested that Derrick look at his student handbook or college website, as they sometimes detail the process for taking time off. This information can be difficult to find in some cases, so the next step was to confirm anything he had discovered and run his ideas by a supportive academic administrator.

The procedure for taking a medical leave is different for every college. Sometimes it can be arranged by talking with a dean. Other times, the student needs to submit a petition through a dean, after which their request goes to another deliberative body. Some of the questions that you and your teen need to have clarified are as follows: How long is the leave expected to be? What is the process and documentation for re-enrolling? How does he re-establish housing and financial aid when he returns? Derrick was self-aware and knew that he needed time to rest and regroup so that he did not become clinically depressed. Depression is often a reason for a medical leave from college.

In Derrick's case, we are talking about a medical leave of absence. However, there are other reasons why students take time off. Most schools have different policies in place, depending on whether the leave is medical, personal, or academic. It is a good idea to inquire about those differences so your student can choose the most appropriate option. Some students are just not enjoying college enough and feel stressed. If students continue to feel dissatisfied after they have explored other options, like talking with a dean, getting therapy, and perhaps changing majors or taking a reduced course load, time away may be a good idea. Some students also just feel unready, as if they had been moving on a conveyor belt to the next stage after high school. They may not have the maturity or interest that can provide motivation for academic success. Many of these students, especially those who drink and party too much, get into academic trouble and need time off for a fresh start. For these students, time to reflect and establish better schedules, study skills, and a healthier lifestyle is necessary. Other students take a leave because they have particular interests that they want to pursue before completing their education.

A final reason is that some students feel they had made a "poor match" with their college choice. They never felt that the school was right for them even after a semester or two and need time to think about transferring. In all cases, I encourage students to try to finish the semester in order to get credit for the work they've done. In addition, it's important to keep documentation of their meetings with campus administrators. Staying in touch with campus friends and faculty will make returning much easier. I believe that it is crucially important for students to have a clear plan for readmission in order to make time off worthwhile.

Derrick ended up staying home for two semesters, then returned. He felt re-energized and had worked in therapy with a psychologist in Buffalo to address his perfectionism. We continued with this theme and then began to develop strategies to reduce his overall level of stress.

Many parents put so much energy and hope into their children's college plans that it is hard to accept the idea of time off as a healthy step. I understand the difficulty, but it can be extremely important and may even prove life-changing for a student struggling with depression and other mental health challenges.

- Keep in touch with your teen when you hear that he is having difficulties. Increase the frequency of contact, whether by text, phone, or email, so he knows you are there for him.
- Listen carefully to assess his level of stress and possible symptoms of depression and anxiety.
- If he is having academic problems, suggest he talk with faculty, a dean, or student support services. If he is depressed or has a learning difference, he may be able to take a reduced course load.
- Similarly, most colleges have writing centers and referrals to tutors to help students with academic difficulties.
- Recommend a consultation with the counseling center. Some cover both academic and psychological needs. If depressive and anxious symptoms are prominent, suggest psychological services specifically.
- If your son or daughter has never been assessed for learning differences and is having academic difficulties, think about a neuropsychological assessment. Remember that depression is often associated with other disorders (see Chapter 3).
- If loneliness is prominent, suggest he talk with a resident advisor (RA). The RA often knows other students who also want to expand their social group or may have a possible idea for a "friend match."
- Mindfulness meditation can lessen the symptoms of depression and anxiety, and many colleges offer courses in mindfulness or a mindfulness center where students can learn and practice it.
- In most colleges, there are interest groups and activities of all kinds; joining one may be an easier way than reaching out to students in the cafeteria or classes.
- If, after all these steps, your student wants to take time off, try to listen nonjudgmentally. It is okay to ask questions to see if he has explored his other options, though.
- Suggest he talk to the relevant dean and decision-making body.
- Ask permission to talk to the dean and the therapist so that you can understand the parameters of a leave of absence.
- Discuss the need for structure. Even if your student's needs are related to depression and require time for more intensive psychotherapy, too much free time is not a good idea. Taking classes or getting a job, even a part-time one, will give him some structure and boost self-confidence.
- If necessary, help him find a therapist skilled in CBT or another evidence-based therapy (see Chapter 14).

- Check on continued health insurance. If your student is on a university-sponsored plan, the university may have a policy regarding how long a student can remain on the plan while away from campus.
- Verify future financial aid and housing.
- If your home is not the best place for your son or daughter to take time off, assist in identifying a safe and comfortable environment in a location where close friends or other family members are nearby.
- Staying in the same location as the college while on leave has advantages and disadvantages. Access to friends, ongoing therapy if he has been in treatment, and job opportunities are all advantages. The feelings of alienation that often develop when friends are not available because of their college commitments can, however, prove to be a significant disadvantage, one that can lead to feelings of stigma and alienation. In general, I believe that the disadvantages outweigh the advantages; if possible, a leave should really be a leave and taken away from campus.
- Review plans for return, transfer, or additional time away from college.
- Most of all, try to check your own ego and fear. You may feel disappointed or embarrassed if your son or daughter returns home. It is not shameful to take time off. If the reason is psychological, it is about health. Your child may return to the same college, decide to transfer, or completely change plans. The best role for a parent is to listen and help him find his way by looking at his strengths, weaknesses, and true interests, not to insist that he follow a predetermined career path. In addition to the students I have seen, I have heard many stories from deans and student support personnel about how a medical leave was a valuable experience. Remember that if your student gets into treatment early in the leave, he will likely begin to feel better as depression and anxiety subside and may then be interested in seeking new experiences through a job or volunteer work. This will be a source of enrichment in ways that may not be apparent at the moment. Time away often promotes growth and leads to a better college experience in the long run.

CHAPTER 19

Can We Change the Culture to Promote Psychological Health?

The process of education is profoundly affected by mental health, especially depression and anxiety. A child cannot thrive, and will therefore be less able to learn, if she is impaired by a mental health condition. At the same time, education can either promote growth or prove to be stressful and stifling, depending on the circumstances. Therefore, we should do everything we can to change the dominant culture, to promote growth through education rather than stress.

Earlier, we posited a basic formula: vulnerability to depression and anxiety plus stress leads to a depressive or anxious episode. Some major stressors are early trauma, the loss of a parent, and family conflict. We addressed these stressors in previous chapters, but now we can add the intensity of the college application process to this list. High school students' (and their parents') perceived need to get into a "good college" is a major source of pressure. But who decides what constitutes a good college? Isn't it true that one college may be good for one student and unhealthy for another? Sometimes the process seems to be a branding exercise in which a number of private colleges struggle to attain a high number on the *US World and News Reports* list and a low acceptance rate. This marketing strategy leads parents and competitive students to push full force in their attempts to secure admission to those colleges, and those colleges alone. The Varsity Blues scandal, where wealthy parents committed fraud in collusion with corrupt college coaches to have their children accepted into "elite colleges" is the logical, outrageous (and illegal) culmination of these "get in at all costs" attitudes. Ironically, many of these teens may well have been admitted to numerous colleges on their own merits, and at least one of them didn't even want to go to college because she was already financially successful, independent of her parents. Now the teens have been embarrassed and expelled and some of the parents have spent time in jail.

An experienced college guidance counselor, Scott White, from a competitive high school commented on the college admissions struggle: "Who started it? 'We expect applicants to take the most demanding schedule available to them'? That is the source of one of the most cruel and truly unnecessary abuses of our children. These words send students, so many students, into depression and despair and hopelessness," he wrote in an email to a group of counselors from the National Association for College Admission Counseling. White's email elicited an enormously positive reaction from his peers.

The pressure is not only to take numerous demanding courses but also to create an application to college that "stands out." This has led to an entire industry of college admission coaches, and some "consultants" who will write personal (*sic*) statements for students from wealthy families. I have also seen parents who push their children at a young age toward a specific sport, musical endeavor, or unusual college interest because they think the college they've targeted favors such students. Even if this process does not directly cause depression by itself, the extreme amount of stress on students is certainly unhealthy. At the high school level, we need to challenge, or at least avoid, the cut-throat college admission process. The marketing of students can easily lead to a superficial, false sense of self that may collapse once college begins.

Another factor is that there is no level playing field. We need to acknowledge to our students and ourselves that certain aspects of the college admissions process are arbitrary and, frankly, kind of rigged against the average student. Once, when we took our son on a college tour, the tour guide for some reason decided to share with us the college's need for varsity athletes, legacies, and orchestra members that needed to be filled every application cycle, leaving only a very small number of admission slots that were truly open. This is one reason why so many students I know, despite having excellent academic credentials, were rejected by many colleges. The intense stress seems like a steep price to pay for such limited chances, especially when there are so many other options available that might offer excellent educational and cultural opportunities without the intense and likely unfair competition of certain elite universities. These options include often overlooked lower-profile colleges and state universities with honors programs and specialized areas of study.

Mae is a good example of Scott White's concerns. I first saw Mae with her parents when she was a high school junior. Slim and petite, she played with her shiny black hair as she avoided eye contact. She told me that she was embarrassed by her current situation but did not know what to do. Mae attended a program for gifted teens in a public high school. As Mae's parents described her, she had been an enthusiastic, happy preteen who enjoyed going to church with her family and playing soccer. Mae is Chinese American and has many supports in the community, with an extended family network and weekly cultural events.

When Mae got to high school, however, she focused more on "dressing and dating," but nonetheless continued to study hard and performed in the school orchestra. Always a bit of a perfectionist, she crammed the most demanding AP courses into her schedule. Her parents said that Mae did this on her own, but Mae smiled sadly and said she knew what her parents wanted, and that was to get into an elite college.

At the end of sophomore year, Mae became involved with James and they started spending a lot of time together. Mae told me in private that they had had a sexual relationship and that she was in love with James. Unfortunately, during Thanksgiving break of junior year, James broke up with her with very little explanation. Thus, Mae suffered her first heart-break. She spent a lot of time over the holiday break crying and hanging out with girlfriends. Her parents had never approved of James because he was not Chinese but tried not to say anything. By second semester, Mae was feeling a bit better but stopped doing her homework and her grades began to slip. Her parents' initial reaction was to take her cell phone and driving privileges away and ground her. This led to Mae becoming more iso-lated, and she stopped talking to her parents.

Mae told me that she was just "tired of it all." She knew she had taken on too much but didn't know what to do about it. When we talked in greater depth, I learned that she had some fleeting suicidal thoughts but mainly just felt trapped. I met with Mae's parents and told them that we needed to find a way to reduce the stress. Her parents were initially reluctant because they had been extremely hard workers and had achieved professional suc-cess; her father was a physician and her mother a mathematician. Both of them had a slightly rigid, authoritarian parenting style. To them, Mae's ac-ceptance at a competitive college would guarantee her a better life. I replied that everyone was different, and that Mae was now telling them that the situation was too much for her at the moment. Cutting back now did not mean she would give up on attending a good college.

I suggested that her parents give Mae her cell phone back so that she could stay in touch with her friends. Alone she would spent a lot of time thinking about James. I also suggested that she meet with her high school guidance counselor to see if there was some way to drop one of the extra courses for which she had registered. This was not difficult because it was relatively early in the semester and Mae had taken so many extra courses.

Mae and I then began a course of CBT to help her with her perfectionism and to help her keep her aspirations high, but within a less rigid and demanding schedule. After she came to trust me, I also asked Mae not to take extra courses in the summer but to try and enjoy herself with friends, soccer, and perhaps a part-time job. We also explored the meaning of sexual relationships. Mae had assumed that since she and James were having intercourse, they would have a long-term commitment, certainly into college. I shared that it is better not to make assumptions about relationships but rather to talk about them.

Over time, and with her parents learning more about the negative effects of stress, Mae felt better and even began dating again. She enjoyed taking a summer off, and she and her parents (very reluctantly) decided that she could at least think about a gap year between high school and college. Her parents were reassured that Mae could go through the admission process and then defer for a year, if that was the family's decision.

In many ways, it was fortunate that Mae came to this crisis in high school so that she could have an early intervention before she went to college. I find it disheartening that this precise trajectory takes place so often. You take a happy preteen, throw her into the challenges of adolescence, focus on numerous AP courses, extensive amounts of homework, parental pressure, and then surround her with the additional stress of the college admission process. Very few students escape the pain associated with this process.

WHAT PARENTS CAN DO

Take a Step Back from the Pressure and Look at Your Teen

Changing the college admissions process on a large scale is a complicated task. And it's hard to know where to begin. Given that we, as individual families, have less control over the culture as a whole, and because institutional change is unlikely in the near term, for now we must begin at home. For a start, it is both rewarding and helpful to focus on your student's needs, rather than on a school's pedigree or ranking in *US News and World Reports*. Wouldn't it be better to reverse the process by spending some real time talking with your teen about her aspirations, strengths, needs, and learning style and then find a college that is good match? Wouldn't it be a better idea to replace one of those AP courses with one on reducing stress?

I completely understand the desire for both upward mobility and for your children to receive the best education possible. However, parents can try to resist the temptation of joining this race. It will be difficult, because colleges and the application process form so much of the conversation for parents, and these conversations do not center around the needs of the individual student but get mired in social status. There are many colleges that are overlooked because of the branding exercise described earlier. I think it would be better if we looked at a wide range of colleges with our teens before committing to a very small list.

Mae's parents were challenged by the idea that Mae was stressed and might need a year off. To them the college application process was short-term stress in the hopes of a better future. After first responding with anger, they ultimately saw that the toll taken on their daughter was too much. It was difficult for them to understand but they ultimately accepted Mae's cutting back on her AP courses. Ultimately, the reduction of parental pressure and a slightly easier schedule allowed Mae to regroup, and she did not end up taking a gap year after all.

Think about Their Future

As parents, we also need to acknowledge that the economic situation has changed from when we were young. Even if parents can afford college tuition, for many students, the idea of the liberal arts education followed by graduate school may not be the way to establish a career or even get a job. It is no wonder that many small colleges are eliminating liberal arts majors in favor of science, technology, engineering, and mathematics (STEM), but this trend is tragic to me, because I am a believer in the power of liberal arts as a basis for lifelong education. Moreover, some observers have hypothesized that the heavy investment in STEM isn't even the best preparation for the job market of the future; as phenomena like automation and machine-learning place more and more of the primary production of everything from raw materials to raw data into the hands of machines, businesses may, in the long term, be more likely to require employees with so-called soft skills to interpret raw data, analyze the cultural dimensions of markets, and communicate with one another. These and other critical thinking and communication skills are what the liberal arts teach, and they are precisely what we aren't investing in. That being said, because the shorter-term job market does seem to favor STEM, and because many students and families go into debt in order to afford a college education, it does seem reasonable to research what career paths are usually available to particular majors before committing to them. However, there are no guarantees about the future, so it is also reasonable that students should choose courses that they want to study.

In my state, Rhode Island, we are fortunate now that the state government has enacted the Promise scholarship, making 2 years of in state community college free for all high school graduates. This is an enormous benefit for many families who otherwise could not afford higher education for their children. In the United States, there has been some controversy around the idea of free college for all, but we can start slowly, as we are doing in Rhode Island. At the time of this writing, 17 other states have some sort of free tuition plan and others are actively exploring options.

Be Flexible

Some students are just not ready for college at the end of high school. They may have high levels of cognitive and academic development, but their social development and self-regulation skills may be lagging behind. Many of these students are afraid of talking to their parents about their concerns for fear of disappointing them. I believe that gap years can be extremely beneficial. Some students, like Mae, are so burnt out by academics that they can benefit from a break. There are numerous options, including a part-time job and a course or two at a community college, or a volunteer experience. Some students save their money from work to then take a supervised travel program. Other students' behavior in high school make it clear that they're not ready for college, by drinking too much, coming in late frequently, and not concentrating on academics in high school. For these students, a gap year of work, volunteer work, or part-time education (rather than unsupervised travel, which may make things worse) gives a teen time to learn more about schedules, self-regulation, and responsibility. And it gives them time to grow. I believe that students who have a productive gap year tend to make better use of the opportunities available in college.

WHAT HIGH SCHOOL TEACHERS AND ADMINISTRATORS CAN DO

Many high school teachers have told me that it is difficult for them to reduce the college pressure, not only because students arrive at high school with determination and such strong needs to excel, but also because their parents are pressuring the school, assuming the school's primary responsibility is to get their child into an elite college. However, I think that in terms of values, high school teachers and administrators can encourage students to lead more balanced lives. I would like to see an upper limit on the number of AP courses a student can take and the possibility of a gap year promoted as a positive option. Teachers and administrators can also pay more attention to the students who are very good citizens, and not just the academic or athletic superstars. I am aware that many schools are trying to do just this. Some also have mental health awareness programs and clubs, which is a good first step to creating a culture of support.

Much of the competition over college admissions is a result of the exclusive focus on individual achievement and upward mobility. Victor Schwartz, Chief Medical Officer of The Jed Foundations, points out, "There's a much more radical feeling that you are either a winner or a loser. That puts tremendous pressure on college students and is feeding a lot of the anxiety we're seeing."[1] This anxiety actually starts much earlier and is certainly in place by the teen years.

I would like to see high schools and society in general pay more attention to the common good and collaboration. For this reason, reducing stress at the high school level must involve a zero-tolerance policy toward bullying. I recently spoke to a young man who was short and had been bullied for all of his years in school because of his small stature. He recently transferred to a school that had a zero-tolerance policy toward bullying, led by strong teachers. He suddenly felt like he could go to school with a clear mind and lightness in his heart. It is also worth bearing in mind that bullying in high school is not so much being physically attacked as it is being ostracized, teased, humiliated, and shunned. It is troubling to talk to so many people in their 20s and even 30s whose high school experiences were almost ruined by being bullied. High schools cannot force students to be friends, but they can monitor and discipline those who harm others psychologically. In addition, it's important for high school staff to know that some bullies are very charming to teachers. Bullies often learn the art of deception early on, so it's important for everyone to have "eyes on the ground" and listen carefully to students who come to an adult for help. We also know that some of the bullies have been bullied themselves, so attention to them is a secondary goal. This is a culture we can change, and many schools are doing so.

---

1. Victor Schwartz, cited in in Wolverton, B. As students struggle with stress and depression, colleges act as counselors. *The New York Times,* February 21, 2019.

Remember that the goal of adolescence is developing an identity, or a sense of self. They are going through a process of individuation, or becoming a distinct and unique person. (I am using the word here in a general sense, and not as the technical Jungian term that refers to a much longer and more opaque process that includes unconscious motivation.) We must strive to eliminate those major stressors on teens that interfere with or prevent individuation. When you are not allowed to show aspects of yourself owing to harassment, stigma, or disapproval, growth and mental health will suffer. Some of the examples we have explored in this book are gender nonconformity, racial or ethnic minority status, and feeling trapped by gender roles.

THE SOCIETAL LEVEL

On a larger scale, I believe we should care for all our children, especially those who are marginalized or living in poverty. If I were in charge of national policy, I would refocus resources on creating excellent public schools with strong, well-paid teachers and collaborative efforts with a mental health system for all that focuses on early identification, treatment, and prevention of depression and other psychological conditions.

On a public policy level, 2 years of national service followed by financial support for college makes perfect sense and would have many advantages. Philosopher Martha Nussbaum suggests that we "send [young people] to do work that urgently needs doing all over America: eldercare, childcare, infrastructure work but always sending people into different regions both geographically and economically. . . . The idea that we owe our country some of our work and our time is a very compelling idea if expressed well."[2] Nussbaum adds that this plan accomplishes two goals: "It promotes the common good and exposes young people to the diversity of people and geography of the country." It would also allow emerging adults to mature more before continuing their education. It would create more upward mobility for those who could not afford college otherwise. In *Tribe*, Sebastian Junger, asks, "How do you become an adult in a society that doesn't ask for sacrifice?"[3] There is a historical precedent for national service and tuition assistance; the G.I. Bill was based on a similar idea. Passed in 1944,

2. Martha Nussbaum. *The Monarchy of Fear: A Philosopher Looks at Our Political Crisis.* New York: Simon & Schuster, 2018, p. 242.
3. Sebastian Junger. *Tribe: On Homecoming and Belonging.* New York: Twelve, 2016, p. xiv.

it provided veterans who had seen at least 90 days of active duty and were honorably discharged with tuition for high school, vocational school, or college, as well as other benefits. The benefits were not taxable as income. The GI Bill has been a political and economic success.

I wish for a society where being lesbian, gay or transgender is okay; where being overweight is okay; where having a disability is OK; where teenage girls can be free to embrace their bodies, not strive for some unrealistic ideal; and where teenage boys could have the freedom of emotional expression, not stifle their emotions with repression or alcohol. The good news is that younger generations are more open and accepting of difference. But these generations are not yet in charge, we are.

I also wish for a society where children do not have to fear gun violence when they go to school and fear for their future because of the lack of efforts to stop climate change. And I wish for equal access to all healthcare, including mental health services.

FIGHT TO REDUCE THE STIGMA

Finally, when depression or another mental health problem occurs, we must take it out of the realm of shame. We need to continue the process of destigmatizing mental health conditions. The stigma is one reason that so few teens get treatment, with estimates of only 30–40%. Stigma makes teens feel worse; not only do they suffer from the depression itself, but they are afraid of being humiliated if they reveal their problems. If we could accept depression as medical illness or condition, then young people and their parents would be more open to treatment and we would all benefit.

Some organizations in the United States combating stigma include the National Alliance on Mental Illness (https://www.nami.org), which includes campus chapters and shares anti-stigma information; The Jed Foundation (https://www.jedfoundation.org), which we discussed earlier; the American Foundation for Suicide Prevention, which sponsors Out of the Darkness walks (https://afsp.org/); Make It OK, which helps people have conversations about mental illness (https://makeitok.org); and Active Minds, an organization devoted to supporting mental health awareness and education for students (https://www.activeminds.org).

In response to suicide prevention month in September, Representative Susan Wild of Pennsylvania took to the floor of the US House of Representatives to reveal that the death of her longtime partner was a result of suicide. She called for better mental health treatment and reducing the stigma. "We still have such a stigma in this society, not only about suicide .. but also about mental health care," Wild said. "I felt like if I use my public platform to talk about it, and also if I sort of took . . . the risk of talking about something so personal . . . it would make others feel like it was more accepted to talk about it and to acknowledge, whether it's them or their family member."[4]

In the UK, through their Royal Foundation, the Duke and Duchess of Cambridge and the Duke and Duchess of Sussex (respectively better known as Prince William and Kate Middleton and Prince Harry and Meghan Markle) have supported the Heads Together initiative, to raise awareness about mental health and destigmatize psychological conditions. They have formed a partnership with their Secretary of Defense to include women and men in military service (https://www.headstogether.org.uk). It is, however, noteworthy that Prince William reported that when they began the organization in 2016, not one celebrity offered to join the mental health campaign, confirming the existence of stigma. Another UK-based organization, Time to Change, aims to end mental health discrimination and sponsors a Time to Talk day (https://www.time-to-change.org.uk). Similar organizations exist in Canada, with Mind Your Mind, (https://mindyourmind.ca), in Scotland, with Seeme Scotland (https://www.seemescotland.org), and in many other countries.

WHAT WE CAN ALSO DO

- Monitor and eliminate stigmatizing language. For example, don't say, "Are you crazy?" when you strongly disagree with an idea. Don't describe self-contradictory behavior as "schizophrenic," which is both stigmatizing and an incorrect understanding of schizophrenia. Don't suggest that a depressed person may just be "lazy" or merely needs to "get going!"
- Write letters to the editor when you see stigma, especially in the media.
- Support education about mental health in the schools.
- Advocate for legislation to improve mental health treatment.

DISCONNECTION AND THE EMPATHY GAP

In all education, a real danger of the current environment worldwide is disconnection and an empathy gap. Connection is a basic human need, yet

4. Rachel Bade. Freshman Rep. Wild turns grief from partner's suicide into a new purpose. *Washington Post*, September 8, 2019.

many current social and political forces are pulling us apart and, in some ways, so is the educational system. Teens feel this lack of trust and connection deeply, as they would prefer to be idealistic. The empathy gap is evident when Western cultures minimize the pain of "others" and view them as enemies, creating fear of them. UCLA Professor of Education Pedro Noguera writes, "The crisis of connection, like the empathy gap, can be characterized as a type of myopia in that it distorts our vision and prevents us from seeing the world as a coherent whole. It is also a form of self-centeredness . . . especially when suffering occurs among people of a different race, religion, gender sexual orientation or nationality."[5] A focus on connection would not only offer us closeness to one another but also a more meaningful sense of self in the world and a common sense of humanity. With respect to education, I hope for more collaborative and less competitive educational experiences and more attention to understanding and communicating with the "other." Education should not be just about improvement of the individual but a process for appreciating and learning from a wide variety of sources of knowledge. As Michel Foucault stated, "My job is making windows where there were once walls."[6]

5. Pedro Noguera, in Way, N. Ali, A., Gilligan, C., & Noguera, P. *The Crisis of Connection: Roots, Consequences, and Solutions.* New York: New York University Press, 2018, p. 154.
6. Foucault, M. (1994) An Interview with Simon Riggins in P. Rabinow (Ed.) Michel Foucault: Ethics: The Essential Works. London: Penguin. p. 132.

Depression Checklist*

Most of the day or nearly every day do you feel one or all of the following?

- Sad
- Empty

or

- Angry, cranky, or frustrated, even at minor things

You may also:

- Not be interested in things or activities you used to enjoy.
- Have weight loss when you are not dieting or a change in your appetite.
- Have trouble falling asleep or staying asleep, or sleep much more than usual.
- Move or talk more slowly.
- Feel restless or have trouble sitting still.
- Feel very tired or like you have no energy.
- Feel worthless or very guilty.
- Have trouble concentrating, remembering information, or making decisions.
- Think about dying or suicide.

If you are sad, empty, hopeless, or irritable most of the day for 2 weeks and have checked off more than one or two of the other symptoms, talk to your primary care professional or a mental health professional. If you can't see

* Adapted from *Teen Depression*. National Institute of Mental Health (NIMH), 2015. Retrieved from https://www.nimh.nih.gov/health/publications/teen-depression/index.shtml

someone right away, talk with your family, exercise, schedule a pleasant activity with a friend, get enough sleep, and eat healthy foods.

If you are feeling suicidal, call 1-800-27-TALK ASAP or go to your nearest hospital emergency department.

Remember, depression is

- Not your fault.
- Nothing to be ashamed of.
- Not something you can just "snap out of."
- VERY TREATABLE!

Anxiety Checklists

SOCIAL ANXIETY DISORDER (FORMERLY SOCIAL PHOBIA)*

Do you:

Have a persistent fear of one or more social or performance situations?

Fear or avoid situations with unfamiliar people or potential scrutiny by others?

Fear that you will act in a way (or show anxiety symptoms) that will be embarrassing and humiliating?

And

Have these fears lasted for more than 6 months and interfered with your daily functioning?

GENERALIZED ANXIETY DISORDERS*

Do you:

Worry a lot about everyday issues, school, or sports performances?

Have trouble controlling worries or feelings of nervousness?

Know that you worry much more than you should?

Feel restless and have trouble relaxing?

Have a hard time concentrating?

Feel easily tired or tired all the time?

Tremble or are easily startled, irritable, or "on edge"?

Sweat a lot?

* Adapted from *Anxiety Disorders*. National Institute of Mental Health (NIMH), 2018. Retrieved from https://www.nimh.nih.gov/health/topics/anxiety-disorders/index.shtml

Have to go to the bathroom a lot?

Experience physical symptoms that make it hard to function and that interfere with daily life?

And

Have these fears lasted for at least 6 months and interfered with your daily functioning?

If you answered Yes to several of these questions.

And they have lastered for 6 months or more, talk to your primary care professional or a mental health professional.

APPENDIX 3
LGBTQ Vocabulary*

LGBTQ is shorthand for lesbian, gay, bisexual, transgender, and questioning (or queer). **Questioning** is an identity label for a person who is exploring their sexual orientation or gender identity and is in a state of moratorium in terms of identity formation. **Queer** is an umbrella term that individuals may use to describe a sexual orientation, gender identity, or gender expression that does not conform to dominant societal norms.

Coming out is the process of openly identifying oneself as LGBTQ––first to oneself, and then to others. This is not a one-time event. It is a process and it continues throughout one's lifetime.

"In the closet" means to hide one's identity. To be **"outed"** means to have one's identity exposed by another without consent. According to recent studies, including one by Cornell University, the average coming-out age for a gay or lesbian person in the United States today is around 14 or 15––significantly younger than the average age of 19 to 23 during the late 1970s and early 1980s.

GENDER

Gender refers to the attitudes, feelings, and behaviors that a given culture associates with a person's biological sex. Behavior that is compatible with cultural expectations is referred to as gender-normative; behaviors that are viewed as incompatible with these expectations constitute

* Adapted from *Key Terms and Concepts in Understanding Gender Diversity and Sexual Orientation among Students*. American Psychological Association, Divisions 16 and 44, (2015). Retrieved from https://www.apa.org/pi/lgbt/programs/safe-supportive/lgbt/key-terms.pdf

gender nonconformity. Western society has traditionally recognized two genders, male and female. This is referred to as the **gender binary**.

Cis-gender refers to individuals whose personal identities are in line with the sex (male or female) and the gender identity (boy/man or girl/woman) assigned at birth.

Cross-dresser refers to a person who, for relaxation, fun, sexual gratification, or employment, wears clothing that conflicts with the traditional gender expression of their sex and gender identity. These are very often persons who identify as "straight." *Transvestite* is an outdated term for someone who practices cross-dressing.

Gender-affirming surgery refers to surgery that "affirms" a person's gender by altering their bodily characteristics to better conform to the gender with which they identify. *Sex change* is an outdated term for a basically comparable set of medical procedures.

Gender expression refers to an individual's outward presentation that communicates aspects of their gender identity or gender role, including physical appearance, choice of clothing and accessories, and behavior. Gender expression may or may not conform to a person's gender identity.

Gender identity is a person's *internal* sense of their gender (e.g., *feeling* male, female, or neither). Gender identity doesn't necessarily align with the sex assigned at birth.

Gender nonconforming is an adjective that serves as an umbrella term to describe individuals whose gender expression, gender identity, or gender role differs from gender norms associated with their assigned birth sex.

Intersex is a general term used for a variety of conditions in which a person is born with a reproductive or sexual anatomy that doesn't seem to fit the typical definitions of female or male. Intersex conditions can affect the genitals, the chromosomes, and/or secondary sexual characteristics. *Hermaphrodite* was previously used to describe these individuals, but it is now regarded as an outdated term associated with non-affirming attitudes.

Mx. is the gender-neutral title that some non-gender-binary people, as well those who do not want to be categorized, prefer.

Trans refers to a member of the gender nonconforming community without referring to whether they are transsexual, transgender, etc.

Transgender is an umbrella term for those people whose gender identity, expression, or behavior is different from those typically associated with their assigned sex at birth.

Transition refers to the myriad actions a person may take to transition from one gender to another. These may include social, psychological, and/or medical processes. Transitioning is a complex process that occurs over a long period of time; it is not a one-time event.

Transsexual is an outdated term, originating in the medical and psychological communities, that historically referred to people whose gender identity was not aligned with their sex assigned at birth. Many of these individuals pursue some form of transition.

Two-Spirit is a term used by some Native American people to recognize individuals who possess qualities or fulfill roles of both genders.

SEXUAL ORIENTATION

Asexual describes a person who generally does not experience sexual attraction (or very little) to any group of people.

Bisexuality refers to attraction to people of both sexes.

Gay or lesbian people are primarily attracted to people with the same gender identity as their own.

Heterosexuals are those people whose attraction is primarily to members of the opposite sex; often referred to as "straight."

Pansexual describes a person who experiences sexual, romantic, physical, and/or spiritual attraction for members of all gender identities or expressions.

Same-gender loving is a phrase coined by the African American/Black queer communities used as an alternative for *gay* and *lesbian,* to be more culturally affirming.

RESOURCES

CHAPTER 1
Online Resources
The Jed Foundation and National Alliance on Mental Illness. Starting the conversation: College and your mental health. https://www.jedfoundation.org/wp-content/uploads/2017/11/jed-nami-guide-starting-conversation-college-mental-health.pdf

The Jed Foundation (JED) is a nonprofit organization that exists "to protect emotional health and prevent suicide for our nation's teens and young adults." JED provides programs to support schools, students, families, and communities. In partnership with the Steve Fund, JED has created the Equity in Mental Health Framework (EMH Framework) to help colleges and universities support and strengthen their mental health for students of color.

Maryland Collaborative for Using Evidence-Based Strategies to Reduce College Drinking and Related Problems. http://www.collegeparentsmatter.org/

This site promotes ongoing conversations between college students and parents and includes helpful scripts of conversations.

CHAPTER 2
Books
Lisa Damour. *Untangled: Guiding Teenage Girls through the Seven Stages of Development.* New York: Ballantine, 2017.

Michael Gurian. *Saving Our Sons: A New Path for Raising Healthy and Resilient Boys.* New York: Gurian Institute, 2017.

Frances E, Jensen and Amy Ellis Nutt. *The Teenage Brain: A Neuroscientist's Survival Guide to Raising Adolescents.* New York: Harper, 2015.

David Walsh and Nat Bennett. *Why Do They Act That Way?: A Survival Guide to the Adolescent Brain for You and Your Teen.* New York: Free Press. 2005.

For a Deeper Dive

Jeffrey Jensen Arnett. *Adolescence and Emerging Adulthood.* New York: Oxford University Press, 2006.

Articles
Elan C. Hope, Lori S. Hoggard, and Alvin Thomas. Becoming an adult in the face of racism. *Monitor on Psychology*, June 2016, Vol. 47, No. 6.

Online Resources

The National Institute of Mental Health (NIMH) is a great place to start for all questions about teens and psychological problems: https://www.nimh.nih.gov

Set to Go: https://www.settogo.org/for-families/

A program of The Jed Foundation, settogo.org guides students, families, and high school educators through the social, emotional, and mental health challenges related to the transition from high school to college and adulthood.

CHAPTER 3
Resources for Depression

Books

Dwight L. Evans and Linda Wasmer Andrews. *If Your Adolescent Has Depression or Bipolar Disorder: An Essential Resource for Parents* (Adolescent Mental Health Initiative). New York: Oxford University Press, 2005.

Leanne Rowe, David Bennett, and Bruce Tonge. *I Just Want You to Be Happy: Preventing and Tackling Teenage Depression*. Sydney: Allen and Unwin, 2012.

Michael E. Thase and Susan S. Lang. *Beating the Blues: New Approaches to Overcoming Dysthymia and Chronic Mild Depression*. New York: Oxford University Press, 2004.

Online Resources

Kathryn DeLonge. Adolescent depression. National Institute of Mental Health, 2018. https://www.youtube.com/watch?v=yKABcJcptBI

National Institute of Mental Health. Depression basics, 2016. https://www.nimh.nih.gov/health/publications/depression/index.shtml

University of Michigan Depression Center. Depression Center Toolkit, 2019. https://www.depressioncenter.org/depression-toolkit

Resources for Anxiety

Books

Martin M. Antony and Richard P. Swinson. *The Shyness and Social Anxiety Workbook: Proven, Step-by-Step Techniques for Overcoming Your Fear*. Oakland, CA: New Harbinger Press, 2017.

Gillian Butler. *Overcoming Social Anxiety and Shyness*. London: Constable Robinson 2016.

Edna Foa and Linda Andrews. *If Your Adolescent Has an Anxiety Disorder: An Essential Resource for Parents* (Adolescent Mental Health Initiative). New York: Oxford University Press, 2006.

Harriet Lerner. *The Dance of Fear: Rising Above Anxiety, Fear, and Shame to Be Your Best and Bravest Self*. New York: William Morrow Paperbacks, 2005.

Online Resources

Social Anxiety Support Forum (https://www.socialanxietysupport.com/) offers a number of informative articles discussing social anxiety diagnoses, how to seek treatment, and the different treatment options available. It also hosts a forum where community members can connect with one another for mutual support and to discuss their experiences with social anxiety and its treatment.

The Andrew Kukes Foundation for Social Anxiety (AKFSA; https://akfsa.org) has compiled a library of videos about social anxiety and treatment options on YouTube (https://www.youtube.com/user/AKFSAFoundation/videos) and has developed a diagnostic questionnaire specifically targeted toward adolescents who may suffer from social anxiety (https://akfsa.org/wp-content/uploads/2012/08/Exam_Sufferers_Adolescents.pdf).

The Anxiety and Depression Association of America has developed an online support group, Anxiety and Depression Support (https://healthunlocked.com/anxiety-depression-support/about), which aims to serve as "a safe space for those affected by anxiety and depression to talk to others who truly understand." In addition to hosting online discussions, Anxiety and Depression Support also publishes a free monthly e-newsletter.

CHAPTER 4
Communication

Amy Alamar and Kristine Schlichting. *The Parenting Project: Build Extraordinary Relationships with Your Kids through Daily Conversation*. Beverly, MA: Fair Winds Press, 2018.

Robert Alberti and Michael Emmons. *Your Perfect Right. Assertiveness and Equality in Your Life and Relationships* (10th ed,). Oakland, CA: Impact Press, 2008.

Michelle Skeen, Matthew McKay, Patrick Fanning, and Kelly Skeen. *Communication Skills for Teens: How to Listen, Express, and Connect for Success*. Oakland, CA: New Harbinger, 2016.

Online Resources

American Academy of Pediatrics. Working parents. https://www.healthychildren.org/English/family-life/work-play/Pages/Working-Parents.aspx

Healthychildren.org is the informative and readable website of the American Academy of Pediatrics. This section is for parents who both work outside the home, with suggestions for dividing family responsibilities and avoiding burnout.

Divorce

JoAnne Pedro Carroll. *Putting Children First: Proven Parenting Strategies for Helping Children Thrive through Divorce*. New York: Avery Press, 2010.

Nicholas Long and Rex L. Forehand. *Making Divorce Easier on Your Child: 50 Effective Ways to Help Children Adjust*. New York: McGraw Hill, 2004.

Online Resources

The American Psychological Association (APA) is the major organization for US psychologists. With a motto of "a healthy divorce," the APA provides resources for parents with children going through a divorce: https://www.apa.org/helpcenter/healthy-divorce

CHAPTER 5
Books

Caren Baruch-Feldman. The *Grit Guide for Teens: A Workbook to Help You Build Perseverance, Self-Control, and a Growth Mindset*. Oakland, CA: Instant Help, New Harbinger, 2017.

Angela Duckworth. *Grit: The Power of Passion and Perseverance*. New York: Scribner 2016.

Mary Karapetian Alvord, Bonnie Zucker, and Judy Johnson Grados. *Resilience Builder Program for Children and Adolescents: Enhancing Social Competence and Self-Regulation*. Champaign, IL: Research Press, 2011.

Online Resources
American Academy of Pediatrics. Contribution: Building competence, confidence, connection & character. https://www.healthychildren.org/English/family-life/Community/Pages/Contribution-Building-Competence-Confidence-Connection-Character.aspx

Apps
To stay up to date on all mental health apps, check out https://psyberguide.org/about-psyberguide/, a list created by a nonprofit organization with an excellent scientific advisory board. The guide includes ratings on credibility, user experience, and transparency regarding privacy.

In addition, the American Psychiatric Association offers a guide for you to evaluate apps: https://www.psychiatry.org/psychiatrists/practice/ mental-health-apps/app-evaluation-model

SuperBetter is a game focusing on increasing resilience and the ability to remain strong, optimistic, and motivated when presented with challenging obstacles in life. In game form, the player is challenged to conquer "physical, mental emotional and social" challenges.

CHAPTER 6
Books
Susan Alpers. *Eating Mindfully for Teens*. Oakland CA: Instant Help Books, New Harbinger, 2018.
Michael Pollan. *Food Rules*. New York: Penguin, 2009.
Michael Thompson and Monique A. Thompson. *The Insomnia Workbook for Teens: Skills to Help You Stop Stressing and Start Sleeping Better*. Oakland, CA: Instant Help, New Harbinger, 2018.
Carol Whiteley and Helene A. Emsellem. *Snooze . . . or Lose!: 10 "No-War" Ways to Improve Your Teen's Sleep Habits*. Washington, DC: Joseph Henry Press, 2006.

Online Resources
American Academy of Pediatrics. Fitness for teens. https://www.healthychildren.org/English/ages-stages/teen/fitness/Pages/default.aspx
US Department of Health and Human Services. Adolescent health: Think, Act, Grow® (TAG). https://www.hhs.gov/ash/oah/tag/index.html
WebMD. Get kids moving. https://www.webmd.com/parenting/raising-fit-kids/move/get-teens-moving#1

CHAPTER 7
Books
Alison Macklin. *Making Sense of "It": A Guide to Sex for Teens (and Their Parents, Too!)*. Newburyport, MA: Red Wheel Weiser Conari, 2018.
Al Vernacchio. *For Goodness Sex: Changing the Way We Talk to Teens About Sexuality, Values, and Health*. New York: Harper Wave, 2014.

Online Resources

Alcoholics Anonymous. http://www.aa.org. The website includes a location finder for AA meetings and materials.

Childmind Institute. Co-occurring substance abuse and mental health disorders. Childmind.org. https://childmind.org/guide/parents-guide-to-co-occurring-substance-use-and-mental-health-disorders/

Mayo Clinic. Opiate addiction. https://www.mayoclinic.org/diseases-conditions/prescription-drug-abuse/in-depth/how-opioid-addiction-occurs/art-20360372

National Institute on Drug Abuse (NIDA). Family check-up for drug abuse: Positive parenting prevents drug abuse. https://www.drugabuse.gov/family-checkup

NIDA for Teens. Drug & Health Blog. Snuff it, chew it, hookah pipe it. Tobacco by any other name is still tobacco and it causes cancer. October 19, 2015. https://teens.drugabuse.gov/blog/post/tobacco-by-any-other-name-is-still-tobacco

NIDA for Teens. Drug & Health Blog. The real cost of vaping. October 29, 2018. https://teens.drugabuse.gov/blog/post/real-cost-vaping

NIDA for Teens. Teens: Drug use and the brain. November 26, 2019. https://teens.drugabuse.gov/teens

Office of Adolescent Health, US Department of Health & Human Services. Talking with teens about alcohol. https://www.hhs.gov/ash/oah/resources-and-training/for-families/alcohol/index.html

Planned Parenthood (https://www.plannedparenthood.org/). The Planned Parenthood Federation of America (PPFA) works to support Planned Parenthood health centers across the country, educate the public about reproductive and sexual health, and advocate for policy to expand access to healthcare. PPFA and its affiliates are nonprofit health care organizations. Their website provides up-to-date information about sexual health. They also offer a chat room and email newsletter.

Planned Parenthood. For parents. https://www.plannedparenthood.org/learn/parents

CHAPTER 8
Books

Sheri Dan Dijk. *Don't Let Your Emotions Run Your Life for Teens: Dialectical Behavior Therapy Skills for Helping You Manage Mood Swings, Control Angry Outbursts, and Get Along with Others.* Oakland, CA: New Harbinger, 2011.

Jon Kabat-Zinn. *Full Catastrophe Living: Using the Wisdom of Your Body and Mind to Face Stress, Pain, and Illness.* New York: Delacorte, 1990.

Dean Pederson. *The DBT Deck for Clients and Therapists: 101 Mindful Practices to Manage Distress, Regulate Emotions & Build Better Relationships.* Eau Claire, WI: PESI Publishing, 2019.

This is a card deck with skills and exercises.

Jill H. Rathus and Alec L. Miller. *DBT® Skills Manual for Adolescents* (Foreword by Marcia Linehan). New York: Guilford Press, 2014.

Cindy Goodman Stulberg and Ronald Frey. *Feeling Better: Beat Depression and Improve Your Relationships with Interpersonal Psychotherapy.* San Francisco: New World Library, 2018.

Online Resources

Apps

BUDDHiFY: According to the app's description, there is "no need to find time for a formal meditation session every day; [BUDDHiFY] will show you how to bring mindfulness to all parts of your life—challenges including anxiety, stress, sleep pain, and difficult emotions. Different sessions are aimed for people with various levels of experience."

Calm: Ranked by Apple as one of the best apps of 2018. According to its description, "Learn the life-saving skills of meditation, sleep stories, breathing and master classes."

Headspace: One of the most popular apps. According to its description, "Relax with guided meditations and mindfulness techniques to bring come wellness and balanced to your life in just a few minutes a day."

The Mood Meter: According to its developers at Yale Center for Emotional Intelligence, "the Mood Meter can be used to check in regularly on your feelings, expand your emotional vocabulary and discover the nuances and your feelings. It also helps you notice patterns and learn effective strategies to regulate your feelings." This is one of my favorite apps because it is helpful in so many ways. I am even breaking my rule of preferring free apps because it is not quite free, costs $0.99. We can all use help in identifying emotions from time to time. The Mood Meter is a 2 × 2 figure, color coded, with one scale indicating energy level and the other a scale of pleasant versus unpleasant emotions. When you check the type of emotion you are feeling on the grid of the figure it generates a list of vocabulary words. For example, if you indicate higher energy and negative mood, some of the following words will appear: "frustrated," "tense," "stunned," "angry," "nervous," "restless," "worried," or "irritated." If you are feeling less energetic but positive, some of the words that are generated include "easy-going," " content," " loving," "secure," "satisfied," "grateful," "chilled," "restful," and "blessed." In this way, the user can begin to develop a more precise vocabulary of emotions. In addition, the app will provide strategies to change or maintain these moods, images, and relevant quotations. For example, Emerson's "Nothing can bring you peace but yourself" appears for the positive, calm state.

The Mood Meter is part of the Center's "Anchor Tools" for the evidence-based RULER (for the five skills of emotional intelligence: recognizing, understanding, labeling, expressing, and regulating emotions). The larger program aims to improve emotional intelligence in schools and in the workplace. Research by Nathanson and colleagues suggests that students using RULER have better academic performance, emotional intelligence, and social skills, as well as less anxiety and depression, and their schools have a better academic performance.

Documents

Peter Lewinsohn's Pleasant Events Schedule is available online. It includes directions on how to use the schedule to increase reinforcement and provide distraction, among other things. Available at: https://www.healthnetsolutions.com/dsp/PleasantEventsSchedule.pdf

Videos

Children's Mercy Hospital. Progressive muscle relaxation. https://www.youtube.com/watch?v=ihOO2wUzgkc&t=26s

Jon Kabat-Zinn. Benefits of meditation. https://www.youtube.com/watch?v=wjXXvtGEZQQ

CHAPTER 9
Books
Lucie Hemmen. *The Teen Girl's Survival Guide: Ten Tips for Making Friends, Avoiding Drama, and Coping with Social Stress*. Oakland, CA: The Instant Help Solutions Series, New Harbinger, 2015.

Nancy Jo Sales. *American Girls: Social Media and the Secret Lives of Teenagers*. Deckle Edge, 2016.

Jean Twenge. *iGen: Why Today's Super-Connected Kids Are Growing Up Less Rebellious, More Tolerant, Less Happy—And Completely Unprepared for Adulthood—And What That Means for the Rest of Us*. New York: Atria, 2017.

Niobe Way. *Deep Secrets: Boys' Friendships and the Crisis of Connection*. Cambridge, MA: Harvard University Press, 2013.

Online Resources
American Academy of Child and Adolescent Psychiatry. Bullying resource guide. https://www.aacap.org/aacap/families_and_youth/resource_centers/Bullying_ Resource_Center/Home.aspx

American Academy of Pediatrics. How to make a family media plan. Healthychildren. org https://www.healthychildren.org/English/family-life/Media/Pages/How-to-Make-a-Family-Media-Use-Plan.aspx

Stopbullying.gov. Prevention: Teach kids how to identify bullying and how to stand up to it safely. https://www.stopbullying.gov/

This site provides advice for parents, kids, and schools.

CHAPTER 10
Books
Daniel J. Siegel and Mary Hartzell. *Parenting from the Inside Out: How A Deeper Self-understanding Can Help You Raise Children Who Thrive* (10th Anniversary ed.). New York: Tarcher/Penguin Group, 2014.

CHAPTER 11
Books
David D. Burns. *Feeling Good: The New Mood Therapy*. New York: Harper Books, 1992.

Dennis Greenberger and Christine Padesky. *Mind Over Mood: Change How You Feel by Changing the Way You Think*. New York: Guilford Press, 2015.

Russ Harris. *The Happiness Trap: How to Stop Struggling and Start Living: A Guide to ACT*. Boulder, CO: Trumpeter, 2008.

James O. Prochaska, John Norcross, and Carto Di Clemente. *Changing for Good: A Revolutionary Six-Stage Program for Overcoming Bad Habits and Moving Your Life*. Quill, 2007.

For a Deeper Dive
Ellen Frank (Ed.) and Jessica C Levenson. *Interpersonal Psychotherapy (Theories of Psychotherapy)*. Washington DC: American Psychological Association, 2010.

Steven C. Hayes, Kirk D. Strosahl, and Kelly G. Wilson. *Acceptance and Commitment Therapy: The Process and Practice of Mindful Change* (2nd ed.). New York: Guilford Press, 2008.

Holly Rogers and Margaret Maytan. *Mindfulness for the Next Generation: Helping Emerging Adults Manage Stress and Lead Healthier Lives*. New York: Oxford, University Press, 2012.

Zindel V. Segal, Mark Williams, John Teasdale, and Jon Kabat-Zinn
(Foreword). *Mindfulness-Based Cognitive Therapy for Depression* (2nd ed.).
New York: Guilford Press, 2018.

Myrna M. Weissman, John C. Markowitz, and Gerald Klerman. *The Guide to
Interpersonal Psychotherapy: Updated and Expanded Edition*. New York: Oxford
University Press, 2017.

Apps

Pacifica: An Apple Best of 2017, *Pacifica* is an app for help with "stress anxiety and depression. [It provides] psychologist-designed tools based on CBT and mindfulness."

PTSD Coach was developed by the Veterans Administration and is based on treatment for post-traumatic stress disorder (PTSD). It has many other tools for other symptoms of depression and anxiety, provides education, helps with tracking and managing symptoms, offers positive imagery, and provides ways of getting support.

CHAPTER 12
Books

Brené Brown. *The Gift of Imperfection: Let Go of Who You Think You're Supposed to be and
Embrace Who You Are*. Center City, MN: Hazelden, 2010.

Ann Marie Dobosz. *The Perfectionism Workbook for Teens: Activities to Help You
Reduce Anxiety and Get Things Done*. Oakland, CA: Instant Help, New
Harbinger, 2016.

Christopher Germer. *The Mindful Guide to Self-Compassion: Freeing Yourself from
Destructive Thoughts and Emotions*. New York: Guilford Press, 2009.

William Knaus. *Overcoming Procrastination for Teens: A CBT Guide for College-Bound
Students*. Oakland, CA: Instant Help, New Harbinger, 2016.

Kristen Neff. *Self-Compassion: The Proven Power of Being Kind to Yourself*.
New York: William Morrow, 2015.

For a Deeper Dive

Sarah J. Egan, Tracey D. Wade, Roz Shafran, and Martin M. Antony. *Cognitive-
Behavioral Treatment of Perfectionism*. New York: Guilford Press, 2016.

Online Resources

American Academy of Pediatrics. The problem with perfectionism. https://www.
healthychildren.org/English/ages-stages/young-adult/Pages/The-Problem-
with-Perfectionism.aspx

Jack Kornfield. The tyranny of perfection. https://jackkornfield.com/
tyranny-of-perfection/

CHAPTER 13
LGBTQ Issues

Books

Keith Boykin. *For Colored Boys Who Have Considered Suicide When the Rainbow
Is Still Not Enough: Coming of Age, Coming Out, and Coming Home*.
Minneapolis: Magnus Books, 2012.

Diane Ehrensaft. *The Gender Creative Child: Pathways for Nurturing and Supporting
Children Who Live Outside Gender Boxes*. New York: The Experiment, Workman
Press, 2016.

Michael LaSala. *Coming Out, Coming Home: Helping Families Adjust to a Gay or Lesbian Child*. New York: Columbia University Press, 2010.

Elijah C. Nealy. *Transgender Children and Youth: Cultivating Pride and Joy with Families in Transition*. New York: Norton, 2017.

Dan Savage and Terry Miller (Eds.). *It Gets Better: Coming Out, Overcoming Bullying, and Creating a Life Worth Living*. New York: Dutton, 2011.

Online Resources
The Family Acceptance Project, and its booklet, *Supportive Families, Healthy Children: Helping Families with Lesbian, Gay, Bisexual & Transgender Children*, can be found at http://familyproject.sfsu.edu/publications

The Human Rights Campaign offers a report, *Growing Up LGBT in America*, a groundbreaking survey of more than 10,000 LGBT-identified youth ages 13–17. It provides a stark picture of the difficulties they face. Available at: https://www.hrc.org/youth-report/view-and-share-statistics

PFLAG (Parents, Families and Friends of Lesbians & Gays): https://pflag.org/

Youth Pride: https://www.facebook.com/youthpride

The Trevor Project, online at https://www.thetrevorproject.org, is a suicide prevention program that provides a hotline, education, and support, at 1-866-488-7386.

Weight Issues

Books
Linda Bacon. *Health At Every Size: The Surprising Truth About Your Weight*. Dallas: Ben Bella Books, 2010.

Harriet Brown. *Body of Truth: How Science, History, and Culture Drive Our Obsession with Weight––And What We Can Do about It*. Boston: Da Capo Lifelong Books, 2016.

Jason Lillis, JoAnne Dahl, and Sandra Weineland. *The Diet Trap: Feed Your Psychological Needs and End the Weight Loss Struggle Using Acceptance and Commitment Therapy*. Oakland, CA: New Harbinger, 2014.

Sarai Walker. *Dietland*. New York: Houghton Mifflin Harcourt, 2015.

Online Resources
The Rudd Center at the University of Connecticut http://www.uconnruddcenter.org/ is the best overall resource for treatment, support, and advocacy. They address food policy and offer up-to-date statistics, materials for advocacy and fighting weight stigma, and anti-bias training for healthcare professionals.

Association for Size Diversity and Health (ASDAH), at https://www.sizediversityandhealth.org/content.asp?id=76 provides "ongoing opportunities for development, including educational resources, vetted referral opportunities, and an extensive network of like-minded advocates and professionals." They offer webinars and promote balanced eating and physical activity and weight acceptance.

Obesity Action (OAC), at https://www.obesityaction.org/, describes itself as "a more than 58,000 member-strong, national non-profit organization dedicated to giving a voice to the individual affected by the disease of obesity and helping individuals along their journey toward better health through education, advocacy and support."

Video
Full Frontal with Samantha Bee. Fat people have heads. https://www.youtube.com/watch?v=aD9x7_aFsN0

CHAPTER 14
Online Resources
American Academy of Pediatrics. Mental health care: Who's who." https://www.healthychildren.org/English/healthy-living/emotional-wellness/Pages/Mental-Health-Care-Whos-Who.aspx

More from the American Academy of Pediatrics: These pages describe the training and credentials of mental health professionals.

American Psychological Association (APA). How do I find a good therapist? https://www.apa.org/ptsd-guideline/patients-and-families/finding-good-therapist

The APA makes suggestions as to finding a good psychotherapist and questions to ask ahead of time.

Psychology Today. Therapist finder. https://www.psychologytoday.com/us/therapists

Psychology Today's Therapist Finder can help you identify a licensed psychotherapist and search by location, expertise, gender, and specialization.

The US Substance Abuse and Mental Health Services Administration (SAMHSA) provides a National Helpline, 1-800-662-HELP (4357) (also known as the Treatment Referral Routing Service) or TTY: 1-800-487-4889, that is a confidential, free, 24-hour-a-day, 365-day-a-year, information service, in English and Spanish, for individuals and family members facing mental and/or substance use disorders. This service provides referrals to local treatment facilities, support groups, and community-based organizations. Callers can also order free publications and other information.

CHAPTER 15
Books
Adams Media. *The Infographic Guide to College: A Visual Reference for Everything You Need to Know*. New York: Adams Media, 2017.

Loren Pope. *Colleges That Change Lives: 40 Schools That Will Change the Way You Think about Colleges*. New York: Penguin Books, 2012.

CHAPTER 16
Books
Nora Bradbury-Haehl and Bill McGarvey. *The Freshman Survival Guide: Soulful Advice for Studying, Socializing and Everything in Between*. New York: Hachette Book Group, 2016.

Harlan Cohen. *The Naked Roommate for Parents: Not Calling, Roommates, Relationships, Friends, Finances and Everything Else that Really Matters When Your Child Goes to College*. Naperville, IL: Sourcebook, 2012.

Harlan Cohen. *The Naked Roommate and 107 Other Issues You Might Run Into in College*. Naperville, IL: Sourcebook, 2017.

Online Resources
Web MD and The Jed Foundation: Campus life. https://www.jedfoundation.org/wp-content/uploads/2017/10/WebMD-CampusLife-JED.pdf

WebMD. Preparing your teen for college. https://www.webmd.com/special-reports/prep-teens-college/default.htm

Web MD. Your first year: College students share advice. https://www.webmd.com/special-reports/prep-teens-college/video/video-college-freshmen-advice

Hear from college students on this video about what the first year of college is like.

CHAPTER 17
Books

Stephanie Kaplan Lewis, Annie Chandler Wang, and Windsor Hanger Western. *The Her Campus Guide to College Life, Updated and Expanded Edition: How to Manage Relationships, Stay Safe and Healthy, Handle Stress, and Have the Best Years of Your Life!* Avon, MA: Adams Media, 2019.

Marcia Morris. *The Campus Cure: A Parent's Guide to Mental Health and Wellness for College Students.* Lanham, MD: Rowman & Littlefield, 2018.

Online Resources

Activeminds.org. Active Minds has over 450 Chapters on campuses, with peer-to-peer support and advocacy, raising awareness of mental health issues.

Lean on Me (https://lean0n.me/) is an anonymous student-to-student non-crisis texting support service. The service originated at MIT when, after a string of suicides, a group of students decided to create something to support student mental health on campus.

CHAPTER 18
Books

Kristin M. White. *The Complete Guide to the Gap Year: The Best Things to Do Between High School and College.* New York: Jossey Bass, 2009.

Online Resources

Gap Year Association: https://gapyearassociation.org/research.php

Mental Health America. Taking a leave of absence: What you need to know. http://www.mentalhealthamerica.net/taking-leave-absence-what-you-need-know

Princeton Review. Study abroad. https://www.princetonreview.com/study-abroad/college-abroad/gap-year

CHAPTER 19
Books

William Damon. *The Path to Purpose: How Young People Find Their Calling in Life.* New York: Free Press, 2009.

William Deresiewicz. *Excellent Sheep: The Miseducation of the American Elite and the Way to a Meaningful Life.* New York: Free Press, 2014.

Niobe Way, Carol Gilligan, and Pedro Noguera (Eds.). *The Crisis of Connection: Roots Consequences and Solutions.* New York: New York University Press, 2018.

BIBLIOGRAPHY

Adams, G. C., Balbuena, L., Meng, X., & Asmundson, G. J. G. (2016). When social anxiety and depression go together: A population study of comorbidity and associated consequences. *Journal of Affective Disorders, 206*, 48–54.

Adrian, M., Zeman, J., Erdley, C., Lisa, L., & Sim, L. (2011). Emotional dysregulation and interpersonal difficulties as risk factors for nonsuicidal self-injury in adolescent girls. *Journal of Abnormal Child Psychology, 39*(3), 389–400.

Agochiya, D. (2010). *Life Competencies for Adolescents: Training Manual for Facilitators, Teachers and Parents.* New Delhi: SAGE Publications.

Albers, S. (2018). *Eating Mindfully for Teens: A Workbook to Help You Make Healthy Choices, End Emotional Eating, and Feel Great.* Oakland, CA: New Harbinger.

Albert D., Chen J., & Steinberg L. (2013). The teenage brain: Peer influences on adolescent decision making. *Current Directions in Psychological Science, 22*(2), 114–120.

Allison, R., Bird, E., & McClean, S. (2017). Is team sport the key to getting everybody active, every day? A systematic review of physical activity interventions aimed at increasing girls' participation in team sport. *AIMS Public Health, 4*(2), 202–220.

Alvy, L. (2013). Do lesbian women have a better body image? Comparisons with heterosexual women and model of lesbian-specific factors. *Body Image, 10*(4), 524–534.

Amato, P. (2010). Research on divorce: Continuing trends and new developments. *Journal of Marriage and Family, 72*(3), 650–666.

Amato, P., & Parke, R. D. (2001). Children of divorce in the 1990s: An update of the Amato and Keith (1991) meta-analysis. *Journal of Family Psychology, 15*(3), 355–370.

American Academy of Pediatrics. (2012). The case for eating breakfast. *Healthy Children.* Summer, 2009. Retrieved from https://www.healthychildren.org/English/healthy-living/nutrition/Pages/The-Case-for-Eating-Breakfast.aspx

American Academy of Pediatrics. (2014). Policy statement: School start times for adolescents. *Pediatrics, 134*(3), 642–649.

American Civil Liberties Union–Wisconsin. (2019). ACLU sends demand letter to stop sexual harassment in Kenosha Unified School District. Retrieved from https://www.aclu-wi.org/en/press-releases/aclu-sends-demand-letter-stop-sexual-harassment-wisconsin-school-district

American College Health Association. (2011). Fall 2011 Reference Group executive summary. Retrieved from https://www.acha.org/documents/ncha/ACHA-NCHA-II_ReferenceGroup_ExecutiveSummary_Fall2011.pdf

American Psychiatric Association. (2013). *Diagnostic and Statistical Manual of Mental Disorders* (5th ed.). Arlington, VA: American Psychiatric Publishing.

American Psychological Association. (2018, October 30). APA Stress in America(TM) survey: Generation Z stressed about issues in the news but least likely to vote. *PR Newswire.*

Anderson, N. B. (2012). Guidelines for psychological practice with lesbian, gay, and bisexual clients. *American Psychologist, 67*(1), 10–42.

Anderson, N. B., & Kazak, A. E. (2015). Guidelines for psychological practice with transgender and gender nonconforming people. *American Psychologist, 70*(9), 832–864.

Animosa, L., Lindstrom Johnson, S., & Cheng, T. (2018). "I used to be wild": Adolescent perspectives on the influence of family, peers, school, and neighborhood on positive behavioral transition. *Youth & Society, 50*(1), 49–74.

Ardeatine, M., Niknami, S., Hidarnia, A., & Hajizadeh, E. (2015). Predictors of physical activity among adolescent girl students based on the social cognitive theory. *Journal of Research in Health Sciences, 15*(4), 223–227.

Arnett, J., Reynolds, C. R., & Lilienfeld, S. O. (2018). Getting better all the time: Trends in risk behavior among American adolescents since 1990. *Archives of Scientific Psychology, 6*(1), 87–95.

Ask, H., Torgersen, S., Seglem, K. B., & Waaktaar, T. (2014). Genetic and environmental causes of variation in adolescent anxiety symptoms: A multiple-rater twin study. *Journal of Anxiety Disorders, 28*(4), 363–371.

Assari, S., & Caldwell, C. (2015). Gender and ethnic differences in the association between obesity and depression among black adolescents. *Journal of Racial and Ethnic Health Disparities, 2*(4), 481–493.

Auerbach, R. P., Mortier, P., Bruffaerts, R., Alonso, J., Benjet, C., Cuijpers, P., . . . WHO WMH-ICS Collaborators. (2018). WHO World Mental Health Surveys International College Student Project: Prevalence and distribution of mental disorders. *Journal of Abnormal Psychology, 127*(7), 623–638.

Auerbach, R. P., Webb, C. A., & Stewart J. G. (2016). *Cognitive Therapy for Depressed Adolescents: A Practical Guide to Management and Treatment.* New York: Routledge.

Azevedo, V., Simoes, S., Marques, M., Cunha, H., Santo, V., & Espirito Santo, S. (2013). The role of parental rearing styles in the perception of college adolescents' anxiety symptoms. *European Psychiatry, 28*(Suppl. 1), 1.

Ball, L. (2010). Profile: Carol Gilligan. *Psychology's Feminist Voices.* Retrieved from http://www.feministvoices.com/carol-gilligan/

Bámaca-Colbert, M., Umaña-Taylor, A., Gayles, J., & Eccles, J. (2012). A developmental-contextual model of depressive symptoms in Mexican-origin female adolescents. *Developmental Psychology, 48*(2), 406–421.

Bandura, A. (1964). The stormy decade: Fact or fiction? *Psychology in the Schools, 1*(3), 224–231.

Bandura, A. (1988). Self-efficacy conception of anxiety. *Anxiety Research, 1*(2), 77–98.

Bandura, A. (1991). Social cognitive theory of moral thought and action. In W. M. Kurtines & J. Gewirtz (Eds.), *Handbook of Moral Development, Vol. 1.* Mahwah, NJ: Erlbaum.

Bandura, A. (2002). Parenting and children's prosocial and moral development. In M. H. Bornstein (Ed.), *Handbook of Parenting* (2nd ed.). Mahwah, NJ: Erlbaum.

Bandura, A., & Schunk, D. H. (1981). Cultivating competence, self-efficacy, and intrinsic interest through proximal self-motivation. *Journal of Personality and Social Psychology, 41*(3), 586–598.

Barlow, D. H. (2000). Unraveling the mysteries of anxiety and its disorders from the perspective of emotion theory. *American Psychologist, 55*(11), 1247–1263.

Baumrind, D., & Black, A. (1967). Socialization practices associated with dimensions of competence in preschool boys and girls. *Child Development, 38*(2), 291–327.

Beardselee, W. R., Versage, E. E., & Giadstone, T. R. G. (1998). Children of affectively ill parents: A review of the past 10 years. *Journal of the American Academy of Child & Adolescent Psychiatry, 37*(11), 1134–1141.

Becker, S. P., Jarrett, M. A., Luebbe A. M., Garner, A. A., et al. (2018). Sleep in a Large, Multi-University Sample of College Students: Sleep Problem Prevalence, Sex Differences, and Mental Health Correlates. *Sleep Health, 4*(2), 174–181.

Belle, B., Belle, D., Bernard, J., Stress Families Project, & Institute for the Study of Contemporary Social Problems. (1982). *Lives in Stress: Women and Depression* (Sage Focus Editions, Vol. 45). Beverly Hills, CA: Sage Publications.

Bennett, K., Manassis, K., Duda, S., Bagnell, A., Bernstein, G., Garland, E., . . . Wilansky, P. (2015). Preventing child and adolescent anxiety disorders: Overview of systematic reviews. *Depression and Anxiety, 32*(12), 909–918.

Berge, J., Winkler, M., Larson, N., Miller, J., Haynos, A., & Neumark-Sztainer, D. (2018). Intergenerational transmission of parent encouragement to diet from adolescence into adulthood. *Pediatrics, 141*(4), e20172955.

Bersamin, M., Zamboanga, B., Schwartz, S., Donnellan, M., Hudson, M., Weisskirch, R., . . . Caraway, S. (2014). Risky business: Is there an association between casual sex and mental health among emerging adults? *Journal of Sex Research, 51*(1), 43–51.

Bevan Jones, R., Thapar, A., Rice, F., Beeching, H., Cichosz, R., Mars, B., . . . Simpson, S. A. (2018). A web-based psychoeducational intervention for adolescent depression: Design and development of mood. *JMIR Mental Health, 5*(1), E13.

Biddle, S. J., Braithwaite, R., & Pearson, N. (2014). The effectiveness of interventions to increase physical activity among young girls: A meta-analysis. *Preventive Medicine, 62*(05-01), 3119–3131.

Birmaher, B., & Brent, D. (2007). Practice parameter for the assessment and treatment of children and adolescents with depressive disorders. *Journal of the American Academy of Child & Adolescent Psychiatry, 46*(11), 1503–1526.

Blanco, C., Okuda, M., Wright, C., Hasin, D., Grant, B., Liu, S., & Olfson, M. (2008). Mental health of college students and their non–college-attending peers: Results from the National Epidemiologic Study on Alcohol and Related Conditions. *Archives of General Psychiatry, 65*(12), 1429–1437.

Blease, C. (2015). Too many "friends," too few "likes"? Evolutionary psychology and "Facebook depression". *Review of General Psychology, 19*(1), 1–13.

Bouris, A., Everett, B., Heath, R., Elsaesser, C., & Neilands, T. (2016). Effects of victimization and violence on suicidal ideation and behaviors among sexual minority and heterosexual adolescents. *LGBT Health, 3*(2), 153–161.

Breslau, J., Gilman, S., Stein, B., Ruder, T., Gmelin, T., & Miller, E. (2017). Sex differences in recent first-onset depression in an epidemiological sample of adolescents. *Translational Psychiatry, 7*(5), E1139.

Breslau, N., Schultz, L., & Peterson, E. (1995). Sex differences in depression: A role for preexisting anxiety. *Psychiatry Research, 58*(1), 1–12.

Brice, C., Masia-Warner, C., Okazaki, S., Ma, P., Sanchez, W., Esseling, A., & Lynch, P. (2015). Social anxiety and mental health service use among Asian American high school students. *Child Psychiatry & Human Development, 46*(5), 693–701.

Briesmeister, J., & Schaefer, C. (2007). *Handbook of Parent Training: Helping Parents Prevent and Solve Problem Behaviors.* Hoboken, NJ: John Wiley & Sons.

Broderick, P. C. (2013). *Learning to Breathe: A Mindfulness Curriculum for Adolescents to Cultivate Emotion Regulation, Attention, and Performance.* Oakland, CA: New Harbinger.

Broderick, P. C., Jennings, P., & Malti, T. (2012). Mindfulness for adolescents: A promising approach to supporting emotion regulation and preventing risky behavior. *New Directions for Youth Development, 136,* 111–126.

Bronfenbrenner, U. (1979). *The Ecology of Human Development: Experiments by Nature and Design.* Cambridge, MA: Harvard University Press.

Brown, G. W., & Harris T. (1978). *Social Origins of Depression: A Study of Psychiatric Disorders in Women.* London: Tavistock.

Bruni, F. (2016). *Where You Go Is Not Who You'll Be: An Antidote to the College Admissions Mania Paperback.* New York: Grand Central Publishing.

Buboltz, W. C., Brown, F., & Soper, B. (2001). Sleep habits and patterns of college students: A preliminary study. *Journal of American College Health, 50*(3), 131–135.

Buechner, S. D. (2018). Transgender issues. Retrieved from http://saradavisbuechner. com/transgender-issues/

Burnette, J., Davisson, E., Finkel, E., Van Tongeren, D., Hui, C., & Hoyle, R. (2014). Self-control and forgiveness: A meta-analytic review. *Social Psychological and Personality Science, 5*(4), 443–450.

Burrus, B., Krieger, K., Rutledge, R., Rabre, A., Axelson, S., Miller, A., . . . Jackson, C. (2018). Building bridges to a brighter tomorrow: A systematic evidence review of interventions that prepare adolescents for adulthood. *American Journal of Public Health, 108*(S1), S25–S31.

Campbell, T., & Campbell, D. (1997). Faculty/student mentor program: Effects on academic performance and retention. *Research in Higher Education, 38*(6), 727–742.

Campos, B., & Kim, H. (2017). Incorporating the cultural diversity of family and close relationships into the study of health. *American Psychologist, 72*(6), 543–554.

Cara, E. (2016, August 3). Depression and anxiety symptoms: How mental health disorders affect the human body. *Medical Daily.* Retrieved from https://www. medicaldaily.com/depression-and-anxiety-symptoms-how-mental-health-disorders-affect-human-body-393713

Center on Addiction. (2009). CASA 2009 teen survey reveals: Teens likelier to get drunk, use marijuana, smoke cigarettes if they see parent drunk. Retrieved from https://www.centeronaddiction.org/newsroom/press-releases/ 2009-teen-survey-xiv

Centers for Disease Control and Prevention. (2018). Obesity & overweight. Retrieved from https://www.cdc.gov/obesity/index.html

Centers for Disease Control and Prevention, CDC Healthy Schools. (2018). Physical activity facts. Retrieved from https://www.cdc.gov/healthyschools/ physicalactivity/facts.htm

Chand, S. P., Ravi, C., Chakkamparambil, B., Prasad, A., & Vora, A. (2018). CBT for depression: What the evidence says. *Current Psychiatry*, *17*(9), 14–55.

Chen, E., Brody, G., Miller, G., Kazak, A. E., & Smith, T. W. (2017). Childhood close family relationships and health. *American Psychologist*, *72*(6), 555–566.

Cherry, K. (2018, November 22). 10 influential psychologists. *Very Well Mind*. Retrieved from https://www.verywellmind.com/most-influential-psychologists-2795264

Cheung, A., Zuckerbrot, R., Jensen, P., Laraque, D., & Stein, R. (2018). Guidelines for adolescent depression in primary care (GLAD-PC): Part II. Treatment and ongoing management. *Pediatrics*, *141*(3), e20174082.

Chickering, A., & Reisser, L. (1993). *Education and Identity* (2nd ed.). San Francisco: Jossey-Bass.

Choi, E., & Choi, I. (2016). The associations between body dissatisfaction, body figure, self-esteem, and depressed mood in adolescents in the United States and Korea: A moderated mediation analysis. *Journal of Adolescence*, *53*, 249.

Clark, L., & Watson, D. (1991). Tripartite model of anxiety and depression: Psychometric evidence and taxonomic implications. *Journal of Abnormal Psychology*, *100*(August), 316–336.

Clarke, G., & Harvey, A. G. (2012). The complex role of sleep in adolescent depression. *Child and Adolescent Psychiatric Clinics of North America*, *21*(2), 385–400.

Conklin, A. J., Yao, C. A., & Richardson, C. G. (2018). Chronic sleep deprivation and gender-specific risk of depression in adolescents: A prospective population-based study. *BMC Public Health*, *18*(1), 1–7.

Conley, C. S., Travers, L. V., & Bryant, F. B. (2013). Promoting psychosocial adjustment and stress management in first-year college students: The benefits of engagement in a psychosocial wellness seminar. *Journal of American College Health*, *61*(2), 75–86.

Conway, J. (1994). *True North: A Memoir*. New York: Alfred A. Knopf.

Cornelius, J. B., & Clark, D. B. (2008). Depressive disorders and adolescent substance use disorders. In Y. Kaminer (Ed.), *Adolescent Substance Abuse: A Comprehensive Guide to Theory and Practice* (pp. 222–242). New York: Springer Science.

Costello, E., Mustillo, S., Erkanli, A., Keeler, G., & Angold, A. (2003). Prevalence and development of psychiatric disorders in childhood and adolescence. *Archives of General Psychiatry*, *60*(8), 837–844.

Crone, E., & Konijn, E. (2018). Media use and brain development during adolescence. *Nature Communications*, *9*(1), 588.

Cross, T. L. (2013). Uncharted territory: Growing up gifted amid a culture of social media. *Gifted Child Today*, *36*(2), 144–145.

Cuijpers, P., Beekman, A. T. F., & Reynolds, C. F. (2012). Evaluation of a group cognitive-behavioral depression prevention program for young adolescents: A randomized effectiveness trial, *JAMA*, *307*(10), 1033–1034.

Cuijpers, P., Munoz, R. F., Clarke, G. N., & Lewinsohn, P. M. (2009). Psychoeducational treatment and prevention of depression: The "Coping with Depression" course thirty years later. *Clinical Psychology Review*, *29*(5), 449–458.

Cuijpers, P., Weitz, E., Karyotaki, E., Garber, J., & Andersson, G. (2015). The effects of psychological treatment of maternal depression on children and parental functioning: A meta-analysis. *European Child & Adolescent Psychiatry*, *24*(2), 237–245.

Cummings, C., Caporino, N., Kendall, P., & Hinshaw, S. P. (2014). Comorbidity of anxiety and depression in children and adolescents: 20 years after. *Psychological Bulletin, 140*(3), 816–845.

Cuncic, A. (2018). Treating social anxiety disorder with interpersonal therapy. Retrieved from https://www.verywellmind.com/interpersonal-therapy-for-social-anxiety-3024897

Curran, T., & Hill, A. (2019). Perfectionism is increasing over time: A meta-analysis of birth cohort differences from 1989 to 2016. *Psychological Bulletin, 145*(4),410–429.

Dacher, E. S. (2014). A brief history of mind-body medicine. *International Journal of Transpersonal Studies, 33*(1), 148–157.

Dassen, F., Houben, K., & Jansen, A. (2015). Time orientation and eating behavior: Unhealthy eaters consider immediate consequences, while healthy eaters focus on future health. *Appetite, 91*, 13–19.

Dastagir, A. (2017, March 31). Men pay a steep price when it comes to masculinity. *USA Today.* Retrieved from https://www.usatoday.com/story/news/2017/03/31/masculinity-traditional-toxic-trump-mens-rights/99830694/

Deblois, M., & Kubzansky, L. (2015). Childhood self-regulatory skills predict adolescent smoking behavior. *Psychology, Health & Medicine, 21*(2), 1–14.

Degges-White, S., & Borzumato-Gainey, C. (2013). *College Student Mental Health Counseling: A Developmental Approach*. New York: Springer.

Del Vecchio, P. (2018). The good news about preventing adolescent depression. *Prevention Science, 19*(Suppl. 1), S112–S114.

Deresiewicz, W. (2011). *The Death of Friendship*. Newbury, NH: New Word City.

Derubeis, R., Hollon, S., Amsterdam, J., Shelton, R., Young, P., Salomon, R., . . . Gallop, R. (2005). Cognitive therapy vs. medications in the treatment of moderate to severe depression. *Archives of General Psychiatry, 62*(4), 409–416.

Dewey, J. (1897). My pedagogic creed. *School Journal, 54*, 77–80.

Dewey, J. (1998). Analysis of reflective thinking. In L. A. Hickman & T. M. Alexander (Eds.), *The Essential Dewey: Vol. 2. Ethics, Logic, Psychology*. Bloomington: Indiana University Press. pp. 137–144.

Dickson, J., & Moberly, M. (2013). Goal internalization and outcome expectancy in adolescent anxiety. *Journal of Abnormal Child Psychology, 41*(3), 389–397.

Draper, C., Grobler, L., Micklesfield, L., & Norris, S. (2015). Impact of social norms and social support on diet, physical activity and sedentary behaviour of adolescents: A scoping review. *Child: Care, Health and Development, 41*(5), 654–667.

Dreisbach, S. (2011, February 3). Shocking body-image news: 97% of women will be cruel to their bodies today. *Glamour.* Retrieved from https://www.glamour.com/story/shocking-body-image-news-97-percent-of-women-will-be-cruel-to-their-bodies-today

Dreisbach, S. (2014, October 9). How do you feel about your body? *Glamour.* Retrieved from https://www.glamour.com/story/body-image-how-do-you-feel-about-your-body

Duke, M. (2012, October 7). Starting college: A guide for parents. *Huffington Post.* Retrieved from https://www.huffingtonpost.com/marshall-p-duke/college-guide_b_1750951.html

Dulaney, E. S., Graupmann, V., Grant, K. E., Adam, E. K., & Chen, E. (2018). Taking on the stress-depression link: Meaning as a resource in adolescence. *Journal of Adolescence, 65*, 39–49.

Dweck, C. (2016). *Mindset: The New Psychology of Success*. New York: Random House.

Dyson, F. (1988). *Infinite in All Directions: Gifford Lectures Given at Aberdeen, Scotland, April–November 1985* (1st ed., Gifford lectures, 1985). New York: Harper & Row.

Egan, S. J., Wade, T. D., & Shafran, R. (2011). Perfectionism as a transdiagnostic process: A clinical review. *Clinical Psychology Review*, 31(2), 203–212.

Ehrenreich-May, J., Kennedy, S., Sherman, J., Bennett, S., & Barlow, D. (2017). *Unified Protocol for Transdiagnostic Treatment of Emotional Disorders in Adolescents: Workbook*. New York: Oxford University Press.

Enns, M., Cox, B., & Clara, I. (2002). Adaptive and maladaptive perfectionism: Developmental origins and association with depression proneness. *Personality and Individual Differences*, 33(6), 921–935.

Enns, M., Cox, B., Sareen, J., & Freeman, P. (2001). Adaptive and maladaptive perfectionism in medical students: A longitudinal investigation. *Medical Education*, 35(11), 1034–1042.

Erikson, E. H. (1959). *Identity and the Life Cycle: Selected Papers*. Oxford: International Universities Press.

Erikson, E. H. (1966). Eight ages of man. *International Journal of Psychiatry*, 2(3), 281–307.

Evans, D., & Andrews, L. W. (2005). *If Your Adolescent Has Depression or Bipolar Disorder: An Essential Resource for Parents*. New York: Oxford University Press.

Evans, D., Foa, E., Gur, R., Hendin, H., O'Brien, C., Seligman, M., & Walsh, B. (2005). *Treating and Preventing Adolescent Mental Health Disorders* (1st ed.). New York: Oxford University Press.

Fagan. K. (2017). *What Made Maddy Run: The Secret Struggles and Tragic Death of an All-American Teen*. New York: Little Brown.

Ferrari, M., Yap, K., Scott, N., Einstein, D., Ciarrochi, J., & Van Amelsvoort, T. (2018). Self-compassion moderates the perfectionism and depression link in both adolescence and adulthood. *PLoS ONE*, 13(2), e0192022.

Fife, J., Svetaz, M., & Allen, M. (2018). Assessing multicultural parenting values and practices in prevention programs for Latino youth. *Journal of Youth Development*, 13(3), 61–75.

Fish, J., Pollitt, A., Schulenberg, J., & Russell, S. (2018). Measuring alcohol use across the transition to adulthood: Racial/ethnic, sexual identity, and educational differences. *Addictive Behaviors*, 77, 193.

Fisher, M., Worth, K., Garcia, J., & Meredith, T. (2012). Feelings of regret following uncommitted sexual encounters in Canadian university students. *Culture, Health & Sexuality*, 14(1), 45–57.

Fitts, S., Gibson, P., Redding, C., & Deiter, P. (1989). Body dysmorphic disorder: Implications for its validity as a DSM-III-R clinical syndrome. *Psychological Reports*, 64(2), 655–658.

Flannery, K., Vannucci, A., & Ohannessian, C. (2018). Using time-varying effect modeling to examine age-varying gender differences in coping throughout adolescence and emerging adulthood. *Journal of Adolescent Health*, 62(3S), S27–S34.

Foret, M. M., Scult, M., Wilcher, M., Chudnofsky, R., Malloy, L., Hasheminejad, N., & Park, E. R. (2012). Integrating a relaxation response-based curriculum into a public high school in Massachusetts. *Journal of Adolescence*, 35(2), 325–332.

Franki, L. (2018). Female to male transgender teens most likely to attempt suicide. *Pediatric News*, 52(10), 2.

Friedrichs, E. (2017, September 18). What is the average age to come out? *Live About*. Retrieved from https://www.liveabout.com/what-is-the-average-age-to-come-out-1415428

Frost, H., Campbell, P., Maxwell, M., O'Carroll, R. E., Dombrowski, S. U., Williams, B., . . . Pollock, A. (2018). Effectiveness of motivational interviewing on adult behaviour change in health and social care settings: A systematic review of reviews. *PLoS ONE, 13*(10), e0204890.

Fuligni, A., Pedersen, S., & Dannemiller, J. L. (2002). Family obligation and the transition to young adulthood. *Developmental Psychology, 38*(5), 856–868.

Galla, B. (2016). Within-person changes in mindfulness and self-compassion predict enhanced emotional well-being in healthy, but stressed adolescents. *Journal of Adolescence, 49*(C), 204–217.

Garcia, J., Reiber, C., Massey, S., Merriwether, A., Candland, D. K., Fisher, M. L., & Salmon, C. (2012). Sexual hookup culture: A review. *Review of General Psychology, 16*(2), 161–176.

Gaultney, J. F. (2010). The prevalence of sleep disorders in college students: Impact on academic performance. *Journal of American College Health, 59*(2), 91–97.

Geisner, I., Mallett, K., Varvil-Weld, L., Ackerman, S., Trager, B., & Turrisi, R. (2018). An examination of heavy drinking, depressed mood, drinking related constructs, and consequences among high-risk college students using a person-centered approach. *Addictive Behaviors, 78*, 22.

Gibbs, N. (2006, June 4). The magic of the family meal. *Time*. Retrieved from http://content.time.com/time/magazine/article/0,9171,1200760,00.html

Gillham, J. E., Reivich, K. J., Brunwasser, S. M., Freres, D. R., Chajon, N. D., Kash-MacDonald M., . . . Seligman, M. E. P. (2012). Evaluation of a group cognitive-behavioral depression prevention program for young adolescents: A randomized effectiveness trial. *Journal of Clinical Child and Adolescent Psychology, 41*(5), 621–639.

Gilligan, C. (1982). *In a Different Voice*. Cambridge, MA: Harvard University Press.

Gillison, F. B., Standage, M., & Skevington, S. M. (2011). Motivation and body-related factors as discriminators of change in adolescents' exercise behavior profiles. *Journal of Adolescent Health, 48*(1), 44–51.

Gladstone, T. R. G., Beardslee, W. R., & O'Connor, E. E. (2011). The prevention of adolescent depression. *Psychiatric Clinics of North America, 34*(1), 35–52.

Goniu, N., & Moreno, M. (2013). Increased risk for anxiety among college students with ADHD. *Journal of Adolescent Health, 52*(2), S81.

Goodyer, I. (2018). Editorial perspective: Antidepressants and the depressed adolescent. *Child and Adolescent Mental Health, 23*(3), 137–140.

Gopnik, A. (2016). *The Carpenter and the Gardener*. New York: Farrar, Straus and Giroux.

Gosselink, C., Cox, D., Mcclure, S., & De Jong, M. (2008). Ravishing or ravaged: Women's relationships with women in the context of aging and Western beauty culture. *International Journal of Aging and Human Development, 66*(4), 307–327.

Gottman, J., & Silver, N. (1999). *The Seven Principles for Making Marriage Work*. New York: Three Rivers Press.

Grello, C., Welsh, D., & Harper, M. (2006). No strings attached: The nature of casual sex in college students. *Journal of Sex Research, 43*(3), 255–267.

Gross, J., Salovey, P., Rosenberg, E. L., & Fredrickson, B. L. (1998). The emerging field of emotion regulation: An integrative review. *Review of General Psychology*, 2(3), 271–299.

Gross, T. (2007, July 19). Adam Shankman, putting new moves on "Hairspray" [Interview]. *Fresh Air*. Retrieved from https://www.npr.org/templates/story/story.php?storyId=12093815

Gross, T. (2018, March 30). For Bill Hader, sketch comedy sprung from a "need to be doing something creative" [Interview]. *Fresh Air*. Retrieved from https://www.npr.org/2018/03/30/597972897/for-bill-hader-sketch-comedy-sprung-from-a-need-to-be-doing-something-creative

Guttmacher Institute. (2017). Adolescent sexual and reproductive health in the United States. Retrieved from https://www.guttmacher.org/sites/default/files/factsheet/adolescent-sexual-and-reproductive-health-in-united-states.pdf

Häberling I., Baumgartner, N., Emery, S., Keller, P., Strumberger, M., et al. (2019). Anxious depression as a clinically relevant subtype of pediatric major depressive disorder. *Journal of Neural Transmission*, 126(9), 1217–1230.

Hadland, S. E., & Harris, S. K. (2014). Youth marijuana use: State of the science for the practicing clinician. *Current Opinion in Pediatrics*, 26(4), 420–427.

Hall, G. (1904). *Adolescence: Its Psychology and Its Relations to Physiology, Anthropology, Sociology, Sex, Crime, Religion and Education* (Francis A. Countway Library of Medicine–Medical Heritage Library digitization project). New York: D. Appleton and Company.

Han, B., Compton, W., Eisenberg, D., Milazzo-Sayre, L., McKeon, R., & Hughes, A. (2016). Prevalence and mental health treatment of suicidal ideation and behavior among college students aged 18–25 years and their non–college-attending peers in the United States. *Journal of Clinical Psychiatry*, 77(06), 815–824.

Hermann, K. M., Benoit, E. N., Zavadil, A. (2013). The myriad faces of college student development. In S. Degges-White & C. Borzumato-Gainey (Eds.), *College Student Mental Health Counseling: A Developmental Approach*. New York: Springer.

Herring, M. P., O'Connor, P. J., & Dishman, R. K. (2014). Self-esteem mediates associations of physical activity with anxiety in college women. *Medicine & Science in Sports & Exercise*, 46(10), 1990–1998.

Hewitt, P., Flett, G., & Mineka, S. (1991). Dimensions of perfectionism in unipolar depression. *Journal of Abnormal Psychology*, 100(1), 98–101.

Hill, N., Wang, M., & Eccles, J. S. (2015). From middle school to college: Developing aspirations, promoting engagement, and indirect pathways from parenting to post high school enrollment. *Developmental Psychology*, 51(2), 224–235.

Himmelstein, M., Incollingo Belsky, A., & Tomiyama, A. (2015). The weight of stigma: Cortisol reactivity to manipulated weight stigma. *Obesity*, 23(2), 368–374.

Hoffman, E. (2003). *The Wisdom of Carl Jung*. London: Kensington Publishing Corporation, Citadel Press.

Hoffman, P. D., Fruzzetti, A. E., Buteau, E., Emily R., Neiditch, E. R., Penney D., Bruce, M. L., Hellman F., & Struening, E. (2005). Family Connections: A Program for Relatives of Persons With Borderline Personality Disorder. *Family Process*, 44(2), 217–225.

Holland, G., & Tiggemann, M. (2016). A systematic review of the impact of the use of social networking sites on body image and disordered eating outcomes. *Body Image*, 17, 100–110.

Hollon, S. (2003). Does cognitive therapy have an enduring effect? *Cognitive Therapy and Research*, 27(1), 71–75.

Holt-Lunstad, J., Robles, T., Sbarra, D., Kazak, A. E., & Smith, T. W. (2017). Advancing social connection as a public health priority in the United States. *American Psychologist*, 72(6), 517–530.

Horowitz, J., & Graf, N. (2019). Most U.S. teens see anxiety and depression as a major problem among their peers. Pew Research Center. Retrieved from https://www.pewsocialtrends.org/2019/02/20/most-u-s-teens-see-anxiety-and-depression-as-a-major-problem-among-their-peers/

Hurrelmann, K. (1990). Health promotion for adolescents: Preventive and corrective strategies against problem behavior. *Journal of Adolescence*, 13(3), 231–250.

Hyde, L. (1998). *Trickster Makes this World: Mischief, Myth, and Art*. New York: Farrar, Straus and Giroux.

Jackson, C., Geddes, R., Haw, S., & Frank, J. (2012). Interventions to prevent substance use and risky sexual behaviour in young people: A systematic review. *Addiction*, 107(4), 733–747.

Jackson, C., Henderson, M., Frank, J., & Haw, S. (2012). An overview of prevention of multiple risk behaviour in adolescence and young adulthood. *Journal of Public Health*, 34(Suppl. 1), I31–I40.

Jackson, P. (1968). *Life in Classrooms*. New York: Holt, Rinehart and Winston.

Jahren, H. (2016). *Lab Girl*. New York: Alfred A. Knopf.

Jakobsen, J. C., Hansen, J. L., Simonsen, S., Simonsen, E., & Gluud, C. (2012). Effects of cognitive therapy versus interpersonal psychotherapy in patients with major depressive disorder: A systematic review of randomized clinical trials with meta-analyses and trial sequential analyses. *Psychological Medicine*, 42(7), 1343–1357.

Jaschi, S. (2018, January 15). Are colleges pushing students to do too much in high school? *Inside Higher Ed*. Retrieved from https://www.insidehighered.com/admissions/article/2018/01/15/counselor-issues-critique-college-admissions-demands-are-pushing-high

Jed Foundation. (2006). MTV Network increasing mental health awareness at college campuses. Retrieved from https://www.jedfoundation.org/mtv-network-increasing-mental-health-awareness/

Jennings, A. (2010, October 21). Drunkorexia: Alcohol mixes with eating disorders. *ABC News*. Retrieved from https://abcnews.go.com/Health/drunkorexia-alcohol-mixes-eating-disorders/story?id=11936398

Johnson, A. B., & Wong-Bailey, H. (2019). Busted: The model minority myth and mental health—Understanding Asian and Asian-American college students. Presented at the Eighteenth Annual Diversity Challenge Making Race and Culture Work in the STEM Era: Bringing all People to the Forefront, Boston College, Boston, MA, October 19, 2019.

Johnson, K., & Taliaferro, L. (2011). Relationships between physical activity and depressive symptoms among middle and older adolescents: A review of the research literature. *Journal for Specialists in Pediatric Nursing*, 16(4), 235–251.

Junger, S. (2016). *Tribe: On Homecoming and Belonging*. New York: Twelve.

Juvonen, J., & Graham, S. (2014). *Peer Harassment in School: The Plight of the Vulnerable and Victimized*. New York: Guilford Press.

Kabat-Zinn, J. (2013). *Full Catastrophe Living: Using the Wisdom of Your Body and Mind to Face Stress, Pain, and Illness* (Revised and updated ed.). New York: Bantam Books.

Kadison, R., & DiGeronimo, T. (2004). *College of the Overwhelmed: The Campus Mental Health Crisis and What To Do about It.* San Francisco: Jossey-Bass.

Karasz, P. (2019, January 24). In Davos, Prince William calls for action on mental health. *New York Times.* Retrieved from https://www.nytimes.com/2019/01/24/world/europe/prince-william-mental-health.html

Keddie, A. (2003). Little boys: Tomorrow's macho lads. *Discourse: Studies in the Cultural Politics of Education, 24*(3), 289–306.

Kelada, L., Hasking, P., & Melvin, G. A. (2017). School response to self-injury: Concerns of mental health staff and parents. *School Psychology Quarterly, 32*(2), 173–187.

Kennard, B., Stewart, S., Hughes, J., Patel, P., Emslie, G., & Nagayama Hall, G. G. (2006). Cognitions and depressive symptoms among ethnic minority adolescents. *Cultural Diversity and Ethnic Minority Psychology, 12*(3), 578–591.

Kessler, R. C., Amminger, G. P., Aguilar-Gaxiola, S. B., Alonso, J., Lee, S., & Üstün, T. (2007). Age of onset of mental disorders: A review of recent literature. *Current Opinion in Psychiatry, 20*(4), 359–364.

Kessler, R. C., Berglund, P., Demler, O., Jin, R., Koretz, D., Merikangas, K., . . . Wang, P. (2003). The epidemiology of major depressive disorder: Results from the National Comorbidity Survey Replication (NCS-R). *JAMA, 289*(23), 3095–3105.

Kimmel, M. (2018). Masculinity and our common humanity: "Real" men versus "good" men. In N. Way, C., Gilligan, & P. Noguera (Eds.), *The Crisis of Connection: Roots Consequences and Solutions.* New York: New York University Press, pp. 173–188.

Klerman, G. L., Weissman, M. M., Rounsaville, B. J., & Chevron, E. S. (1984). *Interpersonal Psychotherapy of Depression.* New York: Basic Books.

Kohlberg, L. (1972). Moral stages and moralization: The cognitive developmental approach. In T. Lickona (Ed.), *Moral Development and Behavior.* New York: Holt, Rinehart and Winston.

Kohlberg, L. (1981). *The Philosophy of Moral Development: Moral Stages and the Idea of Justice.* San Francisco: Harper & Row.

Kornfield, J. *The Tyranny of Perfection.* JackKornfield.com. https://jackkornfield.com/?s=tyranny+perfection

Kross, E., Verduyn, P., Demiralp, E., Park, J., Lee, D. S., Lin, N., . . . Ybarra, O. (2013). Facebook use predicts declines in subjective well-being in young adults. *PLoS ONE, 8*(8), e69841.

Kuffel, F. (2013, June 30). Don't talk to your overweight teen—Act! The shame and pain of being an overweight teen. *Psychology Today.* Retrieved from https://www.psychologytoday.com/us/blog/what-fat-women-want/201306/dont-talk-your-overweight-teen-act

Kuo, M. (2018, April 14). How to disobey your tiger parents, in 14 easy steps. *New York Times.* Retrieved from https://www.nytimes.com/2018/04/14/opinion/sunday/disobey-your-tiger-parents.html

Kyeyune, S. *Imparted Wisdom in Troubled Times: Making Sense of the Senseless Situation.* Author House, 2018.

Laird, Y., Fawkner, S., Kelly, P., McNamee, L., & Niven, A. (2016). The role of social support on physical activity behaviour in adolescent girls: A systematic review and meta-analysis. *International Journal of Behavioral Nutrition and Physical Activity*, *13*(1), 79.

Lambert, A., Terenzini, P., & Lattuca, L. (2006). More than meets the eye: Curricular and programmatic effects on student learning. *Research in Higher Education*, *48*(2), 141–168.

Lerner, R. M., Lerner, J. V., Von Eye, A., Bowers, E. P., & Lewin-Bizan, S. (2011). Individual and contextual bases of thriving in adolescence: A view of the issues. *Journal of Adolescence*, *34*(6), 1107–1114.

Lesure-Lester, G. E., & King, N. (2004). Racial-ethnic differences in social anxiety among college students. *Journal of College Student Retention: Research, Theory & Practice*, *6*(3), 359–367.

Levine, R., Kern, B., & Wright, D. (2008). The impact of prompted narrative writing during internship on reflective practice: A qualitative study. *Advances in Health Sciences Education*, *13*(5), 723–733.

Lewandowski, R., O'Connor, B., Bertagnolli, A., Beck, A., Tinoco, A., Gardner, W., . . . Horwitz, S. (2016). Screening for and diagnosis of depression among adolescents in a large health maintenance organization. *Psychiatric Services*, *67*(6), 636–641.

Lewinsohn, P., Larson, M., & Muñoz, D. (1982). The measurement of expectancies and other cognitions in depressed individuals. *Cognitive Therapy and Research*, *6*(4), 437–446.

Lewis, M., Granato, A., Blayney, H., Lostutter, J., & Kilmer, T. (2012). Predictors of hooking up sexual behaviors and emotional reactions among U.S. college students. *Archives of Sexual Behavior*, *41*(5), 1219–1229.

LeViness, P., Bershad, C., Gorman, K. P., Braun, L., & Murray, T. (2018). The Association for University and College Counseling Center Directors Annual Survey—Public Version 2018. https://www.aucccd.org/assets/documents/Survey/2018%20AUCCCD%20Survey-Public-June%2012-FINAL.pdf

Li, N. N., & Li, L. (2012). Study on the invention effect of the cognitive-behavioural group counseling on college students' social anxiety. *International Journal of Psychology*, *47*, 196.

Linden, A., Lau-Barraco, C., & Milletich, R. (2013). Protective behavioral strategies in a model of anxiety and college student drinking. *Alcoholism-Clinical and Experimental Research*, *37*(S2), 92A.

Linehan, M. (1993). *Skills Training Manual for Treating Borderline Personality Disorder*. New York: Guilford Press.

Lipari, R. N., Hedden, S., Blau, G., & Rubenstein, L. (2016). Adolescent mental health service use and reasons for using services in specialty, educational, and general medical settings. In *The CBHSQ Report*: May 5, 2016. Rockville, MD: Substance Abuse and Mental Health Services Administration, Center for Behavioral Health Statistics and Quality.

Logan, D., Marlatt, G., & Tatarsky, A. (2010). Harm reduction therapy: A practice-friendly review of research. *Journal of Clinical Psychology*, *66*(2), 201–214.

Long, E., Lockhart, G., Cruz, R., Deberard, S., Dotterer, A., & Geiser, C. (2018). *Using Social Network Analysis to Examine the Intersection of Adolescent Friendships and Health Behavior*. ProQuest Dissertations and Theses.

Luan, Z., Poorthuis, A., Hutteman, R., Asendorpf, J., Denissen, J., Van Aken, M., . . . Gerstorf, D. (2018). See me through my eyes: Adolescent–parent agreement in personality predicts later self-esteem development. *International Journal of Behavioral Development*, *42*(1), 17–25.

Luoma, J., Hayes, S., & Walser, R. (2007). *Learning ACT: An Acceptance and Commitment Therapy Skills-Training Manual for Therapists*. Oakland, CA: New Harbinger.

Macdonald, D., Dimitropoulos, G., Royal, S., Polanco, A., & Dionne, M. (2015). The Family Fat Talk Questionnaire: Development and psychometric properties of a measure of fat talk behaviors within the family context. *Body Image, 12*(1), 44–52.

Mahalik, J. R., Burns, S. M., & Syzdek, M. (2007). Masculinity and perceived normative health behaviors as predictors of men's health behaviors. *Social Science & Medicine, 64*(11), 2201–2209.

Malti, T., & Buchmann, M. (2010). Socialization and individual antecedents of adolescents' and young adults' moral motivation. *Journal of Youth and Adolescence, 39*(2), 138–149.

Markowitz, J. C., Lipsitz, J., & Milrod, B. (2014). Critical review of outcome research on interpersonal psychotherapy for anxiety disorders. *Depression and Anxiety, 31*(4), 316–325.

Martin, C. (2007). *Perfect Girls, Starving Daughters: The Frightening New Normalcy of Hating Your Body*. New York: Free Press.

Martinson, V., Holman, T., Larson, J., & Jackson, J. (2010). The relationship between coming to terms with family-of-origin difficulties and adult relationship satisfaction. *American Journal of Family Therapy, 38*(3), 207–217.

Maryland Collaborative to Reduce College Drinking and Related Problems. (2018). 21st birthday. *College Parents Matter*. Retrieved from http://www.collegeparentsmatter.org/birthday.html

Mastrotheodoros, S., Van der Graaff, J., Deković, M., Meeus, W. H., & Branje, S. J. (2019). Interparental conflict management strategies and parent–adolescent relationships: Disentangling between-person from within-person effects across adolescence. *Journal of Marriage and Family, 81*(1), 185–203.

Mclaughlin, K. A., & Nolen-Hoeksema, S. (2011). Rumination as a transdiagnostic factor in depression and anxiety. *Behaviour Research and Therapy, 49*(3), 186–193.

Merikangas, K. R., He, J-p., Burstein, M., Swanson, S. A., Avenevoli, S., Cui, L., . . . Swendsen, J. (2010). Lifetime prevalence of mental disorders in U.S. adolescents: Results from the National Comorbidity Survey Replication-Adolescent Supplement (NCS-A). *Journal of the American Academy of Child & Adolescent Psychiatry, 49*(10), 980–989.

Meyer, I. H. (1995). Minority stress and mental health in gay men. *Journal of Health and Social Behavior, 36*, 38e56.

Meyer, R. (2016, September 1). How Instagram opened a ruthless new chapter in the teen photo wars. *The Atlantic*. Retrieved from https://www.theatlantic.com/technology/archive/2016/09/how-one-teen-uses-instagram-and-snapchat-stories/498254/

Miech, R., Johnston, L. D., & O'Malley, P. M. Bachman, J. G., & Patrick, M. E. (2019). Adolescent vaping and nicotine use in 2017–2018: U.S. national estimates. *New England Journal of Medicine, 380*, 192–193.

Miech, R., Johnston, L., O'Malley, P., Bachman, J. D., & Patrick, M. E. (2019). Trends in adolescent vaping, 2017–2019. *New England Journal of Medicine, 381*, 1490–1491.

Miller, A., Glinski, J., Woodberry, K., Mitchell, A., & Indik, J. (2002). Family therapy and dialectical behavior therapy with adolescents: Part I: Proposing a clinical synthesis. *American Journal of Psychotherapy, 56*(4), 568–584.

Miller, T., Levy, D., Spicer, R., & Taylor, D. (2006). Societal costs of underage drinking. *Journal of Studies on Alcohol, 67*(4), 519–528.

Miller, W., Rose, G., & Anderson, N. B. (2010). Motivational interviewing in relational context. *American Psychologist, 65*(4), 298–299.

Moe, J. (Host) (2017, January 30). Baron Vaughn and his inadvisable all-Cheerio diet [Audio podcast]. The Hilarious World of Depression. Retrieved from https://www.apmpodcasts.org/thwod/2017/01/baron-vaughn-and-his-inadvisable-all-cheerio-diet/

Moe, J. (Host). (2017, October 2). Margaret Cho works out a lot and makes people upset in New Jersey [Audio podcast]. The Hilarious World of Depression. Retrieved from https://www.apmpodcasts.org/thwod/2017/10/margaret-cho-works-out-a-lot-and-makes-people-upset-in-new-jersey/

Moller, H., Bandelow, B., Volz, H., Barnikol, U. B., Seifritz, E., & Kasper, S. (2016). The relevance of "mixed anxiety and depression" as a diagnostic category in clinical practice. *European Archives of Psychiatry and Clinical Neuroscience, 266*(8), 725–736.

Moyers, B. (1993). Meditate! For stress reduction, inner peace, or whatever! (Interview with Jon Kabat-Zinn, founder and director of the Stress Reduction Clinic, University of Massachusetts Medical Center). *Psychology Today, 26*(4), 36–41.

Mrug, S., King, V., & Windle, M. (2016). Brief report: Explaining differences in depressive symptoms between African American and European American adolescents. *Journal of Adolescence, 46*, 25.

Mubayi, S. (2011). I claim the right to choose my ultimate gender. In Boston Women's Health Collective, *Our Bodies Ourselves*. New York: Simon and Schuster.

Mueller, M. K., Phelps, E., Bowers, E. P., Agans, J. P., Urban, J., & Lerner, R. M. (2011). Youth development program participation and intentional self-regulation skills: Contextual and individual bases of pathways to positive youth development. *Journal of Adolescence, 34*(6), 1115–1125.

Mufson, L. (2004). *Interpersonal Psychotherapy for Depressed Adolescents* (2nd ed.). New York: Guilford Press.

Munoz, R. F., Beardslee, W. R., Leykin Y. (2012). Major depression can be prevented. *American Psychology, 67*(4), 285–295.

Muzaffar, N., Brito, E., Fogel, J., Fagan, D., Kumar, K., & Verma, R. (2018). The association of adolescent Facebook behaviours with symptoms of social anxiety, generalized anxiety, and depression. *Journal of the Canadian Academy of Child and Adolescent Psychiatry, 27*(4), 252–260.

Napolitano, C. M., Bowers, E. P., Gestsdottir, S., Depping, M., Von Eye, A., Chase, P., & Lerner, J. V. (2011). The role of parenting and goal selection in positive youth development: A person-centered approach. *Journal of Adolescence, 34*(6), 1137–1149.

Nathanson, L., Rivers, S. E., Flynn, L. M., & Brackett, M. A. (2016). Creating emotionally intelligent schools with RULER. *Emotion Review, 8*(4), 1–6.

National Alliance on Mental Illness & The Jed Foundation. (2016). *Starting the Conversation: College and Your Mental Health*. Arlington County, VA: National Alliance on Mental Illness.

National Center for Education Statistics. (2015). Number of faculty in degree-granting postsecondary institutions, by employment status, sex, control, and level of institution: Selected years, fall 1970 through fall 2013. *Digest of Education Statistics*. Retrieved from https://nces.ed.gov/programs/digest/d15/tables/dt15_315.10.asp?current=yes

National Center on Addiction and Substance Abuse at Columbia University. (2012). *The Importance of Family Dinners VIII*. New York: Columbia University.

National Institute on Alcohol Abuse and Alcoholism. (2009). *Make a Difference: Talk to Your Child About Alcohol*. Washington, DC: U.S. Department of Health and Human Services.

National Research Council and Institute of Medicine, Prevention Committee. (2009). *Preventing Emotional and Behavioral Disorders among Young People: Progress and Possibilities*. Washington, DC: National Academies Press.

National Sleep Foundation. (2018). School start time and sleep. Retrieved from https://www.sleepfoundation.org/articles/school-start-time-and-sleep

Niemiec, C. P., Lynch, M. F., Vansteenkiste, M., Bernstein, J., Deci, E. L., & Ryan, R. M. (2006). The antecedents and consequences of autonomous self-regulation for college: A self-determination theory perspective on socialization. *Journal of Adolescence, 29*(5), 761–775.

Nolen-Hoeksema, S. (1993). *Sex Differences in Depression*. Palo Alto, CA: Stanford University Press.

Nolen-Hoeksema, S., Wisco, B., & Lyubomirsky, S. (2008). Rethinking rumination. *Perspectives on Psychological Science, 3*(5), 400–424.

Nussbaum, M. (2018). *The Monarchy of Fear: A Philosopher Looks at Our Political Crisis*. New York: Simon & Schuster.

Oakley, B. (2018, August 7). Make your daughter practice math. She'll thank you later. *New York Times*. Retrieved from https://www.nytimes.com/2018/08/07/opinion/stem-girls-math-practice.html

Obama, M. (2018). *Becoming*. New York: Crown.

O'Keeffe, G., & Clarke-Pearson, K. (2011). The impact of social media on children, adolescents, and families. *Pediatrics, 127*(4), 800–4.

Oliver, J. (Writer). (2018, June 24). June 24, 2018 [Television series episode]. *Last Week Tonight*. HBO.

Onwuachi, K. (2019). *Notes from a Young Black Chef: A memoir*. New York: Knopf.

Opie, R., O'Neil, A., Jacka, F., Pizzinga, J., & Itsiopoulos, C. (2018). A modified Mediterranean dietary intervention for adults with major depression: Dietary protocol and feasibility data from the SMILES trial. *Nutritional Neuroscience, 21*(7), 487–501.

Oransky, M., & Marecek, J. (2009). "I'm not going to be a girl": Masculinity and emotions in boys' friendships and peer groups. *Journal of Adolescent Research, 24*(2), 218–241.

Oshri, A., Tubman, J., Morgan-Lopez, A., Saavedra, L., & Csizmadia, A. (2013). Sexual sensation seeking, co-occurring sex and alcohol use, and sexual risk behavior among adolescents in treatment for substance use problems. *American Journal on Addictions, 22*(3), 197–205.

Owen, J., & Fincham, F. (2011). Young adults' emotional reactions after hooking up encounters. *Archives of Sexual Behavior, 40*(2), 321–330.

Owen, J., Rhoades, J., Stanley, G., & Fincham, K. (2010). "Hooking up" among college students: Demographic and psychosocial correlates. *Archives of Sexual Behavior, 39*(3), 653–663.

Owens, J. (2014). Insufficient sleep in adolescents and young adults: An update on causes and consequences. *Pediatrics, 134*(3), e921–e932.

Owens, J. A., Dearth-Wesley, T., Lewin, D., Gioia, G., & Whitaker, R. C. (2016). Self-regulation and sleep duration, sleepiness, and chronotype in adolescents. *Pediatrics, 138*(6), e20161406–e20161406.

Panagiotakopoulos, L., & Neigh, G. N. (2014). Development of the HPA axis: Where and when do sex differences manifest? *Frontiers in Neuroendocrinology, 35*(3), 285–302.

Pappas, S. (2019). APA issues first-ever guidelines for practice with men and boys. *Monitor on Psychology, 50*(1), 34.

Parent, M., & Bradstreet, T. (2018). Sexual orientation, bullying for being labeled gay or bisexual, and steroid use among US adolescent boys. *Journal of Health Psychology, 23*(4), 608–617.

Pascarella, E. (1980). Student–faculty informal contact and college outcomes. *Review of Educational Research, 50*(4), 545–595.

Pascarella, E., & Terenzini, P. (1991). *How College Affects Students: Findings and Insights from Twenty Years of Research*. San Francisco: Jossey-Bass.

Pascarella, E., & Terenzini, P. (2005). *How College Affects Students. Vol. 2. A Third Decade of Research*. San Francisco: Jossey-Bass.

Pasupathi, M., Hoyt, T., & García Coll, C. (2009). The development of narrative identity in late adolescence and emergent adulthood: The continued importance of listeners. *Developmental Psychology, 45*(2), 558–574.

Paul, M. (2012). What shields gay youth from suicide? *Northwestern Now*. Retrieved from https://news.northwestern.edu/stories/2012/02/gay-youth-suicide/

Pedersen, G., Grønhøj, A., & Thøgersen., J. (2015). Following family or friends. Social norms in adolescent healthy eating. *Appetite, 86*(C), 54–60.

Penny, L. (2017). *Glass Houses: A Novel*. New York: Minotaur Books.

Perel, E. (2019) cited in Dockett, L., & Simon, R. The Masculinity Paradox: *What Does It Mean to Be a "Real" Man Today? Psychotherapy Networker, January/February 2019*. Retrieved from https://www.psychotherapynetworker.org/magazine/article/23

Pino, N., Tajalli, H., Smith, C., & Desoto, W. (2017). Nonmedical prescription drug use by college students for recreational and instrumental purposes: Assessing the differences. *Journal of Drug Issues, 47*(4), 606–621.

Pires, G. N., Bezerra, A. G., Tufik, S., & Andersen, M. L. (2016). Effects of acute sleep deprivation on state anxiety levels: A systematic review and meta-analysis. *Sleep Medicine, 24*, 109–118.

Plan International. (2018). The state of gender equality for US adolescents. Plan International USA. Retrieved from https://www.planusa.org/docs/state-of-gender-equality-summary-2018.pdf

Planned Parenthood. (2019). For parents. Retrieved from https://www.plannedparenthood.org/learn/parents

Pollan, M. (2009). *Food Rules: An Eater's Manual*. New York: Penguin Books.

Priest, N., Paradies, Y., Trenerry, B., Truong, M., Karlsen, S., & Kelly, Y. (2013). A systematic review of studies examining the relationship between reported racism and health and wellbeing for children and young people. *Social Science Medicine, 95*, 115–127.

Puhl, R. M., Andreyeva, T., & Brownell, K. D. (2008). Perceptions of weight discrimination: Prevalence and comparison to race and gender discrimination in America. *International Journal of Obesity, 32*(6), 992–1000.

Puhl, R. M., Himmelstein, M., & Watson, R. (2019). Weight-based victimization among sexual and gender minority adolescents: Findings from a diverse national sample. *Pediatric Obesity*, *14*(7), E12514.

Queen, A. H., Barlow, D. H., & Ehrenreich-May, H. (2014). The trajectories of adolescent anxiety and depressive symptoms over the course of a transdiagnostic treatment. *Journal of Anxiety Disorders*, *28*(6), 511–521.

Queen, A. H., Stewart, L. M., Ehrenreich-May, J., & Pincus, Donna B. (2013). Mothers' and fathers' ratings of family relationship quality: Associations with preadolescent and adolescent anxiety and depressive symptoms in a clinical sample. *Child Psychiatry and Human Development*, *44*(3), 351–360.

Radhu, N., Daskalakis, Z. J., Arpin-Cribbie, C. A., Irvine, J., & Ritvo, P. (2012). Evaluating a web-based cognitive-behavioral therapy for maladaptive perfectionism in university students. *Journal of American College Health*, *60*(5), 357–366.

Raes, F., Griffith, J., Gucht, W., & Williams, K. (2014). School-based prevention and reduction of depression in adolescents: A cluster-randomized controlled trial of a mindfulness group program. *Mindfulness*, *5*(5), 477–486.

Ramírez García, J., Manongdo, J., Ozechowski, T., & Zarate, Michael A. (2014). Depression symptoms among Mexican American youth: Paternal parenting in the context of maternal parenting, economic stress, and youth gender. *Cultural Diversity and Ethnic Minority Psychology*, *20*(1), 27–36.

Rasing, S. P. A., Creemers, D. H. M., Janssens, J. M. A. M., & Scholte, R. H. J. (2013). Effectiveness of depression and anxiety prevention in adolescents with high familial risk: Study protocol for a randomized controlled trial. *BMC Psychiatry*, *13*(1), 316.

Rasing, S. P. A., Creemers, D. H. M, Janssens, J. M. A. M., & Scholte, R. H. J. (2017). Depression and anxiety prevention based on cognitive behavioral therapy for at-risk adolescents: A meta-analytic review. *Frontiers in Psychology*, *8*, 1066.

Ratanasiripong, P., Sverduk, K., Prince, J., & Hayashino, D. (2012). Biofeedback and counseling for stress and anxiety among college students. *Journal of College Student Development*, *53*(5), 742–749.

Raudsepp, L. (2016). Brief report: Longitudinal associations between sedentary behaviours and depressive symptoms in adolescent girls. *Journal of Adolescence*, *51*, 76–80.

Read, J. P., Wardell, J. D., & Bachrach, R. L. (2013). Drinking consequence types in the first college semester differentially predict drinking the following year. *Addictive Behaviors*, *38*(1), 1464–1471.

Rees, R., & Thomas, J. (2013). The views of young people in the UK about obesity, body size, shape and weight: A systematic review [IOE Research Briefing N°47]. Institute of Education, University of London.

Reynolds, C. R., & Kamphaus, R. W. (2013). Persistent depressive disorder (dysthymia). In American Psychiatric Association. *Diagnostic and Statistical Manual of Mental Disorders* (5th ed.). Washington, DC: American Psychiatric Association.

Richards, D., Rhodes, S., Ekers, D., McMillan, D., Taylor, R., Byford, S., . . . Woodhouse, R. (2017). Cost and Outcome of Behavioural Activation (COBRA): A randomised controlled trial of behavioural activation versus cognitive–behavioural therapy for depression. *Health Technology Assessment*, *21*(46), 1–366.

Richter, M., & Grady D. (2019, September 6). Cases of vaping related illnesses surge, health officials say. *New York Times*.

Roane, B., Seifer, R., Sharkey, K., Van Reen, E., Bond, T., Raffray, T., & Carskadon, M. (2015). What role does sleep play in weight gain in the first semester of university? *Behavioral Sleep Medicine, 13*(6), 491–505.

Rodkin, P., Espelage, D., Hanish, L., & Anderson, N. B. (2015). A relational framework for understanding bullying. *American Psychologist, 70*(4), 311–321.

Rollnick, S., & Miller, W. (1995). What is motivational interviewing? *Behavioural and Cognitive Psychotherapy, 23*(4), 325–334.

Rosenthal, G. T., Domangue, T. J., Folse, E. J., Cortez, N. G., Soper, W. B., & Von Bergen, C. W. (2000). The one-to-one survey: Students with disabilities versus students without disabilities satisfaction with professors during one-on-one contacts. *Journal of Instructional Psychology, 27*(2), 90.

Russek, L. G., & Schwartz, G. E. (1997). Feeling of parental caring predict health status in midlife: A 35-year follow-up of the Harvard Mastery of Stress Study. *Journal of Behavioral Medicine, 20*(1), 1–13.

Rutledge, P. C., Park, A., & Sher, K. J. (2008). 21st birthday drinking: Extremely extreme. *Journal of Consulting and Clinical Psychology, 76*(3), 511–516.

Ryan, C. (2009). *Supportive Families, Healthy Children: Helping Families with Lesbian, Gay, Bisexual & Transgender Children*. San Francisco: San Francisco State University.

Sabina, C., Wolak, J., & Finkelhor, D. (2008). The nature and dynamics of Internet pornography exposure for youth. *CyberPsychology & Behavior, 11*(6), 691–693.

Salk, R., & Engeln-Maddox, H. (2012). Fat talk among college women is both contagious and harmful. *Sex Roles, 66*(9), 636–645.

Sanders, M. R., & Mazzucchelli, T. G. (2011). The promotion of self-regulation through parenting interventions. In V. Barkoukis (Ed.), *Psychology of Self-Regulation* (pp. 103–119). Hauppauge: Nova Science.

Sandler, I., Schoenfelder, E., Wolchik, S., & MacKinnon, D. (2011). Long-term impact of prevention programs to promote effective parenting: Lasting effects but uncertain processes. *Annual Review of Psychology, 62*(1), 299–329.

Schickedanz, A., Halfon, N., Sastry, N., & Chung, P. J. (2018). Parents' adverse childhood experiences and their children's behavioral health problems. *Pediatrics, 142*(2), pii: e20180023.

School Mental Health Resource Training Center. (2018). Fast facts: NYS mental health education in schools law. Retrieved from https://www.mentalhealthednys.org/wp-content/uploads/2018/09/Fast-Facts-Education-Law.docx-1.pdf

Schweitzer, A. (2015). *The Light Within Us*. New York: Philosophical Library.

Seiffge-Krenke, I. (2017). Does adolescents' psychopathology change in times of change? *Journal of Adolescence, 61*, 107.

Seligman, M. E. P., Schulman, P., DeRubeis, R. J., & Hollon, S. D. (1999). The prevention of depression and anxiety. *Prevention & Treatment, 2*(1), 8a.

Senra, C., Merino, H., & Ferreiro, F. (2018). Exploring the link between perfectionism and depressive symptoms: Contribution of rumination and defense styles. *Journal of Clinical Psychology, 74*(6), 1053–1066.

Shain, B. (2016). Suicide and suicide attempts in adolescents. *Pediatrics, 138*(1), 1.

Segal, Z. V., Williams, M. G., & John, D. (2012). *Teasdale Mindfulness-Based Cognitive Therapy for Depression*, Second Edition. New York: Guilford Press.

Siegel, D. (2013). *Brainstorm: The Power and Purpose of the Teenage Brain*. New York: Jeremy P. Tarcher/Penguin.

Silverthorne, N. (2013, May 15). 5 signs your child has a mental-health issue. *Today's Parent*. Retrieved from https://www.todaysparent.com/family/parenting/5-signs-your-child-has-a-mental-health-issue/

Singh, S., & Sharma, N. R. (2018). Self-regulation as a correlate of psychological well-being. *Indian Journal of Health & Wellbeing, 9*(3). 441–444.

Singleton, R., & Wolfson, A. (2009). Alcohol consumption, sleep, and academic performance among college students. *Journal of Studies on Alcohol and Drugs, 70*(3), 355–363.

Sirois, F., Kitner, R., Hirsch, J., & Kazak, A. E. (2015). Self-compassion, affect, and health-promoting behaviors. *Health Psychology, 34*(6), 661–669.

Skarupski, K., Tangney, A., Li, C., Evans, H., & Morris, D. (2013). Mediterranean diet and depressive symptoms among older adults over time. *Journal of Nutrition, Health & Aging, 17*(5), 441–445.

Sloan, L. (2018, May 15). Aidea Downie: Let's be honest here. *Brown Alumni Magazine*. Retrieved from https://news.brown.edu/articles/2018/05/downie

Smith, L. (2016, October 9). World Mental Health Day: What are the dangers of high-functioning depression and anxiety?. *International Business Times*. Retrieved from https://www.yahoo.com/news/world-mental-health-day-dangers-230101384.html

Spence, S. H., Donovan, C. L., March, S., Gamble, A., Anderson, R. E., Prosser, S., & Kenardy, J. (2011). A randomized controlled trial of online versus clinic-based CBT for adolescent anxiety. *Journal of Consulting and Clinical Psychology, 79*(5), 629–642.

Spielman, A., Caruso, L., & Glovinsky, P. (1987). A behavioral perspective on insomnia treatment. *Psychiatric Clinics of North America, 10*(4), 541–53.

Stein, M. D., & Galea, S. (2018). On our minds: The downside of drinking. *Public Health Post*. Retrieved from https://www.publichealthpost.org/the-publics-health/the-downside-of-drinking/. December 19, 2018.

Stevelos, J. (2019). Bullying, bullycide and childhood obesity. Obesity Action Coalition. Retrieved from https://www.obesityaction.org/community/article-library/bullying-bullycide-and-childhood-obesity/

Stone, A. L., Becker, L. G., Huber, A. M., & Catalano, R. F. (2012). Review of risk and protective factors of substance use and problem use in emerging adulthood. *Addictive Behaviors, 37*(7), 747–775.

Substance Abuse and Mental Health, Services Administration, Center for Behavioral Health Statistics and Quality. (2016). *The CBHSQ Report: May 5, 2016*. Rockville, MD: US Department of Health and Human Services.

Tak, Y. R., Brunwasser, S. M., Lichtwarck-Aschoff, A., & Engels, R. C. M. E. (2017). The prospective associations between self-efficacy and depressive symptoms from early to middle adolescence: A cross-lagged model. *Journal of Youth and Adolescence, 46*, 744–756.

Terenzini, P., & Pascarella, E. (1980). Student/faculty relationships and freshman year educational outcomes: A further investigation. *Journal of College Student Personnel, 21*(6), 521–528.

Terry, M., & Leary, M. (2011). Self-compassion, self-regulation, and health. *Self and Identity, 10*(3), 352–362.

Thompson, M. (2001). Informal student–faculty interaction: Its relationship to educational gains in science and mathematics among community college students. *Community College Review, 29*(1), 35–57.

Tompkins, T. L., Hockett, A. R., Abraibesh, N., & Witt. J. L. (2011). A closer look at co-rumination: Gender, coping, peer functioning and internalizing/externalizing problems. *Journal of Adolescence, 34*(5), 801–811.

Townsend, J., & Wasserman, M. (2011). Sexual hookups among college students: Sex differences in emotional reactions. *Archives of Sexual Behavior, 40*(6), 1173–1181.

Trudeau, G. (2019, February 17). Doonesbury. *GoComics.* Retrieved from https://www.gocomics.com/doonesbury/2019/02/17

Tsang S. K. M., Hui, E. K., & Law, C. P. M. (2012). Self-efficacy as a positive youth development construct: A conceptual review. *Scientific World Journal, 452327.*

Twenge, J. M. (2013). Does online social media lead to social connection or social disconnection? *Journal of College and Character, 14*(1), 11–20.

Twenge, J. (2017). *iGen: Why Today's Super-Connected Kids Are Growing Up Less Rebellious, More Tolerant, Less Happy—and Completely Unprepared for Adulthood—And What That Means for the Rest of Us.* New York: Atria.

University of Michigan Institute for Social Research, Monitoring the Future. (2018, December 17). National adolescent drug trends in 2018 [Press release]. Retrieved from http://monitoringthefuture.org//pressreleases/18drugpr.pdf

US Department of Education. (2018). Federal TRIO Programs. Retrieved from https://www2.ed.gov/about/offices/list/ope/trio/index.htm

Weil, Andrew. Three Breathing Exercises and Techniques. Retrieved from https://www.drweil.com/health-wellness/body-mind-spirit/stress-anxiety/breathing-three-exercises/

Van der Kolk, B. (2019). The politics of mental health. *Psychotherapy Networker.* May-June, 33–54.

Vannucci, A., & McCauley Ohannessian, C. (2018). Self-competence and depressive symptom trajectories during adolescence. *Journal of Abnormal Child Psychology, 46*(5), 1089–1109.

Viana, A., Woodward, E., Hanna, A., Raines, E., Alfano, C., & Zvolensky, M. (2018). The moderating role of anxiety sensitivity in the co-occurrence of anxiety and depression symptoms among clinically anxious children. *Journal of Experimental Psychopathology, 9*(3), 1–12.

Wald, H. (2015). Refining a definition of reflection for the being as well as doing the work of a physician. *Medical Teacher, 37*(7), 696–699.

Wald, H. S., Davis, S. W., Reis, S. P., Monroe, A. D., & Borkan, J. M. (2009). Reflecting on reflections: Enhancement of medical education curriculum with structured field notes and guided feedback. *Academic Medicine, 84*(7), 830–837.

Way, N., Ali, A., Gilligan, C., & Noguera, P. (2018). *The Crisis of Connection: Roots, Consequences, and Solutions.* New York: New York University Press.

Wei, M., Heppner, P., Russell, D., Young, S., & Mallinckrodt, Brent. (2006). Maladaptive perfectionism and ineffective coping as mediators between attachment and future depression: A prospective analysis. *Journal of Counseling Psychology, 53*(1), 67–79.

Wei, M., Mallinckrodt, B., Russell, D., Abraham, W., & Hansen, Jo-Ida C. (2004). Maladaptive perfectionism as a mediator and moderator between adult attachment and depressive mood. *Journal of Counseling Psychology, 51*(2), 201–212.

Weissman, A. N., & Beck, A. T. (1978). Development and validation of the Dysfunctional Attitude Scale: A preliminary investigation. Paper presented at the Association for the Advancement of Behavior Therapy, Chicago.

Weissman, D. G., Bitran, D., Miller, A. B., Schaefer, J. D., Sheridan, M. A., & McLaughlin, K. A. (2019). Difficulties with emotion regulation as a transdiagnostic mechanism linking child maltreatment with the emergence of psychopathology. *Developmental Psychopathology*, 31(3), 899–915.

Weller, B. E., Blanford, K. L., & Butler, A. M. (2018). Estimated prevalence of psychiatric comorbidities in U.S. adolescents with depression by race/ethnicity, 2011–2012. *Journal of Adolescent Health*, 62(6), 716–721.

Weyandt, L. L., White, T. L., Gudmundsdottir, B. G., Nitenson, A. Z., Rathkey, E. S., De Leon, K. A., & Bjorn. S. A. (2018). Neurocognitive, autonomic, and mood effects of Adderall: A pilot study of healthy college students. *Pharmacy*, 6(3), 58.

What We Know. (2019). What does the scholarly research say about the link between family acceptance and LGBT youth well-being? What We Know: The Public Policy Research Portal. Cornell University. Retrieved from https://whatweknow.inequality.cornell.edu/topics/lgbt-equality/what-does-the-scholarly-research-say-about-the-acceptancerejection-of-lgbt-youth-2/

White, R. (1959). Motivation reconsidered: The concept of competence. *Psychological Review*, 66, 297–333.

Williamson, D. E., Birmaher, B., Frank, E., Anderson, B. P., Matty, M. K., & Kupfer, D. J. (1998). Nature of life events and difficulties in depressed adolescents. *Journal of the American Academy of Child & Adolescent Psychiatry*, 37(10), 1049–1057.

Wolverton, B. (2019, February 21) As students struggle with stress and depression, colleges act as counselors. *New York Times*.

Wood, J. (2018, April). Bisexual teens at highest risk of bullying and suicide. *PsychCentral News*.

Woodberry, K. A., Miller, A. L., Glinski, J., Indik, J., & Mitchell, A. G. (2002). Family therapy and dialectical behavior therapy with adolescents: Part II: A theoretical review. *American Journal of Psychotherapy*, 56(4), 585–602.

Yap, M., Lawrence, K., Rapee, R., Cardamone-Breen, M., Green, J., & Jorm, A. (2017). Partners in parenting: A multi-level web-based approach to support parents in prevention and early intervention for adolescent depression and anxiety. *JMIR Mental Health*, 4(4), E59.

Young Park, S. (2018). Social support mosaic: Understanding mental health management practice on college campus. In *Proceedings of the ACM Conference on Designing Interactive Systems Conference (DIS)*, pp. 121–133.

Yousaf, O., Popat, A., & Hunter, M. S. (2015). An investigation of masculinity attitudes, gender, and attitudes toward psychological help-seeking. *Psychology of Men & Masculinity*, 16(2), 234–237.

Zeiss, A., Lewinsohn, P., & Muñoz, R. (1979). Nonspecific improvement effects in depression using interpersonal skills training, pleasant activity schedules, or cognitive training. *Journal of Consulting and Clinical Psychology*, 47, 427.

Zhou, X., Zhu, H., Zhang, B., & Cai, T. (2013). Perceived social support as moderator of perfectionism, depression, and anxiety in college students. *Social Behavior and Personality*, 41(7), 1141–1152.

Zitek, E., & Hebl, M. (2007). The role of social norm clarity in the influenced expression of prejudice over time. *Journal of Experimental Social Psychology*, *43*(6), 867–876.

Zlomuzica, A., Preusser, F., Schneider, S., & Margraf, J. (2015). Increased perceived self-efficacy facilitates the extinction of fear in healthy participants. *Frontiers in Behavioral Neuroscience*, 16, 205.

Zuckerbrot, R., Cheung, A., Jensen, P., Stein, R., & Laraque, D. (2007). Guidelines for Adolescent Depression in Primary Care (GLAD-PC): I. Identification, assessment, and initial management. *Pediatrics*, *120*(5), e1299–e1312.

INDEX

For the benefit of digital users, indexed terms that span two pages (e.g., 52–53) may, on occasion, appear on only one of those pages.

Wilde, Oscar, 181
Williams, Mark, 166
Wolchik, Sharlene, 65–66
Women's Project in Family
 Therapy, 60
World Health Organization, 33
writing for self-reflection, 154–55

Yampolsky, Victor, 163
yoga, 123–24
young men
 body dissatisfaction, 137–38, 139
 masculinity, 24–28, 60–61
 reactions to hookups, 236

social competence, 72
 weight bias, 197–98
young women
 body dissatisfaction in, 23, 44
 body shaming, 136–37
 reactions to hookups, 236
 social competence, 71–72
 weight bias, 197
Your Perfect Right (Alberti and Emmons),
 56–57, 58, 59
Yousaf, Omar, 61

zero-tolerance policy toward bullying,
 261